THE LADY TARS:
The Autobiographies of Hannah Snell, Mary Lacy and Mary Anne Talbot

by

Hannah Snell,
Mary Lacy and Mary Anne Talbot
with Forward by Tom Grundner

Fireship Press
www.FireshipPress.com

THE LADY TARS: The Autobiographies of Hannah Snell, Mary Lacy and Mary Anne Talbot - Copyright © 2008 by Fireship Press

ISBN-13: 978-1-934757-35-2
ISBN-10: 1-934757-35-7

BISAC Subject Headings:
    BIO008000   BIOGRAPHY & AUTOBIOGRAPHY / Military
    BIO006000   BIOGRAPHY & AUTOBIOGRAPHY / Historical

This work is based on:

Snell, Hannah. *The Female Soldier or The Surprising Life and Adventures of Hannah Snell*. London: R. Walker, 1750.

Lacy, Mary *The History of the Female Shipwright*. London: M. Lewis, 1773

Talbot, Mary Anne. *Life and Surprising Adventures of Mary Ann Talbot in the Name of John Taylor*. London: R.S. Kirby, 1809.

Address all correspondence to:
Fireship Press
P.O. Box 68412
Tucson, AZ 85737

Or access our website at:
www.FireshipPress.com

THE LADY TARS:
The Autobiographies of Hannah Snell, Mary Lacy and Mary Anne Talbot

Contents

FORWARD

The Female Soldier or The Surprising Life and
Adventures of Hannah Snell
(1723-1792)
Page 1

The Female Shipwright or Life and Extraordinary
Adventures of Mary Lacy
(1740-1773+)
Page 53

Life and Surprising Adventures of
Mary Ann Talbot in the Name of John Taylor
(1778-1808)
Page 141

Forward

It was the last thing that Paolo Gallo expected to find. The Italian archeologist had been working on Nelson's Island in Aboukir Bay, Egypt for almost two years, excavating some Hellenistic structures that were to be found there. In October 2001, his workers unearthed some British military buttons, a few clasps and an unfired musket ball, all dating from the Napoleonic period. Then came the graves.

It was clear that he had come across a graveyard containing the remains of men killed at the Battle of the Nile. It was Nelson's tremendous victory in 1798 that pinned Napoleon in Egypt and helped to foiled his plans for conquest there.

Gallo expected to find sailor's graves. What he didn't expect to find were the graves of an infant and a woman. The infant was buried in a wooden coffin, wrapped carefully in a shroud held together with several small bronze pins and packed in wood shavings. Next to the infant, and probably its mother, was a woman in a dress with a delicate handkerchief placed over her face.

Who was this woman?

Nick Slope of The Nelson Society was called in and a research effort begun. It will never be known with complete confidence, but the Nelson Society's findings are quite persuasive. They located an old diary belonging to John Nicol, a sailor aboard the HMS *Goliath* and who fought at the Battle of the Nile. He tells of a woman from Leith, Scotland who was injured while serving the *Goliath's* guns during the battle. She died several days later and was "buried on a small island in the Bay."

A woman serving the guns? How weird was that? It turns out— not very. It seems that women played an important role in many of the ships in the Napoleonic navy.

Officially the Admiralty was quite clear about women on board ship: "...no women be ever permitted to be on board but such as are really the wives of the men they come to, and the ship not too much pestered even with them. But the indulgence is only to be tolerated in Port and not under Sailing Orders." The first such injunction appeared in 1587; but it, and every similar regulation for the next 250 years, was routinely ignored.

There were four general categories of women aboard ship. The first consists of civilian passengers. Naval ships at that time were forever being asked to transport civilian government officials, or military passengers transferring stations, along with their wives. A second category was the hordes of prostitutes that attended any Royal Navy ship that put into port and sometimes went to sea with the ship.

For our purposes, however, these two groups are of less interest than the women who actively served on board a Royal Navy ship, either in disguise as a man, or in their own right. Unfortunately there are two problems in writing about them.

The first is that no Admiralty record exists of these women because they were not officially carried on any ship's books. Nevertheless, we know that there are at least written 20 accounts of females serving aboard Royal Navy ships that appear to be authentic. In addition, there are at least another 15 cases which are mentioned in newspaper and other sources of women serving as sailors on board merchant and fishing vessels.

There was "William Brown," a black woman who served for 11 years as captain of the maintop aboard the *Queen Charlotte*; or "Tom Bowling" who served as a bosun's mate on various ships for over 20 years. And women serving as men aboard ship were not limited to the British Navy.

Jeanette Colin was serving aboard the French ship *Achille* at the Battle of Trafalgar. She jumped overboard just before the *Achille* blew up and was fished out, stark naked, by the crew of the *HMS Pickle*. Apparently, when the French fleet left Cadiz she decided to stay with her husband. She dressed as a male and served with him in the battle until he was killed and she jumped over. The British crew supplied her with the means to make some clothes (dresses!) and gave her passage to Gibraltar where she disappeared and was never heard from again.

Besides the fact that Ms. Colin represents the grist for a heck of a good book, she also represents a most interesting category: wives who accompany their men to sea.

It was not uncommon for the wives of warrant and commissioned officers to accompany their husbands. There is one account of a Royal Navy ship in 1800 that went to sea with the wives of the captain, the master, the bosun, the sergeant of marines, six sailors, the bosun's daughter and the maid of the captain's wife. One captain took his new wife with him because he found out after marrying her that she couldn't control her spending and he was afraid she would squander all his savings if he left her ashore. These women, however, were not mere passengers.

It was not uncommon for them, including the captain's wife, to participate in the operation of the ship by serving as nurses and surgeon's assistants, or to do mending, cooking, washing and cleaning. Admiral John Jervis—a dominant figure in the Royal Navy at that time—was known to complain because these women tended to use too much fresh water in doing the wash; but it seems there wasn't much he could do about it.

But it was during battle that their more heroic side was presented. At a minimum, we know that women participated as identified women in combat roles at the Battle of the Nile and later at Trafalgar. We know this from applications for commemorative medals made by them for having fought in each of those battles. And we know it from a grave in Egypt in which a women is laid to rest in a dress, with a handkerchief over her face; but who died of wounds suffered in combat while a part of Nelson's Navy.

Unfortunately, what little we know of these women is based largely on second- and third-hand accounts and deductions, which brings us to our next problem.

In general, few seamen (and even fewer sea-women) in those days knew how to write. As a result, there exists few autobiographical accounts... with three exceptions.

Three women—three lady tars—left memoirs of their experiences serving *as men* in the Royal Navy. They were Hanna Snell (1723-1792), Mary Lacy (1740-1773+), and Mary Ann Talbot (1778-1808).

Hannah Snell: In 1746, when her husband left her and her child died, Hannah Snell borrowed a suit of clothes from her brother, James Gray, assumed his name, and began to search for her missing spouse. She joined the army of the Duke of Northumberland, but deserted over what she felt was an unjust punishment.

From there she moved to Portsmouth and joined Colonel Fraser's regiment of marines where she saw action at the Battle of Pondicherry, and where she received multiple wounds in the legs and one in her groin area. She allowed the doctors to treat the leg wounds, but didn't tell them about the ball in her groin. This she extracted herself.

In 1750 she returned to England, where she learned her husband had been executed for murder and she finally revealed her true identity. She then petitioned for a pension based on her war injuries, which was granted to her *as a woman*. At this time she also wrote her autobiography, *The Female Soldier*, which is presented here. The popularity of this book allowed her to supplement her pension with a stage career where she would appear in her uniform, doing military drills and singing songs.

Eventually she retired to the Midlands where she was remarried, widowed, married again and had a son. After many years as a street pedlar, selling buttons, lace, etc., she was committed to Bedlam, the infamous lunatic asylum, with "the most deplorable infirmity that can afflict human nature" [probably tertiary syphilis received from her first husband].

She died on February 8th, 1792 at the age of 86.

Much of Hannah Snell's life story can be verified. She was indeed on stage, she was married, she did have children, she was a street pedlar, she did die at Bedlam Hospital, and she did indeed receive a lifetime military pension for her wounds at Pondicherry. Unfortunately, some of the details in her account appear to be embellished—especially the flogging episodes. This lessens the perceived accuracy of the whole, but enough verifiable facts remain to give the tale over-all credibility.

The story of Mary Lacy, however, although less action-packed, is even more verifiable.

Mary Lacy: At age 19 Mary Lacy ran away from home, disguised herself as a man, assumed the name William Chandler, and joined the Royal Navy as a carpenter's servant. After nearly four years of service afloat, a bad case of rheumatism forced her to seek employment ashore; and, in 1763 she became an apprentice carpenter where she served for seven years.

At one point a friend of the family from her hometown in Ash came to live in Portsmouth where Mary was working. Instead of keeping Lacy's sexual identity a secret, this lady made it known far and wide that she was a female. This caused some of the other apprentices to want to examine her to determine the truth. Fortunately, two of the shipwrights took her aside where, in private, she admitted her disguise. Even more fortunately, these men decided to cover for her, assuring everyone that s/he was in fact not only a man but "...a man and a half to a great many." This coupled with "William Chandler's" reputation as a "ladies man" got her off the hook, and in 1770 she was granted her certificate as a fully qualified shipwright.

In 1771, however, her rheumatism returned with a vengeance, and she could no longer do the work. She applied to the Admiralty for a pension—but she did so under her true name, Mary Lacy. After some incredulity, the Admiralty granted her claim and she was awarded a pension of £20 per year.

Shortly thereafter she began work on her autobiography, *The Female Shipwright*. Unfortunately, after its publication she disappeared from sight. The exact location and date of her death is unknown, although we know it had to be after July 1, 1773 when she wrote the preface to her book.

Of the three accounts presented here, Mary Lacy's seems to be the most truthful—or perhaps I should say "unembellished," as all three accounts have verifiable facts in them. In her 1996 book, *Female Tars*,[1] Suzanne Stark checked out Mary Lacy's story with numerous ship's muster books and other 18th Century admiralty documents and pronounced her account as being accurate in all the key details.

Mary Ann Talbot: Ms. Talbot was allegedly an illegitimate child of Lord William Talbot, Baron of Hensol, but was cheated out of an inheritance that was due her.

In 1792 she wound up as the mistress of a Captain Bowen who took her aboard his ship disguised as his "footboy" under the name John Taylor. She saw service at the siege of Valenciennes, where Captain Bowen was killed. After his death she deserted the army, made her way to the coast, joined a French privateer, and was captured by a British Navy ship. The Royal Navy being chronically short of manpower, she was quickly pressed into service as a cabin boy aboard the *HMS Brunswick*. In this capacity, in 1794, she took part in the Battle of the Glorious First of June where she almost lost her leg to two serious wounds.

Upon discharge from the hospital she joined the HMS *Vesuvius*, a bomb ketch, where she was captured by the French and spent 18 months in Dunkirk Prison.

She returned to London in 1796, but was soon seized by a press-gang. She decided she had had enough. She revealed her identity and applied for a pension based on her service and wounds, which was eventually granted.

Her luck, however, went downhill after that. She soon found herself destitute and working as a household servant for publisher Robert S. Kirby. Astonished at her story, Kirby wrote it down and published it as the *Life and Surprising Adventures of Mary Ann Talbot in the Name of John Taylor*, which is the book presented here.

---

[1] For readers wishing more information on these topics, I highly recommend the following: Suzanne J. Stark's *Female Tars: Women Aboard Ship in the Age of Sail* (Naval Institute Press, 1996) and David Cordingly's *Women Sailors and Sailor's Women: An Untold Maritime History* (Random House, 2001).

She died on February 4, 1808.

Unfortunately, much of Mary Ann Talbot's story does not check out. In cases where there *should* be records, there simply is no mention of many of the people whose names she invokes. In addition, some of the events, dates, unit names, and so forth, are simply wrong. Does this mean that the story was a fabrication? No, not necessarily.

It is entirely possible that Mary Anne Talbot *did* serve time in the army and navy. It is equally possible that, in so doing, she *was* wounded in the leg, and very probably did time as a prisoner of war. Whether these wounds were sustained at "The Glorious First of June," for example, or whether she really served on the *Vesuvius,* or was captured and taken specifically to Dunkirk Prison, is another matter.

It is entirely possible that Mary Anne Talbot found herself in later life, like tens of thousands of her fellow veterans, without a job, without hope, and in desperate straits. If so, it is quite possible that she wrote her account—based on truth—simply to make enough money to survive. If that is the case, and if she concluded that a little story-line embellishment might make her book sell better, then I for one will not blame her.

* * * * *

Fireship Press is proud to make available—for the first time—the original text of all three of these astonishing autobiographies in one volume.

Enjoy!

Tom Grundner
Tucson, AZ

Hannah Snell

THE FEMALE SOLDIER

or

THE SURPRISING LIFE AND ADVENTURES

of

HANNAH SNELL

Born in the City of Worcester

Who took upon herself the name of James Gray; and, being deserted by her husband, put on men's apparel, and travelled to Coventry in quest of him, where she enlisted in Colonel Guise's Regiment of Foot, and marched with that regiment to Carlisle in the time of the rebellion in Scotland, showing what happened to her in that city, and her desertion from that regiment.

also

A full and true account of her enlisting afterwards into Fraser's Regiment of Marines, then at Portsmouth, and her being drafted out of that regiment and sent on board the Swallow sloop-of-war, one of Admiral Boscawen's squadron then bound for the East Indies. With the many vicissitudes of fortune she met with during that expedition, particularly at the siege of Pondicherry, where she received twelve wounds; likewise the surprising accident by which she came to hear of the death of her faithless husband, whom she went in quest of.

The whole containing

The most surprising incidents that have happened in any preceding age, wherein is laid open all her adventures, in men's clothes, for near five years without her sex being ever discovered.

LONDON

Printed for and sold by R. WALKER, the corner of Elliot's Court, in the Little Old Bailey, 1750.

TO THE PUBLIC

Notwithstanding the surprising adventures of this our British heroine, of whom the following pages fully and impartially treat, yet the oddity of her conduct for preserving her sex from being discovered, by which she preserved her virtue, was such that it demands not only respect but admiration; and as there is nothing to be found in the following sheets but what is matter-of-fact, it merits the countenance and approbation of every inhabitant of this great isle, especially the fair sex, for whom this treatise is chiefly intended; and the truth of which being confirmed by our heroine's affidavit made before the Right Hon. the Lord Mayor of the City of London, the said affidavit is hereunto annexed in order to prevent the public from being imposed upon by fictitious accounts.

Hannah Snell *born in the City of Worcester, in the year of our Lord 1723, and who took upon her the Name of James Gray, maketh oath, and saith, That she this Deponent served his present Majesty King George, as a Soldier and Sailor, from the 27th of November, One Thousand Seven Hundred and Forty-five, to the 9th of this instant June, and entered herself as a Marine in Capt.* Graham's *Company in Colonel* Fraser's *Regiment, and went on board the* Swallow, *his Majesty's Sloop of War, to the East* Indies, *belonging to Admiral Boscawen's Squadron, where this Deponent was present at the Siege of Pondicherry, and all the other Sieges during that Expedition, in which she received Twelve Wounds, some of which were dangerous, and was put into the Hospital for cure of the same, and returned into* England *in the* Eltham *Man of War, Capt.* Lloyd *Commander, without the least Discovery of her Sex.*

And this Deponent further maketh Oath, and saith, That she has delivered to Robert Walker, *Printer, in the* Little Old Bailey, London, *a full and true Account of the many surprising Incidents, and wonderful Hardships she underwent during the Time she was in his Majesty's Service as aforesaid, to be by him printed and published.*

And this Deponent lastly saith, That she has not given the least Hint of her surprising Adventures to any other Person, nor will she, this Deponent, give the least Account thereof, to any Person whatsoever, to be printed or published, save and except the above-mentioned Robert Walker.

Sworn before me this 27th day
 of June, 1750, at Goldsmith's
 Hall, London.

      J. Blachford, Mayor.

Witness   Her
 Susannah Gray,   Hannah + Snell.
Sister of the said Hannah Snell.   Mark
 T. Edwards.

The Life and Adventures of Hannah Snell

IN this dastardly age of the world, when effeminacy and debauchery have taken place of the love of glory and that noble ardour after warlike exploits which flowed in the bosoms of our ancestors, genuine heroism, or rather an extraordinary degree of courage, are prodigies among men. What age, for instance, produces a Charles of Sweden, a Marlborough, or a Prince Eugene? These are *rara aves in terris*, and when they appear they seem particularly designed by Heaven for protecting the rights of injured nations against oppression, securing the privileges of innocence from the dire assault of prey and rapine, and, in a word, vindicating the common prerogatives of human nature from the fatal effects of brutal rage, the love of conquest, and an insatiable lust after power. The amazing benefit arising to mankind from such illustrious and exalted characters is perhaps the principal reason why they attract the eyes and command the attention of all who hear them, even in quarters of the world far remote from their influence and sphere of action, why they are the subjects of the poet's song, the founders of the historian's narration, and the objects of the painter's pencil, all which have a tendency to transmit their names with immortal glory to the latest ages, and will for ever eternise their memories when their bodies are mouldered into dust and mingled with their parent earth. Perhaps their rarity may also contribute in a great measure to the esteem and veneration which the world thinks fit to pay them, but sure if heroism, fortitude, and a soul equal to all the glorious acts of war and conquest

1

are things so rare and so much admired among women! In short, we may on this occasion, without any hyperbole, use the words of Solomon and say, "One man among a thousand have I found, but among women not." However, though courage and warlike expeditions are not the provinces by the world allotted to women since the days of the Amazons, yet the female sex is far from being destitute of heroism. Cleopatra headed a noble army against Mark Anthony, the greatest warrior of his times. Semiramis was not inferior to her in courage. The Arcadian shepherdesses are as memorable for their contempt of danger as their darling and beloved swains. But among all our heroines none comes more immediately under our cognisance, nor perhaps more merits our attention, than the remarkable Hannah Snell, whose history is highly interesting, both on account of the variety of amazing incidents and the untainted veracity with which it is attended. Some people, guided by the suggestions of reason and a sound understanding, have foolishly imagined that persons of low and undistinguished births hardly ever raised themselves to the summit of glory and renown; but they will find themselves widely mistaken when they reflect on a Kouli-Kan, a Cromwell, and many others I could mention. But if this observation had the smallest foundation either in nature or in the course of human experience, from the most remote to the present age, yet its force does by no means extend to Hannah Snell, the heroine of the subsequent narrative; for though her immediate progenitors were but low in the world, when compared with dukes, earls, and generals, yet she had the seeds of heroism, courage, and patriotism transferred to her from her ancestors, as will appear from the following account of her genealogy.

Hannah Snell was born in Fryer Street, in the parish of St. Hellen's, in the city of Worcester, on the 23rd day of April, 1723. Her parents, though not immensely rich by the hereditary gifts of fortune, yet secured a competency which not only placed them above contempt, but also enabled them to bring up and educate a numerous family, none of whom have miscarried for want either of sufficient learning from masters or salutary advices and virtuous examples from their parents. And though Mrs. Hannah Snell did not while she was at school learn to write, yet she made a tolerable progress in the other part of education common to her sex, and could read exceeding well.

Though the father of our heroine was no more than a hosier and dyer, yet he was the son of the illustrious Captain-Lieutenant Sam Snell, for so I may, or rather must, call him, since with intrepidity he stood the brunt of the wars in the latter end of King William's reign, signalised himself at the taking of Dunkirk, and served faithfully in the English army during Queen Anne's wars.

This Captain-Lieutenant Snell, the grandfather of our heroine, entered as a volunteer in King William's reign, and was at the taking of Dunkirk; there his captain-lieutenant was killed by a shot fired through the wicket by the Governor, upon which he fired and killed the Governor. When the general of the army was informed thereof he called him and asked him what preferment he desired. His answer was that he chose to accept of that commission which was become vacant by the death of the captain-lieutenant, which he was immediately preferred to, and took upon him the command as such. After the surrender of Dunkirk, where he received several dangerous wounds, he returned to England, where he had the proffer of a very handsome pension in Chelsea College; but coveting fresh glory and new trophies of conquest, he entreated his Grace the Duke of Marlborough to let him go abroad at the beginning of Queen Anne's wars, which was complied with, and he was accordingly preferred to be captain-lieutenant in the regiment of Welsh Fusiliers, and was present at the battle of Blenheim, where he received several wounds; but at the end of that campaign he came over to England.

After he was perfectly cured of all his wounds, he requested of the Duke of Marlborough that he might make another campaign in Flanders, which request his Grace complied with, and at the battle of Malplaquet he received a mortal wound, from whence he was carried to Ghent, where he died; this last was the twenty-second bloody battle in which he had been engaged, and which he generously launched out into upon the sublime motives, liberty and property. This gentleman's character must appear the more conspicuous when we observe how he advanced himself by merit from a private cadet to the rank he held at his death; and had it not been for his over-modest and generous sentiments he might have been preferred to a much higher rank; but the Englishman prevailed above self-interest.

The son of this illustrious man of whom we have here treated, and father of our heroine, was possessed of many excellent gifts, particularly courage, for which he was distinguished; yet never had an opportunity of displaying his bravery in the field of battle, his genius leading him another way, to wit, trade, into which he entered very young, and prospered in the world, married to his liking, and in a few years saw himself the father of nine promising children, three of which were sons and six daughters, all of whom, save one daughter, were either soldiers or sailors or intermarried with them. The eldest of the sons, Samuel Snell, incapable of re-straint and void of all fear, enlisted himself a soldier in Lord Robert Manners's company in the First Regiment of Foot Guards, commanded by his Royal Highness the Duke of Cumberland, when he was drafted to go for Flanders, where he received his mortal wound at the battle of Fontenoy, and being sent to the hospital at Doway, he there expired.

Though the daughters were by those who knew them accounted genteel, amiable women, both on account of their persons and their virtue, yet I shall pass over the characters of five of them in silence, and only take notice of that of Hannah, the youngest of them but one, who is the heroine of this subject. It is a common thing to observe a family dispersed, when the heads of that family are either laid in their graves or by accidental calamities rendered incapable of supporting it longer. Accordingly, when the father and mother of Hannah died, she came up to London, and arrived in town on Christmas Day, 1710, and resided for some time with her sister in Ship Street, Wapping.

There is one thing so very remarkable in the martial disposition of Hannah Snell, even in her juvenile years, the account of which, being so facetious, shall recommend it to the perusal of the reader.

Hannah, when she was scarce ten years of age, had the seeds of heroism, as it were, implanted in her nature, and she used often to declare to her companions that she would be a soldier if she lived; and as a preceding testimony of this truth she formed a company of young soldiers among her playfellows, and of which she was chief commander, at the head of whom she often appeared, and was used to parade the whole city of Worcester. This body of young volunteers were admired all over the town, and they were styled "Young Amazon Snell's Company." And this martial spirit grew up with her, until it carried her through the many scenes and vicissitudes she encountered for nigh five years, as is fully and impartially related in this treatise of her adventures.

Some time after she came to London she contracted an acquaintance with one James Summs, a sailor, who was a Dutchman; this acquaintance was gradually improved into a familiarity, and this familiarity soon created a mutual though not a criminal passion, for in a little time Summs made his addresses to her as a lover, and gained her consent and was married to her at the Fleet on the 6th day of January, 1743-44. But all his promises of friendship proved instances of the highest perfidy, and he turned out the worst and most unnatural of husbands; since, though she had charms enough to captivate the heart and secure the affection of any reasonable man, yet she was despised and contemned by her husband, who not only kept criminal company with other women of the basest characters, but also made away with her things in order to support his luxury and the daily expenses of his whores. During this unlucky period of the husband's debauchery she, poor woman, proved with child, and at that time felt all the shocks of poverty without exposing her necessities to her nearest friends. But at last her pregnancy laid the foundation for her passing through all the scenes through which she has wandered; for when she was seven months gone with child, her perfidious husband, finding himself deeply involved in debt, made an elopement from her. Notwithstanding these her calamities, she patiently bore herself up under them, and in two months after her husband's departure was delivered of a daughter, which lived no more than seven months, and was decently interred at her own expense at St. George's parish, in Middlesex.

From the time of her husband's elopement till the time she put on man's clothes she continued with her sister, who is married to one James Gray, a house carpenter, in Ship Street, Wapping, and from whence she took her departure unknown to any, and was never heard of until her return, and with whom she now dwells.

As she was now free from all the ties arising from nature and consanguinity, she thought herself privileged to roam in quest of the man who, without reason, had injured her so much, for there are no bounds to be set either to love, jealousy, or hatred in the female mind. That she might execute her designs with the better grace and the more success, she boldly commenced a man—at least in her dress—and no doubt she had a right to do so, since she had the real soul of a man in her breast. Dismayed at no accidents, and giving a full scope to the genuine bent of her heart, she put on a suit of her brother-in-law Mr. James Gray's clothes, assumed his name, and set out on the 23rd of November, 1745, and travelled to Coventry with a view of finding her husband, where she enlisted on the 27th of the said month of November in General Guise's regiment, and in the company belonging to Captain Miller.

When she left London she had a sufficiency of money to bear her expenses to Coventry, where she arrived about three in the afternoon the fourth day after she left her sister's house; and as she walked through the street, the first observation she made was a crowd of people who stood where there was a drum beating up for soldiers, on which she stood to look at them, when a corporal, whose name was Samuel Bishop, seeing her stand in the street came to her (not knowing but she was a man, being in that apparel) and asked her if she would not go for a soldier, with all the other delusive speeches used on such occasions. However indifferent this proposal was to her, he by force put a piece of money into her hand, and insisted she should drink with him. This astonished her much, and she would have returned him his money, but he insisted she should go with him to his captain; and accordingly they went to the place of their rendezvous, which was "The Bear and Bagged Staff," where Captain Miller was. When she appeared before him, he examined her of her occupation, etc., but she, not willing to discover herself, said but little; whereupon, he insisted she should go before a magistrate; and the corporal being called for, he said he had given her the king's picture, therefore she was liable to serve his Majesty. She, not affrighted at their threats, told them she was as ready and as willing as any of them to serve her king and country, and then boldly enlisted with Captain Miller, and took from him one guinea and five shillings in silver, and was the next day, November 27th, sworn in before a magistrate.

Being now a soldier, she was billeted on one Mr. Lucas, in Little Park Street, Coventry, and was attended there by Corporal Bishop and some other of the soldiers, where she was civilly used. After they had drank together and the reckoning called, the new recruit was to pay all, which she readily complied with, and they all took their leave for that night.

Being now alone in her quarters she sat down near the fire, where she spent some time in reflecting on what had passed, as also what might be the event of this her new enterprise. But a new and unexpected accident happened. Her foot being near the fire, a coal fell out of the grate into her shoe, which so burned her foot that she was not able to put her shoe on for many days, which accident prevented her attending on the drum (as is usual for new recruits) whilst in Coventry.

She stayed in this city about three weeks, during which time she made it her chief care to inquire for her husband (only as an old acquaintance), but could hear nothing of him, which disappointment animated her spirits and made her resolve to pursue her fate, let whatever should befall her, and fully determined to keep her sex concealed. And as the North was then the seat of war, and the regiment being at Carlisle, she, in company with seventeen other recruits from Coventry, marched under the care of Corporal Bishop, and carried with them two standards and colours. During this march she was in all appearance as cheerful and as little weary as any of her fellow-travellers, and performed that long journey in twenty-two days.

On her arrival at Carlisle she was instructed in the military exercise, which she now performed with as much skill and dexterity as any sergeant or corporal in his Majesty's service. But here, as Fortune is often a foe to the distressed, she met with a very discouraging circumstance; for her sergeant, whose name was Davis, having a criminal inclination for a young woman in that town, looked upon this our female heroine (a common soldier in the company) as a proper person for assisting him in this his vicious intrigue, therefore disclosed to her this bosom secret, and desired her endeavours in promoting this end. However, this open discovery caused a sudden emotion in her mind, her virtuous soul abhorred with a becoming detestation the criminal intention; yet to prevent the ill consequences that she foresaw must ensue from her refusal of complying with his request, she promised to use her endeavours in his behalf. But instead of acting the pimp, she went and disclosed the whole matter to the young woman, and warned her against the impending danger; which act of virtue and generosity in a soldier gained her the esteem and confidence of this young woman, who took great delight in her company, and seldom a day passed but they were together, having cultivated an intimacy and friendship with each other. Davis, going one day to make his addresses to his mistress, met with an unexpected repulse, which unusual treatment made him suspect our female soldier. Jealousy that moment took possession of his guilty breast, and he imagined that instead of befriending him in his amours, she had become his rival, and had gained her over to her inclinations. These reflections troubled him much; revenge reigned triumphant in his breast, and how to punish her was his chief aim. He took hold of the earliest opportunity, and accused her before the commanding officer for neglect of duty, upon which she was sentenced to receive six hundred lashes, five hundred of which she received, having her hands tied to the castle gates, for a crime which Nature put it out of her power to perpetrate, and had undergone the punishment of the other hundred had it not been for the intercession of some of the officers. Though this severe punishment was, doubtless, very unjustly inflicted upon her, yet that jealous-pated fellow, Davis, still looked upon her with an eye of anger and resentment, and used his utmost endeavours to mortify her by putting her on such duties as he imagined would be most difficult and disagreeable to her. To compensate, however, in some measure, for these numerous testimonies of his partial spleen and ill-nature, her female friend looked upon her with an eye of tenderness and affection, and cheerfully embraced every opportunity that offered of being serviceable to her, and to testifying a grateful sense of all the favours and acts of friendship that she had shown her.

It was not long, however, after this unhappy adventure before another accident occurred that was entirely unforeseen, and gave our heroine no small uneasiness. A fresh recruit, it seems, came into the regiment, and who should this happen to be but one George Beck, a brisk, lively young fellow, a carpenter by profession, who was born in the city of Worcester, and had travelled up to London in hopes of better employment than what he could meet with in the country. And where should this young runaway take up his first quarters but at her brother's and sister's house, and who was actually a lodger with them at the very time that our heroine brushed off the ground in masquerade. Upon the first sight of him she grew restless and uneasy, and lived for some time under the dreadful apprehensions of being blown, and exposed to public ridicule.

This, however, was nothing more than mere conjecture, for the fellow had, in reality, no notion of who she was; but this occurrence, together with the severe treatment that she had met with from the sergeant, made her come to an absolute determination within herself to desert at all adventures, for no dread of punishment was equal to that of shame, which she must have unavoidably undergone had her sex been once discovered.

Having taken all the prudent measures imaginable for the accomplishment of her secret intentions, she very ingeniously communicated the important secret to the young woman with whom she had contracted such an intimate acquaintance as has been related,

Though her friend expostulated with her for some time on the dangers to which she would be exposed, in case of her being retaken by any of her comrades, and used all the arguments she could think of to prevail on her to stay where she was, and decline all thoughts of so rash a resolution, and though she was still the more strenuous, as she was very loth to lose the conversation of so worthy a friend and agreeable companion, yet, upon mature deliberation, she at last not only consented to her flight, but furnished her with all the money she could conveniently spare, that she might enjoy herself on the road, and not be at a loss for the conveniences of life till she had secured herself some proper place of shelter and protection.

Well, the dangerous project is now actually carried into execution. But, alas, with what anxieties of mind must it be attended!

What pain must she unavoidably feel upon a retrospection of all the past scenes of her life! But a recapitulation of incidents, though doubtless very affecting, would be a too tedious digression, and a kind of imposition on the reader. We shall therefore, without any farther preamble, resume the story of this our female adventurer.

No sooner had she taken her final adieu of her affectionate and benevolent friend, but she steered her course on foot for Portsmouth, and determined to embrace the first opportunity for exchanging her regimentals for any other habiliments, however mean and despicable, that she might in her travels be less suspected to be a deserter.

When she had got about a mile out of Carlisle she observed some people picking and bagging peas in a field. And seeing their clothes lying at a distance, she pulled off her own regimental coat, and left it there, and took an old coat for it belonging to one of the men, and then she proceeded to Portsmouth, that being the place she designed to go for.

She was about a month in travelling from Carlisle to Portsmouth, but nothing material happened, except her being very much fatigued and tired in her long journey, and the dread of being pursued by a party from the regiment or suspected as a deserter.

During her residence at Portsmouth, which was not a month, she contracted an intimate acquaintance with one Catherine, an honest tailor's daughter of the place, whose sister was bedfellow, by marriage, with one Mr. Cunningham, who happened to be drum-major of the very regiment to which she last belonged.

Here she took up her place of abode for some time, and as Mrs. Catherine had no nun's flesh about her, she had by consequence no aversion to the conversation of one who seemed to cast an amorous glance on her now and then, and treated her with the utmost decency and good manners. Some particular circumstances occurred during our Hannah's residence at Portsmouth in this family, that were humorous enough, and worthy of the reader's attention; but we shall refer to them for his amusement in some more proper place.

Our heroine, however, disdaining a life thus led at home in indolence and ease, resolved still to go abroad. And in order thereto once more boldly enlisted herself for a marine in Captain Graham's company, belonging to Colonel Fraser's regiment.

She had not been enlisted above three weeks in this regiment of marines, but a draft was made out of the same to go on board

Admiral Boscawen's fleet to the East Indies; upon which many of those who were ordered for that draft deserted, and went off; so that she, though so young in the regiment, was ordered on board the Swallow, sloop-of-war, Captain Bosier, to go on that expedition.

She had not been long on board before she made herself remarkable by her dexterity and address. As she was very tractable, sprightly, and willing, she soon was caressed by her messmates, for whom she would very readily either wash or mend their linen, or stand cook, as occasion required. By these little good offices, cheerfully and frequently performed, she distinguished herself so far that Mr. Wyegate, one of the lieutenants of the marines, took notice of her and asked her in a very kindly manner to become one of their mess.

As this offer could be no ways disagreeable, the reader may easily imagine it was readily complied with; and from thenceforward she acted in the capacity of their boy, and by her knack in cookery and her care in washing their linen and mending their shirts, etc., whenever they wanted repairing, she became a favourite amongst them all, and was looked upon as the most handy boy belonging to the sloop.

In case of an engagement, she was to be stationed upon the quarter-deck, and, as one of the after-guard, her business was to fight and do what mischief she could with the small arms which they had on board, so that she was always in readiness in case of an attack.

Young as she was she was obliged to keep her watch every other four hours, and though never on board any ship before, through her natural intrepidity and peculiar sprightliness she became, with a very little instruction, a little tar of note.

When they first weighed anchor the ship was as serene and the wind as favourable for their intended voyage as ever hearts could wish. Fortune, however, is as fickle as she is fair, for the weather began to alter and the wind turned against them so that all the fleet were obliged to put into Torbay; but the next day after they had put into this bay, the wind coming somewhat more favourable, Admiral Boscawen's ship fired a gun as a signal for all the fleet to get ready to sail, and accordingly, on the 11th of November, the whole fleet set sail, and next day passed the Start Point, and got into the Bay of Biscay.

The second day after they had got into the Bay of Biscay a hurricane came and separated the fleet, and the danger they were in must be apparent to every reader from the following circumstance; for notwithstanding the Swallow sloop, which our heroine was on board of, was as tight and well built a vessel as any one that ever belonged to his Majesty's navy of her burthen, yet the weather was so tempestuous and the water beat so hard upon her that she sprung her mainmast, and, moreover, not only lost her jib-boom, but her two topmasts also. In this tattered and forlorn condition, however, through the goodness of Providence, they arrived at last, though with abundance of difficulty, in safety at the port of Lisbon.

After a storm, we say, comes a calm; and after fatigue and sorrow ensues a scene of mirth. In this port they were apprehensive of no manner of danger, and here they indulged themselves in all the amusements the place could afford for about three weeks or a month successively, it requiring that time at least to repair the damages which the sloop had sustained in her passage, to render her capable of pursuing her intended voyage,

At their arrival in this port they found the Vigilant and Pembroke, men-of-war, which had likewise sustained great damages by the hurricane they had met with in the before-mentioned Bay of Biscay, and where two of the fleet that accompanied them from Portsmouth had put in for shelter and refitment some time before them.

Though our heroine went ashore with her master, and was quartered at one Mrs. Poor's, who kept a kind of tavern or punch-house, for three weeks successively, yet during all that time, it seems, our Hannah lived very reserved; and though the maid of the house was a very pretty lass, yet no private amour was carried on, or any other adventure occurred that is worth inserting into this our narrative. Here, indeed, she lived at ease, and wanted for nothing the house afforded. Pleasure, however, never comes sincere to man, for whilst Jove holds him out the bowl of joy, 'tis dashed (as Mr. Dryden tells us) with gall, by some left-handed god.

The Swallow being now new rigged, she, with our heroine and the rest of the crew, sailed from Lisbon in company with the Vigilant in order to join the admiral's squadron.

They were all alive and merry at their setting out, and had quite forgot the fatigues of the storm that they had weathered with so much danger; but what has been may happen again, and the very first night after their departure a fresh storm arose as violent as the former, wherein the Swallow not only lost sight of her companion the Vigilant, but sprung her new mainmast likewise. In short, she lost the best part of her new rigging, and was damaged to that degree, even in her hold, that all hands were obliged to be busy, and the pump was for ever going. Whatever idea some people may have of such work, we can assure them it is laborious enough of all conscience; but all took their turns with great readiness and indefatigable industry, as they were sensible there was no other remedy reserved for their preservation.

Such a series of misfortunes, some would imagine, was sufficient to shake the resolution and cool the courage of the most able and experienced sailor, but this had no such influence on our intrepid heroine; it proved only a motive for her being more active and industrious both for her own safety and that of her fellow-sufferers. In short, as the vessel, to all outward appearance, was in a sinking condition, she pumped in her turn with as much vigour as any of them; and at other times, where the judgement of the sailor required to be exerted, no office, howsoever dangerous, would she decline; and, in a word, she rendered herself so conspicuous both by her skill and intrepidity, that she was allowed to be a very useful hand on board.

The Pembroke, man-of-war, who was with her and the Vigilant at Lisbon, and refitted, they left there, she having received fresh damage in the Tagus in weighing her anchors, in order to proceed on her voyage with them.

After this narrow escape the Swallow made the best of her way to Gibraltar; and as soon as they arrived at that port our heroine went on shore with her master, Mr. Richard Wyegate, lieutenant of the marines, who was very greatly indisposed, in order to attend him, and to do him all the good offices that lay within her power. Though this stay on shore was but short, yet while they did tarry there they took up their quarters at one Mr. Davis's, on the hill, there by the great tenderness of the landlady, and the additional attendance of our heroine, Mr. Wyegate, though not absolutely recovered, was out of all danger before their departure from that port.

No sooner was the ship refitted here but she set sail for the Madeira Islands, where she took in such a quantity of wines and other provisions as was thought requisite for the immediate pursuit of her intended voyage. Though thus plentifully supplied with all the conveniences they could well wish for with respect to eating and drinking, yet they had but a few hands on board, and as Fortune favours the bold and daring, that deficiency likewise was happily supplied by the accidental arrival of the Sheerness, privateer, belonging to Bristol, through the generous assistance of the commander.

From this port they made the best of their way for the Cape of Good Hope, but in their passage they met with such hard weather, and other unforeseen misfortunes, that, notwithstanding all their supplies, they were reduced to short allowance, and within a small compass of time to a deduction of one-half part. But what was still worse than all the rest, the residue or remainder of their provisions was very salt and very bad. And to render bad still worse, there was such a scarcity of water on board that for some considerable time their quota was reduced to the short pittance of a pint a day, which though doubtless was a sore mortification yet our heroine was no ways dejected, but sat down contented, as she had neighbour's fare; and no sooner were they arrived at the Cape, but to their great satisfaction, they met with the admiral there on board the Namur, and all the rest of the fleet.

As soon as the Swallow sloop arrived safe at the Cape, the admiral as well as all the rest of the fleet were exceedingly overjoyed, as she was expected to have been a lost ship; and in a few days they all set sail for the French islands, on the east of Madagascar.

But before I proceed any further I think it proper to inform the reader that while they were ashore at St. Jago, one of the Cape de Verd islands, they were supplied with great plenty of poultry, goats, hogs, etc., where old clothes, and mere rags too, together with a few halfpenny rings, knives, and scissors, which could not cost in England about twopence apiece, being given in exchange for eight, ten, or a dozen fowls, and a turkey for a halfpenny ring.

But now to proceed. Dangers and distress when once over are seldom much reflected on afterwards. And as our heroine could not prove so happy as to meet with her perfidious husband, and as she had now the pleasure of seeing the fleet all riding together, she was determined, if possible, to acquire some honour in the expedition, and so distinguish herself by her intrepid behaviour. And a favourable opportunity soon offered itself; for it was not long after they set sail from the Cape before they arrived at Morusus, where they made their first attack. And our Hannah, though then but a raw marine, exerted herself so far that she procured the love and esteem of all her fellow-soldiers.

This attack, however, proved but of short duration; for the admiral, finding their utmost efforts altogether ineffectual and having a tender regard for his men as well as his ships, abandoned the place and set sail directly for Fort St. David's, where they safely arrived in a very short time.

There the marines were disembarked, and, having joined the English army, in about three weeks they arrived at Areacopong, where they directly encamped, with a firm resolution to lay siege to the place, and, if possible, to take it by storm.

This adventure animated our heroine afresh, and gave her a fairer opportunity than before of displaying her intrepidity and thirst after glory, and she embraced it in such a manner as that she gained the applause of all her officers.

For nine days successively they carried on the siege, and met with a very vigourous repulse; but on the 10th, a shell from the English falling very fortunately on the enemy's magazines, it blew up at once, by which means they were reduced to the necessity of surrendering at discretion.

Before we proceed to their march to Pondicherry, which is but a few leagues distant from the place before mentioned, it may not prove, perhaps, any disagreeable digression to the reader to pause awhile in order to reflect on the various hardships, fatigues, and dangers which our young adventurer had run through from her first appearance in masquerade to the time of her arrival in Asia. What a sea of troubles was this unfortunate wanderer involved in, even before her desertion! Imagine her mind harassed and perplexed with the anxious thoughts of a barbarous, ungrateful, and perfidious husband, who had broke through all ties, all obligations both civil and sacred, and had drove her to the very brink of despair. Imagine her tormented with the anxious thoughts of being obliged, contrary to her inclinations, to connive at, and seem, at least, to favour the vicious views of her superior officer, to act as his pimp or pander, in order to carry an immodest and shameful intrigue into execution; though, indeed, being secretly animated by more generous principles, she proved instrumental to his disappointment and the preservation of the young innocent maid, whom he proposed should fall a victim to his brutal passions. Imagine the gratitude of the maid, who, through our Hannah's secret discovery of the snares that were laid to entrap her, to her utter ruin and destruction, found means to avoid the temptation and guard herself against the ravenous wolf that was ready to devour her. Imagine the strict and sincere friendship that was thus contracted between those two virtuous persons, and which in all probability would have lasted till death had not hard fate ordained their involuntary separation. Imagine her labouring under the odious suspicions of her jealous-pated sergeant, and the various marks of infamy, as well as the agonising pains she underwent, as the sole result of his unjust anger and resentment. Imagine, however, in all this her distress, how her female friend not only very generously sympathised with her in the ill-treatment that she met with, but administered all the relief that was in her power under her unhappy dilemma. Imagine the thousand restless and uneasy thoughts that must unavoidably arise in our adventurer's mind when she apprehended a discovery of her sex, and being exposed to the insults and sneers of her comrades by perceiving one in her regiment whom she knew so perfectly well. What agonies of mind must she labour under when she formed the dangerous project of her desertion! And how distracted in her thoughts, even after she had carried her scheme into actual execution, for fear of being re-taken! The recollection of all these perplexing incidents must, we imagine, touch the hearts of our readers in some measure, and incline them, if they have any humanity, to commiserate the deplorable circumstances of our unhappy female adventurer.

Let us once more cast our eye back on the numerous sorrows and afflictions which she laboured under after her second enlisting and becoming a marine. What storms and hurricanes had she weathered! How incessantly did she labour at the pump in hopes to save her life and a poor shattered vessel, to all appearance ready to sink at once down to the bottom of the ocean! What pains must she undergo in regard to hunger and thirst when, for seventeen weeks successively, she lived on short allowance in her passage from the Madeiras to the Cape of Good Hope! Then, again, what fatigues, what dangers must she run through when she and her comrades made their attacks to no manner of purpose on the enemy's fortified towns, some of which were absolutely impregnable; when bombshells and cannons were displaying death every moment! If, now, the reflections on such gloomy occurrences as these are sufficient to shake the temper of the most intrepid soldier that ever appeared in battle, we may easily imagine they must have a much stronger influence over a female mind!

But to quit this long digression, and pursue the thread of our narrative, having marched within three miles of Pondicherry, they encamped, Admiral Boscawen, at that time, being both their admiral and general. Here Major Mountpleasant, the general, and the rest of the commanders, in a council of war, informed them that they were come to a resolution to storm the place; and in order thereto the ships, in the first place, fired upon the fort, a great part of which time they lay middle-deep in water in their trenches.

This bold attack lasted eleven weeks successively, and during a great part of the time they had no bread at all, and their principal subsistence was a little rice. To this misfortune we must add that abundance of their men were both wounded and killed, by reason of the numberless bombs and shells that were thrown in amongst them.

As one of our heroine's comrades could write well, he took a short journal of the siege of Pondicherry, an exact copy of which he gave her, and is here inserted to show the great fatigues and hardships not only our Hannah Snell went through, but the whole army.

A Short but Particular Journal of the Siege of Pondicherry

July 28, 1748: The fleet arrived at Port St. David (an English settlement on the coast of Choromandel, in the East Indies), and on the 30th landed all our soldiers, and the next day all the marines of the squadron, who encamped near the Garden House, about two miles from Fort St. David.

August 10th: Having got all our artillery stores on shore, the army began their march towards Pondicherry, which lies sixteen miles to the northward of Fort St. David, our army consisting of about 2,500 foot and 80 horse, Europeans, and about 1,600 peons and seapies, which are Indians that bear arms, and about 1,600 blacks as porters, to supply the place of wagons—these are called coolies. The next day after our army decamped, the fleet anchored off Areacopong, in sight of our army, who was on their march towards that place.

Areacopong is a fort of twelve guns, in possession of the French, and commands the passage of a river, which we were obliged to ford to get to Pondicherry, from which place it is distant about four miles, betwixt it and Fort St. David, so that the reduction of this fort was of the greatest consequence, as well to cover our passage over the river as to open a communication with Fort St. David and the army. As it was by nature and art surprisingly strong, every one thought we should lose a great many more men to master it than we did.

The next day a detachment of foot, being the piquet guards, supported by the grenadiers of the army, attacked the fort, but were repulsed with the loss of thirty men killed and wounded, amongst whom were killed a captain and lieutenant of grenadiers, and two lieutenants wounded, with Major Goodier of the train, who lost his leg, and afterwards died of the wounds. This repulse showing it impracticable to take the fort without battering cannon,

16

and there being none in the army, two were landed the same evening from the fleet, and next morning 1,100 seamen were put on shore, who had been well disciplined in the firelock exercise, etc. These were formed into eleven companies under the command of their own officers, lieutenants being as captains, and midshipmen as lieutenants and ensigns, and the whole battalion commanded by Captain Lloyd, of the Deal Castle, who acted as colonel.

August 16th: Opened the trenches before Areacopong; the 17th erected a battery; the 18th carried on our approaches near the fort, which the enemy perceiving the morning of the 19th, made a sally of almost the whole garrison, as well horse as foot, but were beat back with great loss; however, we had a major and captain taken prisoners by the indiscretion of their men; otherwise our loss was but small. In the height of this skirmish a battery the enemy had thrown up the opposite side of the river, which flanked our trenches and greatly incommoded us, blew up by accident, and killed forty-eight men, with the officer that commanded them. Those in Areacopong seeing that, and fearing their retreat might be cut off from Pondicherry, our lines being all under arms on their march towards them, quitted the fort and passed the river under their own cannon, leaving only a few men to make a show of defence and to protect the main body's retreat, who likewise quitted the fort as soon as the others had got safe over the river, and blew up the bastion that faced it, to prevent our turning the guns thereof upon themselves. Our forces directly took possession of the fort, but the garrison by this time had passed the river and got safe under the cannon of Pondicherry.

August 23rd: The camp moved under the walls of Areacopong, and lay three or four days to refresh our men, in "which time the fort was repaired by our coolies, and then moved towards Pondicherry, leaving a small garrison in Areacopong, and encamped three miles to the north-west of it, having a communication open with Fort St. David and the fleet, which was anchored to the northward of the town.

August 29th: At night opened the trenches before the town and began our approaches; the 31st the garrison made a great sally, but were beat back with the loss of upwards of one hundred men by their own account, amongst whom was M. Peridie, their principal military officer and chief engineer; on our side a captain and a few private men were killed and wounded.

The French had a barrier about a mile from the walls of the town, composed of redoubts of earth, eighty yards distant from each other, which quite encompassed the town, and betwixt these redoubts the trees grew so thick that made it very difficult to penetrate through them, and must consequently have done us great mischief if the French had defended them; but they, fearing we might cut off their retreat from the town, quitted it on our approach, which we took possession of, and cast up an entrenchment within the gate to secure the guard we from that time kept there.

September 4th: Our Peons intercepted and brought into camp 102 French prisoners, which were coming from Mayor, a settlement they had on the coast of Malabar, to reinforce the garrison of Pondicherry.

September 9th: Erected two small batteries, which soon silenced two mud batteries that the enemy had thrown up on the flanks of our works, and which had greatly incommoded us and killed us a great many men. After these batteries were silenced, our two batteries and a bomb battery of four mortars kept playing on the gates and several parts of the town, which prevented their sallying out and impeding our works.

We having carried on our entrenchment as far as was thought requisite, and indeed as far as we could well do, on account of a standing water which was on our front, began to erect blinds for our batteries, but for want of a greater number of men and the heavy rains which began now to fall and quite filled our trenches, the land being very low, and the incessant fire of shot and shells from the town, it was the 25th before our batteries were finished, in which interim little happened worth notice, only a skirmish or two near the waterside, betwixt the enemy and some parties of ours which were bringing up stores that had been landed from the fleet, in which several men were killed on both sides, amongst whom was Lieutenant Campbell, a brave officer in one of the independent companies.

September 25th: Unmasked two batteries, one on the right of eight guns, the other on the left of four, of 21-pounders each, which, with the bomb batteries, where we had thirty mortars, great and small, mounted, began to play on two bastions and the citadel of the town. The bomb-ketch likewise kept an incessant fire from the time of our first opening the trenches.

The 27th: The fleet, consisting of ten sail-of-the-line, viz., the Namur of 74 guns, the Vigilant 64, the Pembroke 60, the York 60, the Exeter 60, the Deptford 60, the Ruby 50, the Chester 50, the Harwich 50, and the Eltham 40, warped in near the bastions of the town that lay towards the sea, and kept an incessant fire all day; and I believe a greater cannonading was never known, the fleet firing that day upwards of 18,000 shot. Our fire from the ships being so great obliged the enemy to quit the guns, so that they did us little or no damage, we only losing three men in the fleet, of whom one was Captain Adams, a brave young gentleman, related to Lord Anson; but on the land side we did not come off so well, for the enemy's fire being greatly superior to ours, killed us a great many men and dismounted several of our guns, they having thrown up mud batteries on the glacis of the town and mounted a great many guns on the curtain betwixt the bastions; and though we knocked down most of the merlons of two bastions, and dismounted the guns, yet they soon fired from thence again, making use of cotton bags, fascines, gabions, etc., to supply the place of merlons, and the walls were so thick that we made no breach, but just at the top, though we kept a continual firing for upwards of a week, our batteries being at too great a distance to batter in breach (especially with such walls as we had to deal with), and there being, as I said before, a standing water in our front 150 yards, so that we could have no dry ground to erect them on unless we carried our approaches to the very glacis of the town, which was thought to be a work of very great difficulty and hazard, and would take more men than we could spare, after guarding the trenches, especially in the condition they were in, scarce one being free from the flux, and great numbers sent to the hospital at Fort St. David; it was therefore thought impossible to reduce the town this season, the monsoon beginning to set and the rains to fall very heavy, which greatly harassed our men, we being so weakened by deaths and sickness that some were obliged to be on duty two or three days together, and those that mounted in the trenches were obliged to sit all that time up to their breech in water. And accordingly, October 4th, after doing with them all that men could do, brought all our guns, mortars, and ammunition, etc., from the batteries, and burnt the platforms and such carriages as were rendered useless, and next morning, having shipped off everything in safety, the battalion of seamen embarked. And next morning the whole camp moved in great order towards Fort St. David, having blown up Areacopong, where they arrived next day without meeting anything worth notice, more than that the French peons, endeavouring to harass our rear, were beat back by our field-pieces with great loss.

Pondicherry is a large garrison town, five miles in circumference, but the number of buildings are not in proportion to the spaciousness of the place, great part being gardens, which caused the prodigious number of shells we threw into the town not to do the execution they otherwise would. The whole is surrounded by a very fine wall of great thickness, faced with brick, properly guarded with bastions, ravelines, etc., and such parts as are not washed by the sea encompassed with a wet foss, glacis, pallisadoes, counterscarps, etc., according to the modern way of fortification, and in the centre of the town is a citadel, capable of making a good defence after the taking of the town and the garrison, which at our first beleaguering the place consisted of 2,000 Europeans, besides multitudes of Indians, is well supplied with ammunition, provisions, and all manner of necessaries, so that it would take at least 10,000 veteran troops to reduce it, and then be thought a great acquisition, they having upwards of 300 large cannon mounted on the different works of the place, and must have a great number of mortars by the vast quantity of shells they daily throw among us.

Having now given this short though particular account of the siege of Pondicherry, I shall proceed to show in what dangerous situation our female heroine was in at the said siege, as also the many other imminent dangers she was exposed to, and the great hardships she underwent through the whole of that exploit.

James Gray (for that was the name she took upon herself) was one of the party that was ordered under Lieutenant Campbell, of the independent companies, to fetch up some stores from the waterside that had been landed out of the fleet, in doing which they had several skirmishes, and one of the common men was shot dead close on her right side, upon which she fired and killed the very man that shot her comrade, and was very near Lieutenant Campbell when he dropped.

She was also in the first party of the English foot that forded the river to get over to Pondicherry, which took her up to her breast, it being so deep, and was likewise very dangerous, as the French kept continually firing on them from a battery of twelve guns.

On the 11th of August she was put on the piquet guard, and continued on that guard seven nights successively, and was one of a party that lay two days and two nights without any covering in going through the barrier, and she was likewise put on duty in the trenches some part of the siege; she was obliged to sit or stand all the while near middle-deep in water.

At the throwing-up of the trenches she worked very hard for about fourteen days, and was paid five-pence English money per day by one Mr. Melton, who has been at Goodman's Fields Wells to see her since her singing at those wells.

I cannot help here reflecting on the numerous hardships, fatigues, and dangers she had already undergone since her taking upon herself the habit of a man, owing to the cruel usage of a wicked husband, whom vengeance pursued, as the reader will find in a proper place in the following pages; therefore, in order to keep to the story of our heroine, I shall proceed in my history without further digression.

During all this long space of time our heroine still maintained her wonted intrepidity, and behaved in every respect consistent with the character of a brave British soldier; and notwithstanding she stood so deep in water she fired no less than thirty-seven rounds of shot, and during the engagement received six shots in her right leg and five in the left, and, what affected her more than all the rest, one so dangerous in the groin that had she applied for any aid or assistance on that account she must inevitably have discovered what she was resolutely bent at all adventures, if possible, to conceal.

I know the reader will be desirous to know how the ball was extracted out of her groin, and will imagine that it was next to an impossibility it could be performed without a discovery. Now, to rectify the scruples of such, I shall relate this account as attested by herself, which she said was that after she received the twelve wounds, as before mentioned, she remained all that day and the following night in the camp before she was carried to the hospital, and after she was brought there and laid in a kit she continued till next day in the greatest agony and pain, the ball still remaining in the flesh of that wound in her groin; and how to extract it she knew not, for she had not discovered to the surgeons that she had any other wound than those in her legs. This wound being so extremely painful, it almost drove her to the precipice of despair; she often thought of discovering herself, that by that means she might be freed from the unspeakable pain she endured by having the ball taken out by one of the surgeons; but that resolution was soon banished, and she resolved to run all risks, even at the hazard of her life, rather than her sex should be known. Confirmed in this resolution, she communicated her design to a black woman who attended upon her, and could get at the surgeon's medicines, and desired her assistance; and her pain being so very great that she was unable to endure it much longer, she intended to try an experiment upon herself, which was to endeavour to extract the ball out of that wound; but notwithstanding she discovered her pain and resolution to this black, yet she did not let her know she was a woman. The black readily came, and afforded her all the assistance she could by bringing her lint and salve to dress the wound with, which she had recourse to, it being left in the wards where the patients lay, for which act of friendship she made her a present of a rupee at her departure, which is 3s. 4d. of the currency of that country, but here in England it goes for no more than 2s. 6d. Now, the manner in which she extracted the ball was full hardy and desperate. She probed the wound with her finger till she came where the ball lay, and then upon feeling it thrust in both her finger and thumb and pulled it out. This was a very rough way of proceeding with one's own flesh, but of two evils, as she thought, this was the least, so rather choosing to have her flesh tore and mangled than her sex discovered. After this operation was performed she applied some of the healing salves which the black had brought her, by the help of which she made a perfect cure of the dangerous wound.

The reader will here observe the invincible courage and resolution of this woman, who, in the midst of so many inconveniences as she daily encountered, should still be able to guard from a discovery of her sex; but indeed it appears she acted so artfully on every emergency as rendered any attempts of this kind abortive, for notwithstanding the wound, she kept from the knowledge of the surgeons by telling them when they came to examine her that all the wounds she had received were in her legs, which they readily believed, and by that means prevented any farther search.

But now to proceed. As the heavy rains and the violent claps of thunder now came on, it being that part of the year when the monsoons happen (for that is the term they are distinguished by in that country), the siege was entirely broken up.

Our heroine being so dangerously wounded, as we have just mentioned, she had been sent away to a hospital, at a place not far from thence, called Cuddylorum, and was attended by Mr. Belchier and Mr. Hancock, two of as able and experienced surgeons as were in those parts, who always dressed the wounds in her legs; but she was resolutely bent to be her own physician in regard to her secret wound, since she dreaded the discovery of her sex more than death itself.

This heroic resolution of our female adventurer met with the desired success. She extracted the ball from her groin without the knowledge or even suspicion of any one person whomsoever about her, and, by the application of such plasters as she artfully procured, made a perfect cure in that dangerous part. And as to the many wounds she had in both her legs, they were all (through the care and skill of her two attendants) absolutely healed in the compass of three months.

During her residence in the hospital above mentioned, the much greater part of the fleet were sailed off; but as soon as she was perfectly restored to her health and strength, she was sent on board the Tartar Pink, which at that time was riding in the harbour, where she continued till the return of the fleet from Madras, and during the whole time performed the duty of a common sailor.

However, soon after the fleet's return, she was turned over to the Eltham man-of-war, Captain Lloyd commander, and set sail for Bombay, where they arrived in less than a fortnight. But as they wanted hands, having no more than eight in a watch, and she one of them, her fatigue must, doubtless, be very great, especially since the ship had sprung a leak in her larboard bow, and by that means some hands were obliged to be kept without intermission, and she also made one in her turn; but the ship happily got safe to Bombay.

Soon after their arrival at Bombay, which was with great labour and difficulty, they were under the indispensable necessity of heaving the vessel down (as they term it) in order to have her bottom thoroughly and effectually cleaned. It was no less than five weeks before this operation was perfectly accomplished. After the expiration, indeed, of that time, they set sail for Mountserrat, in order to take the Royal Duke, Indiaman, under convoy, and bring her to Fort St. David's, where she was come for provisions.

Our female adventurer being now at Bombay, and her master being on shore, she was obliged, according to custom, to perform her watch in her turn; and as she was one night in particular upon duty, the first lieutenant, who at that time had the command of the ship, the captain being on shore, ordered her to sing a merry song for him; but she desired to be excused, being, as she told him, very much indisposed. But he was naturally of a haughty and imperious temper, and much more so as he was not a little proud (like most other upstarts) of his new post, that of commander, as we hinted before, he peremptorily insisted that she should sing; but she, imagining that he had no authority to lay such injunctions upon her, and resenting with true fire and spirit such an imposition on her will, she peremptorily refused to obey his orders, especially as she was not conscious to herself of lying under the least obligation imaginable to truckle to his humours, or regard the imperious airs which he was pleased to give himself.

This refusal, however, of a trifle, of no matter of importance, proved of very ill consequence to her, and occasioned her more vexation and real affliction than any one could ever imagine to arise from such an idle and trivial circumstance; for a story was trumped up that a shirt was missing of one of her comrades, and that she must be the person who had got it; and notwithstanding she positively denied knowing anything of it, and there being no manner of proof in the least against her, only surmise, the lieutenant, who, as is before said, having the command of the ship in the captain's absence, ordered her, without the least delay, to be clapped in irons; and his orders, however unjust, were instantly obeyed. This act of severity was not all, for she not only lay in irons for five days successively, but was obliged to undergo the discipline of twelve lashes at the gangway, and after that to continue at the foretop masthead for four hours. What pity it is such inhuman, thoughtless creatures should ever be invested with an arbitrary power, when they have not the least regard for justice, nor a Christian compassion for their fellow-creatures! And the shirt, which was the presumed charge against her, was soon after found in a chest belonging to the man whom it was said had lost it.

The ship's crew, who were sensible of the innocence of James Gray, as they called our Hannah, were determined that it should not go altogether unpunished, for they had not arrived in England long before one of the sailors, as they were seemingly very busily employed in unrigging the ship, embraced the first favourable opportunity that offered, and let a large heavy block drop down directly on his head.

Our imperious officer felt the smart of this unlucky accident for some considerable time, but not in the least suspecting that it was any contrivance could blame nobody but himself for standing in the way of danger.

Having now the Royal Duke along with them, they made the best of their way for Fort St. David's, and were there at the time when that remarkable hurricane happened, in which not only the Namur and the Pembroke, but several other vessels were unhappily cast away; nay, the Eltham itself, on which our adventurer was on board, but very narrowly escaped, for though she was in port indeed when the storm arose, yet she broke her cables, and was forced out to sea; Providence, however, so ordered it, that they made shift to reach the port again without receiving any considerable damage.

Whilst the vessel rode at anchor here at St. David's our heroine had just grounds to be alarmed, and doubly on her guard for the concealment of that secret she was so resolutely bent should never be disclosed but with the loss of her life, for she frequently went on shore with one part of the crew or another, where her ears were every moment pierced through with the most execrable oaths that could be invented; neither durst she, though the sounds in reality were ever so disagreeable to her, show the least disgust at their manner of conversation. And notwithstanding she was an eye-witness of a thousand unseemly actions which they were too frequently guilty of, and which almost shocked her, yet, considering she was in masquerade and a brother tar, she was not only forced to connive at, but seemingly to countenance and approve.

As there were but very few white women upon the place, and as she found they were resolutely bent to gratify their lustful appetites at all adventures, she must, doubtless, be under dreadful apprehensions lest her refusal to partake in their vicious pleasures should give grounds of suspicion, and be the means of their making a too narrow search into the motives that induced her to decline the like amorous adventures. However, she had no other way for the protection of her innocence and person than to show that her will was her law, and that if they offered in the least to be rude that she had courage and resolution enough to make them feel the weight of her resentment. By this imperious way of deportment, though only affected, she screened herself from the danger to which she was almost daily exposed.

On the 19th of November, in the year 1749, the Eltham, together with the rest of the fleet, weighed anchor and sailed away from Fort St. David's, and never parted till they arrived in safety at the Cape of Good Hope, at which time the Eltham, in particular, had received express orders for steering her course to the port of Lisbon with the utmost expedition, where she was to take in a very considerable sum of money for the use of some of the merchants then residing at London.

Notwithstanding all the care that our adventurer had taken of her Lieutenant Wyegate, of whose sickness mention has been made before, he unfortunately died the very next day after their departure from Fort St. David's. This loss shocked our heroine greatly, for he was the only sincere friend she had on board, and the only one in case of any insult she could have recourse to for any redress.

This loss, in short, so affected her that she indulged herself once more in reflecting on her wayward fate, and on the original cause of all her sorrows, her faithless and perfidious husband. However, though such gloomy thoughts were sufficient to have overwhelmed the mind of the most intrepid hero, yet she soon roused herself out of this disorder and determined to bear her hard lot with as much patience and resignation to the will of Providence as possibly she could.

Being deprived by death of so valuable a friend, and not knowing where his equal was to be found, she was determined, by a courteous deportment to all her comrades in general, to render herself as acceptable as she could. Accordingly she distinguished herself by spending what time she had either in washing or mending any of the crew's clothes. For these voluntary good offices she met with a great deal of respect amongst her comrades; and, notwithstanding whatever she undertook of that nature she did it very dextrously and in a more artful manner than was common, yet as it is customary to have some fellows on board his Majesty's navy that have been apprentice to tailors, and to handle the needle without the least awkwardness, her services of that nature created no jealousies or suspicions that could give her the least uneasiness.

Distinguishing herself in this manner, by daily acts of good nature, she was taken notice of, soon after the death of her dear friend Mr. Wyegate, by Mr. Kite, who was second lieutenant of the ship, and admitted into his immediate service, in which she continued for about two months, in which she behaved so well that, though he wanted her no longer, having a boy to attend him, he recommended her to Mr. Wallace, the third lieutenant of the ship, who not only took her into his service through his friend's recommendation, but finding her very tractable and handy, proved very kind and indulgent to her during the whole voyage.

Here, however, there was one unavoidable misfortune that she was exposed to, and which she was obliged to struggle with and bear up with courage, though contrary to her inclinations, and that was the insults of the sailors for want of having a rough beard as they had; and upon which score, when she had her head shaved, they would damn her in their familiar way, and stigmatise her with the disagreeable title of Miss Molly Gray. As these taunts, however, were only thrown out in jest, she would return the compliment not only with a smile and an oath, but with a challenge of the best sailor of them all, though not so old as they, to prove herself as good a man as any of them on board, for any wager to be deposited in her master's hands.

Though she seemed not to resent the unlucky nickname they had given her, for very prudential reasons, yet it secretly created her many an uneasy hour. And though by her resolute and manly deportment she prevented them from carrying the joke too far, yet she could not shake off the odious title till they arrived at Lisbon.

Though she said but little, and that without the least resentment, as before observed, in regard to the nickname she had brought with her to Lisbon, she was determined within herself to shake off that odious appellation in Portugal, if possible, and to behave in such a manner that the secret she had hitherto kept locked up in her bosom might still remain altogether safe and unsuspected, that she should be so happy as to arrive once more in her native country.

Whilst this vessel lay at anchor in the port of Lisbon, the ship's crew would frequently go on shore upon parties of pleasure; and when any such proposal was made by her comrades (for the secret purpose above mentioned), she would be one of the most forward to promote the scheme, and would seem to take a peculiar delight in carousing, or in the commission of any other youthful flights, that they were in reality fond of. Though all her compliances were indeed forced, and all she did was the result of necessity, and not choice, yet she played the part of a boon companion so naturally, and so far distant from what bore the least appearance of effeminacy, that she answered the end proposed. The name of Miss Molly was here perfectly buried in oblivion; for as she came into all their wildest measures with the utmost alacrity and readiness, she gave them no grounds to suspect her sex or give her the least uneasiness on that score.

We shall instance of the frolics she was there concerned in, only to give the reader an idea of our young adventurer's being a perfect actor. There was one of her intimate acquaintance, who was not only a marine as well as herself, but one of her messmates likewise, by name Edward Jefferies, who used frequently to go on shore with her in quest of adventures. Amongst other frolics, these two cronies pursued an amour together, by contracting an acquaintance with two young women of the place that had no nun's flesh about them. Though neither of them, it is true, were to compare with our British beauties, yet the handsomest of the two was not only our heroine's favourite, but was as favourably received as her heart could wish. Jefferies, however, would every now and then throw out an amorous glance at his comrade's mistress, and not being over-fond of his own told our adventurer that as they were partners in their amours he thought it was but just and reasonable that he should have a chance at least for a night's lodging with the object of his choice, which, he ingeniously acknowledged, he liked much better than his own; and for that purpose he should think he acted fair and above board would she allow of a toss up to determine the point in debate. Our heroine, in order to comply with her comrade's humour, readily consented to the proposition, notwithstanding she insisted on her absolute right and title, in order to enhance his favour. Accordingly, the moot point was to be determined by throwing up cross or pile. The lot, in short, luckily fell in favour of Jefferies' side; and though our heroine seemed to part with her mistress with some reluctance, yet to show her friendship and impartiality to her messmate, she delivered up her property in a very formal manner into his arms.

Jefferies, highly delighted with his good fortune and the generosity of his messmate, kept up an intimate correspondence with his Portuguese lady as long as the ship rode at anchor in the port, and retained a greater respect than ordinary for his impartial friend till their happy arrival together at the port of London.

When they set sail for England the enamoured Portuguese would fain have quitted their native place to have had the pleasure of a voyage with their sweethearts, but that indulgence could not be procured by reason the captain had given express orders that no women should be admitted on board on any pretence howsoever plausible.

But the reader is here to observe that the reason why this strict order was made was that our female heroine, being in the secret of the intention of the two Portuguese Amazons intending to come on board, had contrived to inform the officers of it; and she declares that her reasons for so doing was, lest by a further intimacy with them it might be the cause of her sex being discovered.

Our heroine, by thus affecting a gaiety of heart which was not sincere, and by acting such parts as in secret gave her the utmost disgust, gave a new turn to her character, and her title to manhood was no more suspected; insomuch that she returned at last to her dear native home as pure as when she first set out.

As to the affair of the generous supply of hands, which the captain of the Sheerness privateer gave them off the island of Madeiras, our female adventurer gives us the following remarkable particulars:

"I could not but observe," said she, "that several of our additional comrades appeared very thoughtful, and seemingly disconsolate, upon their first coming on board our Swallow sloop. Upon which my curiosity prompted me to inquire, as far as decency would permit, into the grounds and secret cause of their uneasiness. They were deeply concerned, I found, because they were sent on board a man-of-war. I was unacquainted with the nature of men being impressed for the sea service, their complaint appeared to me at first altogether groundless, and I endeavoured to convince them that they were in a much more advantageous station than they would have been in any other vessel; but by a more familiar conversation with some of them I perceived that they were sent on board the sloop sorely against their inclination; and as some of them had left behind them loving, indulgent wives, and others wives and children, some in one country, and some in another, the melancholy thoughts of their being absent so long from the dear objects of their wishes, and the more gloomy apprehensions of the danger they were in of never seeing their poor disconsolate families again, were the principal motives of those sorrows which they laboured under and which they had not courage and resolution sufficient to conceal."

At the same time she was giving this melancholy relation, and commiserating their unhappy circumstances, she added, "That she took the first opportunity to withdraw from them to her master's cabin, in order to indulge a few melancholy thoughts on her own unhappy situation. These poor unhappy wretches," said she to herself, "have left, it is true, their wives and children behind them, and, it is probable, they may never have the satisfaction of seeing them again; but then that separation is wholly owing to their misfortune, not their fault, the result of compulsion and not of choice, whereas my false perfidious husband flew from me when I was in the utmost distress, and incapable of helping myself, and, too, with the pleasing hopes of seeing me no more, though I had given no manner of provocation for so unnatural and so barbarous a treatment. How different," she said, "I thought their case was from mine. They are bemoaning the loss of those companions they most affectionately loved, whilst my brute of a husband makes it his whole study to avoid my presence only to indulge his lustful appetites in the embraces of a pack of strumpets without control."

In the midst of these gloomy reflections, however, it was some alleviation to her pain to consider that she had new messmates come on board whose company would be very agreeable, as they were men who were endowed with principles of honour, and who expressed the most passionate regard for their afflicted families. Then again would our female adventurer reflect on the deplorable circumstances of those wives and children from whom their husbands and parents had been so unwillingly divorced, and would often wish that it was in her power to communicate to them the anxieties their poor partners were in on their account, imagining it could not but be a secret pleasure to hear of the sincerity and truth of their affection to them.

When our adventurer first began to converse with them she highly blamed them for going on board a privateer, but when she understood that they had entered into articles but for a short service, and that no motives could have prevailed with them to take those measures but the prospect they had by that means of supporting their poor distressed families, she then looked upon them in quite a different light; she no more thought them blameworthy but rather the just objects of pity and compassion.

As such, therefore, she heartily sympathised with them; and notwithstanding she had sorrows enough of her own to struggle with, yet her heart relented on the thoughts of their unhappy case, and she would study all the arguments that she could think of to alleviate the weight of them, and endeavour to comfort them with the hopes that they, and she too, should return in safety to their native country in a short time, and would frequently tell them that patience and a firm trust in Providence were the best measures they could take to make their minds easy in that station in which they were at present planted.

To these friendly and good-natured admonitions our adventurer would frequently add more substantial consolations; for as she had a free resource to all her master's stores, it was not only in her will but in her power to supply them every now and then with something to refresh their spirits and dispel those gloomy cares, in some measure, which were too apt to overwhelm them.

Having here given the reader a transient idea of the humanity and compassionate disposition of our heroine towards her fellow-sufferers, I cannot, I think, introduce in a more proper place a short detail of the inhumanity and brutal deportment of her husband towards her, by way of contrast.

When her perfidious Dutchman first deserted the embraces of his lawful wife in hopes never to see her more, though he knew he left her plunged in the utmost distress, big with child, and altogether helpless, he entered himself a foremast man, on board a Dutch vessel then at anchor in the river Thames. Here, it is true, he fled for shelter, and with a view to shake off all anxiety of mind, all thoughts of the sorrows in which he left his poor wife involved. This expedient soon failed him, for at intervals his conscience, which, as the proverb says, "needs no accuser," would torment him, and, like a vulture, prey upon his vitals; though he thought, by taking this method, to be for the future free and easy, yet he found himself most miserably mistaken; his mind was for ever harassed and perplexed, and (as Mr. Milton elegantly expresses it) "himself was his own dungeon." And this truth has been manifestly evinced, as will appear from very substantial circumstances, an account of which was very accidentally procured.

[Here follows an account of the sufferings, and final execution for murder, of Hannah's husband, narrated to her by a sailor she chanced to meet, but as the circumstances have no bearing on the biography of our heroine we may omit the gruesome details.]

* * * * * *

No sooner had the sailor finished his long narrative, but Hannah told him that, upon mature deliberation, and comparing every incident of his affecting story, she could not but conclude the unhappy malefactor he had been so long talking of must be the very self-same person with whom he had formerly contracted an intimate acquaintance; and assured him, whenever she should happen to see her native country again, she would make it her business to find out the poor widow of that unfortunate man, and give her a full and true account of the untimely end of her penitent husband, and according as she found her circumstances to be, would either console with her or relieve her.

By saying thus much and no more, she very prudently preserved herself from all suspicion.

Having finished the account of the execution of our adventurer's husband, of which she had the relation in an accidental manner, by which untimely death, however, she was conscious to herself she was now a widow, and under no apprehensions of seeing any more a wretch, whom, if she had casually met with, she might possibly, in the height of her rage and resentment, have murdered with her own hands; I shall waive all farther discourse on that topic and proceed to her voyage from Lisbon to England.

The vessel on which our adventurer went on board set sail from the port of Lisbon on the 3rd day of May; and though they met indeed sometimes with contrary winds, and at other times were becalmed (as it is customary at that season of the year), yet they met with no obstructions of any great consequence, or insults or engagements from any ships, or any other occurrence, indeed, of importance enough to be worth relating during the whole voyage.

On the 1st of June then next following, our female adventurer, to her no small satisfaction, arrived with the rest of her shipmates safe at Spithead.

Overjoyed at the sight once more of her dear native country, she went on shore the very day of her arrival, and took lodgings, together with several of her comrades and fellow-travellers, at the sign of the "Jolly Marine and Sailor " in Portsmouth.

This house was kept by Mr. Cunningham, the drum-major of the regiment, who had been with them through the whole expedition, and where most of the marines that came on shore out of the Eltham man-of-war went to get lodgings, so consequently as this house was full of friends, our heroine could not possibly procure (as she proposed privately before she went on shore to do) a bed to herself, with a secret resolution never to enter between a set of sheets again with any but one of her own sex. In this particular, however, though she was disappointed, yet her even temper and frame of mind made her bear the misfortune with patience, and indeed without any visible reluctance or concern.

The first night, then, that she took up her lodgings here she agreed, with all the cheerfulness and freedom imaginable, to be bedfellow with one John Hutchins, who was one of her brother-marines and a fellow that understood himself, and behaved in somewhat a more decent manner than the rest of her shipmates. Here she made herself as easy as she had done everywhere else, and lived the short time she stayed at Portsmouth (which was but two days and three nights) as gaily as heart could wish, without the least danger of having her sex suspected.

Short as our Hannah's stay was in this town, she roved all over it, and drank almost in every public-house in it. In her rambles who should she meet with but a sister of Mr. Cunningham's, the drum-major's, wife, whom we just mentioned. This sister of his was Miss Catherine that we have before mentioned, with whom our heroine had at the time when she first enlisted herself at Portsmouth contracted a slender acquaintance.

Miss Catherine had all her eyes about her, and soon recollected that our Hannah was the very identical young fellow that had enlisted himself and been sent abroad as a marine with Admiral Boscawen, and in a modest way enough, but with a brisk eye, expressed a kind of joy to see her returned home again alive and well. Upon this, and entering into conversation on many things that passed before her voyage, our Hannah renewed her acquaintance, and, in short, in a few hours they began to grow more intimate, insomuch that at last Miss Catherine, being a very good-natured, tender-hearted girl, became a kind of a sweetheart. Our Hannah gradually stole into her good graces, and being a person of much better address than most of her fellow-shipmates, she became a great favourite, and nothing that Miss Catherine could get was either too hot or too good for her.

Our heroine, or female adventurer, improved this opportunity to the best advantage, for she made her courtship no secret to her brother marines, who all readily excused her not drinking with them so much as she would otherwise, since the wind blew in the love corner, as they termed it; and besides every one of them approved of her choice. She drunk to the successful battering of Miss Catherine's fort, and they advised her to take it by storm. By this stratagem she got rid of her raking, drunken companions without giving the least disgust, and spent her hours less extravagantly, and at the same time more agreeably in the familiar conversation with Mrs. Catherine.

Our Hannah, in short, improved what little time she had to stay so well, and her amorous caresses were so engaging to Miss Catherine that she fell a victim to the young God of Love.

This amour was carried on so far with success by our female soldier that Miss Catherine would have pushed it on to a direct matrimonial contract, and consented that the parson should say grace, and she fall to as soon afterwards as she pleased.

Our Hannah, whose presence of mind, as we have observed before, never failed her, artfully evaded this warm proposition by assuring her mistress that, though nothing was so dear as herself, and though the consummation of their mutual happiness was the thing she had most at heart in this world, yet common prudence obliged her to postpone the march for a short time till she could return to London, and not only get her pay but her discharge.

Miss Catherine, warm as she was for matrimony, upon mature deliberation approved of her sweetheart's good conduct and discretion, and consented (though with tears in her eyes) to her departure for London, provided, nevertheless, that she would be true and constant to her vows, and be as expeditious in her return to Portsmouth as her interest and the situation of her affairs would possibly admit.

Our female adventurer, in order to pacify her and countenance this amorous engagement of hers, assured the imaginary object of her love that as soon as she was safely arrived at the town of London, and had received all the wages that were due to her, she would remit whatever sums she should there receive with the utmost pleasure imaginable as the best proof she could possibly give her of her sincere love and affection, and that after she had paid the visits that common decency required to all her relations and acquaintance she would fly back to Portsmouth on the wings of love, pursuant to the contract that was entered into secretly between them, and that then she would consummate their happy nuptials with as much solemnity as was consistent with the utmost of her abilities.

On Saturday, the 2nd of June, being the second night of their lying on shore, our heroine's bedfellow, John Hutchins, who had lain with her but the night before, was obliged on some private occasion, no ways material to be known, to lie at another place, and one James Moody, a shipmate of hers on board the Eltham from Fort St. David's to England, happened by mere accident to come to refresh himself at our Hannah's quarters, and after some conversation passed he told the landlord of the house that he was destitute of a lodging, and should take it as a favour in case he could with any convenience supply him with a bed, or at least some part of one for that night. The landlord imagining he would prove no bad customer, told him he might lie with James Gray, which was the name our heroine was then known by, if he would accept of him for his bedfellow.

Our Hannah, as they had been cronies and intimate acquaintance for some considerable time, readily acquiesced in her landlord's proposal, and told him without the least hesitation that as she had lost one comrade she should be very proud of the company of another with whom she was so well acquainted.

After having caroused together pretty freely, they very sociably went to bed together for that night; and, as her first partner was detained in another place, they lay together the next night with all the freedom imaginable, without Master Moody's in the least suspecting that he had a young brisk girl for his bedfellow.

Who can sufficiently admire the good conduct and presence of mind of this our female adventurer, who could admit one male bedfellow after another into her lodgings without showing the least reluctance or apprehension of being discovered to be any other person than James Gray, whom she so naturally personated, and more particularly with the last, who had been her comrade and shipmate for fifteen or sixteen months successively and had been one of her assistants in the most dangerous exploits which she had been from time to time engaged in, and one, in short, that valued her above any of his comrades, as being conscious of her intrepidity upon all occasions.

Our female heroine having, as I have said, had Mr. Moody for her bedfellow on Saturday night, so she continued to be his bedfellow again the next night, which was the last she was at Portsmouth, she setting out on Monday morning for London in company with ten more belonging to the same regiment.

We shall now proceed to give our readers a succinct account of her passage from Portsmouth to the long-wished-for port of London.

Before she set out, however, she received five shillings conduct money, which, together with what little she had otherwise preserved, proved sufficient to defray her charges on the road without being put to any straits or difficulties, or without being obliged to any of her comrades for the least aid or assistance.

The first place of any note she came to, after she had turned her back on Portsmouth, was Petersfield, a place of good accommodation in the county of Hampshire. Here she took up her residence all night, and accepted her namesake, one Andrew Gray, a young marine who belonged not only to the same regiment but to the very same company as she did, for her bedfellow.

Here, though they enjoyed themselves till it was pretty late, they mounted again betimes the next morning, in order to proceed on their journey before the sun had well got out of his bed.

Before night they reached Guildford, a noted town in the county of Surrey. Here her namesake and she refreshed themselves pretty freely once more, and spent another night together between a pair of sheets, which was the last male bedfellow she ever had, and both mounted the next morning in order to finish their travels.

Our female adventurer was now under no apprehensions of being discovered in regard to her sex, and she and her comrades reached London before sunset.

After she and her friends had taken a hearty cup or two by the way of refreshment, and congratulated each other on their safe arrival in London, a place they had all longed to see for some considerable time, our Hannah took her leave of her comrades in a very handsome manner, and told them nothing should have parted them that night but that an old sweetheart of hers lived not far off, and that she hoped, as they were all flesh and blood as well as herself, that they would excuse her absence, as she was in some hopes of having a brisk young girl for her bedfellow, that would make amends for all the troubles and fatigues she had hitherto undergone.

They all unanimously applauded her resolution, and wished that her purse might never fail her.

Having thus in a gay manner parted with all her comrades, she made the best of her way to her brother's, Mr. James Gray, whose name she had assumed during her travels.

That Mr. Gray is a carpenter by profession, and has resided for several years in Ship Street, Wapping, and with him it is that our female adventurer has lodged ever since her arrival, and with whom she lodged and lived before she went away after her husband, as is before mentioned.

* * * * * *

Notwithstanding her long absence, and notwithstanding our heroine's appearance in masquerade, her sister knew her almost at the first glance, and ventured, contrary to all seeming decency and good manners, to throw her arms about our young marine's neck, and almost stifled her with kisses.

This joyful interview happened pretty late at night, and though Mrs. Gray was up, and had been so some time, yet her husband, being over-fatigued with business, was in bed.

Our Hannah, being impatient to pay her love and respects where she thought they were more justly due, ran upstairs, and without any ceremony opened his chamber door.

No sooner was she got to the bedside, notwithstanding she perceived he was in a sleep, she flung herself upon the bedside, and with her eager arms caressed him in so warm a manner that he soon waked; and finding such odd and uncommon civilities from a stranger in his regimentals, he started up in a kind of confusion, and in a manner resenting such an unseemly manner of proceeding; but our hero in disguise, perceiving that she was received with a frown and that her caresses were in so apparent a manner disapproved of, she burst out into a fit of laughter, and by discovering herself soon convinced him of the innocence of her intentions.

* * * * * *

As our Hannah was a particular favourite of Mr. Gray's before she had entertained the least notion of making an elopement from her friends, and as he was now overjoyed to see his dear rover, whom he imagined to be lost, returned after so long an absence in health and safety, he jumped out of bed directly; whereupon our female soldier with modesty withdrew in an instant, and waited with patience below stairs till her brother-in-law had dressed himself and come down.

It was not long, the reader may suppose, before he had an interview with her; and after abundance of the most hearty salutations, he sat before her whatever he had in the house for her refreshment.

These first acts of civility over, it is natural to conclude that the remainder of the evening was spent in merriment, and that our Hannah at different times related divers adventures, which sometimes made her brother and sister laugh, but at other times again drew tears from their eyes.

At this time there happened to lodge at Mr. Gray's house a very civil, sober young woman, and a single woman withal. And as Mr. Gray had no other commodious place for the reception of his sister, he requested his young lodger to accept of a female bedfellow, an intimate acquaintance of his, for some few nights, and her compliance in that particular would be looked upon both by his wife and him as a singular favour.

The young maiden assured him, without the least hesitation, that his female friend should be heartily welcome to one-half of her bed.

As the night was far spent, this lodger of theirs had been abed for some time, but lay awake in expectation of Mr. Gray and his wife ushering their friend into her apartment to take her repose after the fatigue of her journey. But when she saw her landlord and landlady introduce a handsome young soldier, to all outward appearance, into her room, she was terribly shocked; and though she did not actually scream out, yet she was ready to faint away, thinking they had some sinister design to injure her reputation. Seeing her thus in a kind of agony through their too rash proceedings, they immediately endeavoured to undeceive her, and assured her upon their honours that she was nothing more than a woman like herself, though in masquerade.

The lodger, however, would not trust to their joint asservations, though ever so solemn, but insisted on ocular demonstration before she could consent to her stripping and coming into bed.

As this was but a modest and very reasonable request, Mr. Gray very decently withdrew, and then our Hannah, without the least reluctance, opened her bosom before her sister and her, and gave her such other testimonies as were altogether satisfactory. This incident, after Mr. Gray was recalled, created a little innocent diversion between them; and the young woman being perfectly recovered of her fright, she received her new bedfellow with abundance of complaisance.

This young maiden was the first stranger to whom she communicated the secret which she had so long artfully concealed. And ever since such ocular demonstration was given, as above mentioned, they have been bedfellows, and contracted a more than common respect for each other.

As the neighbours perceived that this young soldier was very intimate with Mr. Gray's lodger, it was currently reported all over the street that Mrs. _____ was married, and she was almost every day congratulated on that occasion.

With abundance of good nature and cheerfulness, and without the least denial of the fact, she would return them many thanks for their friendly wishes and assured them at the same time, in order to confirm them in their mistake, that she was very happy in her new bedfellow.

Since her living in this manner with her sister and her supposed wife, she has paid several visits to particular friends without their being conscious who she was, or in the least suspecting that she ought to appear in petticoats.

It must be allowed that she plays a man's part to admiration, and that had not she revealed the secret of her sex, since her arrival in England, voluntarily to the public, there is no judge, however discerning, could have discovered the imposture.

However, there are some particular incidents, which we have before related, that may not be altogether so satisfactory to some of our inquisitive readers as they could wish, since they may carry with them an air of improbability—and more particularly those of her being twice whipped, and once very dangerously wounded in the groin, without the secret of her being a woman so much as even suspected. As these circumstances, I say, may possibly be looked upon as romantic, and not matter of fact, we shall beg leave to reconcile those seeming paradoxes by a recapitulation of those incidents, and the addition of some new circumstances, which were, through hurry, omitted in the preceding part of this narrative, in order to show that such misfortunes did in reality attend her, and that so important a secret not only might possibly be concealed from all the world, but actually was so, through her dexterity and address, and through a peculiar presence of mind which never forsook her in the midst of the greatest dangers to which she was exposed.

We shall therefore remind our reader of the artful measure she took to prevent her being blown when she was unjustly punished for neglect of duty at Carlisle, through the accusation of Sergeant Davis, who foolishly imagined her to be his rival, as has been hinted already in the preceding pages. Her method was this, according to her own relation:

At that time her breasts were but very small, and her arms being extended and fixed to the city gates, her breasts were towards the wall, so that then there was little or no danger of her comrades finding out the important secret which she took such uncommon pains to conceal.

At her second whipping on board the ship, when her hands were lashed to the gangway, she was in much greater danger of being discovered; but she stood as upright as possible, and tied a large silk handkerchief round her neck, the ends whereof entirely covered her breasts, insomuch that she went through the martial discipline with great resolution, without being in the least suspected. The fears, indeed, of a discovery gave her more inward uneasiness, in reality, than the lashes that she received; but in the most imminent dangers she still extricated herself out of all the difficulties in which she was involved, by her fruitful inventions.

At this time, it is true, the boatswain of the ship, taking notice of her breasts, seemed surprised, and said they were the most like a woman's he ever saw; but as no person on board ever had the least suspicion of her sex, the whole dropped without any farther notice being taken.

* * * * * *

Though the secret of her being a widow, instead of being an intrepid marine and a merry tar, was still an absolute secret to all the world but her brother-in-law, her sister, and her imaginary spouse—the young woman, a lodger in her brother's house—yet the daily apprehensions of her being blown as to that momentous circumstance before she had received the arrears that were due to her both for her pay and smart-money, from the proper office, gave her no small uneasiness, imagining that in case of any casual discovery of that nature she should be inevitably deprived of a debt that was so justly due to her and which she had earned so dearly, and with such apparent hazards of her life.

Those apprehensions, however uneasy they might possibly make her, were only imaginary and altogether groundless, for no such discovery was made till after actual payment of the whole sum to which she laid her just claim, namely, the sum of fifteen pounds, which demand was very duly and truly discharged (to the entire satisfaction of herself and her friends who had been entrusted with the important secret) on the Saturday after her first appearance in London, that is to say, on the 9th day of June, at which time our female adventurer, under the denomination of James Gray, together, with Sergeant Orley, John Hutchins, James Moody, her namesake Andrew Gray, and several other marines that had been her comrades and boon companions, and who arrived in London at the same time with herself, all went in a body to the house of John Winter, Esq., who was then agent to Fraser's regiment, and lived in Downing Street, Westminster, who very readily and with pleasure paid each of them their full and respective demands.

So reasonable a proposition as this we may easily imagine was readily complied with, and into the alehouse they went accordingly.

There they refreshed themselves pretty plentifully; and after the loyal healths above proposed had gone round, with such additional ones as they thought proper, they closed them very cordially with a health to their most noble selves, and health and good success to all their future undertakings.

In the midst of all their merriment, and some time before they parted by consent, our heroine being conscious to herself that two suits of clothing were due to her from the regiment, proposed to sell them, fearing still she should lose the same if her sex was discovered; upon which she took sixteen shillings for the two suits of regimental clothing.

The money being now paid, and our heroine having been determined to raise all the ready cash she could before she opened a new scene, which she well knew would amuse them—I mean, an open and ingenious discovery of a secret that had been so long kept close, and which she purposed to reveal before they parted, prudently considering that she should never perhaps have so favourable an opportunity again of disclosing her sex to such a number of witnesses at once, who would at any time afterwards be ready to testify the truth of all her merry adventures, as well as the many hardships, fatigues, and imminent dangers she had with so much intrepidity and cheerfulness run through, which, had that important discovery been at that juncture omitted, she wisely reflected that it was very probable that her veracity might be called into question, and that most people might suspect her real adventures, as before particularly related, and look upon the narrative of her life as little better than a romance.

As these motives induced our heroine to make an ingenious discovery of her sex before they parted, as judging it the most seasonable opportunity that could possibly offer itself, she proposed to the company, with her usual freedom and alacrity, to call for the reckoning and discharge that in the first place, share and share alike, or at least she paid her share; and when that was done, she said:

"Now, gentlemen, I have one very material secret to disclose to you, and lend me your ears for one minute. It is very probable, gentlemen, that we may not after this merry meeting be so happy as to meet altogether at one time and at one place any more; and it is very probable, likewise, that not one of you will ever see your friend and fellow-soldier, Jemmy Gray, any more."

This she uttered in a soft, melancholy tone, at which they started, and one and all (as Jemmy was always universally beloved) crying out, "God forbid!" With that she burst out into laughing, and then added, "Why, gentlemen, Jemmy Gray, you will find, will, before we part, cast his skin like a snake and become a new creature." And then, turning to her bedfellow, Mr. Moody, and addressing herself to him more particularly than the rest, said, in her jocose way, "Had you have known, Master Moody, who you had between a pair of sheets with you, you would have come to closer quarters. In a word, gentlemen, I am as much a woman as my mother ever was, and my real name is Hannah Snell." At this sudden and unexpected declaration the whole company stood astonished, but after they had pretty well recovered themselves from, the consternation she had thrown them into, like Thomas of Didymus, they began to grow hard of belief, and insisted that what she had advanced was all a fiction, and nothing but one of Jemmy's merry conceits to amuse them.

Her brother and sister, however, interposed, and assured them that they would attest the truth of this metamorphosis, if the company required it, upon oath.

This serious confirmation being allowed by them all sufficient to convince them of the matter of fact, they one and all expatiated very largely in their way in her commendation. They all applauded her intrepidity and presence of mind as a soldier in the most imminent dangers, even when death itself stared her in the face. In the next place they sounded forth her praise in regard to her peculiar dexterity and address as a sailor, and one who very deservedly was taken notice of and highly respected on that account by her superior officers. They proceeded from that part of her character to be lavish in her praise with respect to her sincerity as a friend, and to her humane and compassionate regard for all fellow-soldiers and sailors in general, when indisposed, or under any other kind of distress, wherein it lay in her power (through the interest she had in some of the superior officers) to procure them such relief as the nature of their case required.

They did not, however, stop here; they expatiated very largely on the evenness of her natural disposition, on the regularity of her conduct, and her peculiar presence of mind when under the most imminent dangers.

They frankly acknowledged that they never heard her in the least murmur or complain at the toils and fatigues which she frequently underwent, and that she never appeared discontented (as ever they could perceive), though her situation was ever so bad, or, in a word, in any way impatient, even when she laboured under such a multiplicity of wounds and felt the most agonising pains.

As soon as these extraordinary encomiums were over, the above-named Mr. Moody, who had been her bedfellow for two nights (as we have hinted before), and the party to whom our Hannah more particularly applied herself at the time of her discovery, was so pleased with the agreeable manner in which she did it and the encomiums which her comrades gave her, which he was very sensible were no more than the just results of her extraordinary merits, carried the testimonies of his respects to a much higher pitch than any of his comrades, for he protested solemnly and seriously that he was become all of a sudden so enamoured with her, on account of her numerous and praiseworthy qualifications, that, if Mrs. Hannah had as favourable opinion of him as he had of her, he was very ready and willing to commit matrimony with her that very hour as an incontestable demonstration of the sincerity of his love and affection.

Though our Hannah made him all the grateful acknowledgments that could be desired for such unexpected and open declaration of his esteem, yet she modestly refused the generous offer upon reflecting upon what unhappy circumstances she had been in, and what miseries and misfortunes she had been reduced to through the hard-heartedness and inhumanity of a former husband, and was fully determined, if she knew her own mind, never to submit herself to the marriage yoke any more.

She assured Moody, however, in the most complaisant terms that could be conceived, that she knew of no man living for whom she had a greater respect, and for whose future friendship she should have a greater regard.

Now, upon this open and public removal of the mask and frank and ingenious acknowledgments of her sex, not only her relations, but some of her most intimate friends and acquaintance, pressed her very closely to make her applications to his Royal Highness, the Duke of Cumberland, to take her extraordinary case into his serious consideration, telling her withal that they did not question in the least but that, if a petition was properly drawn up, with a short recital of all her adventures, but more particularly of the wounds she had received at the siege of Pondicherry in his Majesty's service, that his Royal Highness would be so gracious as to consider her case and make some handsome provision for her, that she might be able, as it was very probable, to spend the remainder of her life in peace and tranquility.

Upon these friendly admonitions of her sincere friends and well-wishers a petition was accordingly drawn up in form, setting forth such of her adventures and such of the hardships she had underwent as were most conducive to procure the relief requested, but more particularly the many and dangerous wounds she had received, and the heroic manner in which she turned her own physician for the better concealment of her sex.

This petition, thus drawn up to the entire satisfaction of herself and her friends, was delivered to his Royal Highness with her own hands, in the same dress and form as the picture which was delivered with the first number of this work; for on Saturday, June 16, 1750, a very favourable opportunity offering, his Royal Highness being in his landau, accompanied by Colonel Napier, and standing still whilst one of his servants was gone on a short errand, our female adventurer had time sufficient to present her memorial into the coach, and, with a modest assurance, carried her project into execution.

His Royal Highness, with his wonted goodness and condescension towards all soldiers in general, not only received it, but, being at leisure, perused the contents, and afterwards delivered it to the colonel, at the same time desiring him to make some inquiry into the merits of the petition, that he might be the better able to form a true state of so uncommon a case, and, if real fact, encourage his female petitioner for her heroic achievements.

Colonel Napier, struck with the novelty of the affair and with the extraordinary intrepidity of the petitioner (in case the contents were really matter of fact), assured his Royal Highness that his orders should he punctually obeyed, and that he would soon acquaint him either with the truth or falsehood of the allegations in the memorial contained.

Accordingly the colonel made all the inquiries that were requisite in a case so extraordinary, and in a short time "was so good and gracious as to represent the affair to the Duke in a very favourable light for the petitioner, which gave his Highness a very agreeable surprise, and thereupon he told the colonel that such an Amazonian lady as Mrs. Snell was deserved some encouragement, and that her heroic achievements should not be altogether buried in oblivion.

What acts of indulgence, however, his Royal Highness, out of his wonted goodness and peculiar regard for the meanest soldier in the army that behaves himself like a man, proposes to show to our heroine is not in our power at present absolutely to determine, but we are in hopes that we shall be able to give a satisfactory account of so important a particular before we come to conclude this narrative; and we are farther in hopes that it will prove not only an annuity for life, but such a one as will (when added to what she can earn by the dint of her own industry and application to business) enable her for the future to spend the remainder of her days in some degree of credit and reputation.

It is demonstrable that our heroine (ever since the discovery of her sex to the public) has generously disdained to lead a life of indolence and ease, but has shown a more than ordinary ambition to render herself conspicuous in the military way; and the amazing success which she met with on her benefit night at the New Wells, in Goodman's Fields, through her common dexterity and address in representing the jovial tar and the well-disciplined marine, is an incontestable demonstration.

What she did that night, and what additional performances she has exhibited since, has induced the manager of the said house to enter into a contract with her to pay her a weekly salary for the season, which is such a stipend that not one woman in ten thousand of her low extraction and want of literature could by any act of industry (howsoever laborious) with any possibility procure.

As we have now brought our heroine on the public stage, and as she, by her wonted presence of mind and unwearied application to that her casual profession for her present maintenance and support, we imagine a particular detail of all her several performances, together with a transcript of the most humorous and entertaining songs, with which she continues to divert the town, and that, too, with universal applause, will be thought no disagreeable amusement.

But before we enter on that detail, give us leave to make a few cursory reflections on her extraordinary merit, which, in our humble opinion, must needs place her on a level with the most celebrated of the ancient heroines. She ought not to be entered on the same list with the late famous Pamela, who for some time alarmed the town with her extraordinary virtues. Those, we are all sensible, were imaginary only, and the result of an artful bookseller, or author's brains, who entertained the public, to his no small emolument, with a fabulous story of a lady of his own creating, one that never in reality had any existence; whereas the virtue and chastity in particular of our heroine, who is no shadow but true flesh and blood, have been amply displayed in one of the remotest corners of the world, and doubtless will now be displayed all over Europe with equal lustre. With what amazing art did she conceal her sex, and by what means preserve her chastity amongst a whole crowd of military men at the famous siege of Pondicherry, of which we have given, we hope, a satisfactory account already? With what intrepidity, with what presence of mind, did she behave when on the stormy ocean in a leaky vessel just ready to sink into the unfathomable abyss? Who, of all the most skilful sailors, was more active and resolute than she was? What marine, howsoever well disciplined, ever exercised his small arms better on the poop and quarter-deck than she did? In a word, who fired his pontoon, who brandished his sword with more bravery, and, in the attack of the enemy, who with more undaunted courage exposed himself to greater dangers than she did, or who testified a greater readiness to lay down her life for the service of her country than our female adventurer? If these, and a thousand other instances too tedious to repeat, will not give our heroine an indisputable right and title to as high a character for her honour and virtue as the famed Pamela, though a fictitious one, I am greatly mistaken, and shall freely submit them to the superior judgement of our impartial readers.

To what I have here said I shall only add one sanguine wish, namely this: May she hereafter meet with as much encouragement as she does at present, and ever remain (if she persists to merit it) the just object of universal admiration!

I hope the reader will excuse this little excursion, by way of encomium.

And as we have here attempted to do her merit justice in plain humble prose, we think we can have no fairer opportunity than this which at present offers itself of introducing an ingenious and sincere, though somewhat ludicrous, panegyric of our female soldier by a young son of Parnassus.

The humorous and good-natured poem, then, in favour of our heroine is, without any farther unnecessary introduction, couched in the following terms, which we have the pleasure of transcribing from one of the public papers; and as it was inserted there for the general amusement of the town, we doubt not but it will be equally acceptable to the readers of these our memoirs in particular.

The title and words, then, of the above-mentioned little facetious poem, or character of our heroine, which, by the way, we may venture to assure our readers has met with universal approbation, are as follows, viz.:

THE FEMALE SOLDIER

Hannah in briggs,[1] behaved so well
That none her softer sex could tell;
Nor was her policy confounded
When near the mark of nature wounded;
Which proves what men will scarce admit,
That women are for secrets fit.
  That healthful blood could keep so long
Amidst young fellows hale and strong
Demonstrates, though a seeming wonder,
That love to courage truckles under.
  Oh, how her bedmate bit his lips,
And marked the spreading of her hips,
And cursed the blindness of his youth,
When she confessed the naked truth!
Her fortitude, to no man's second,
To woman's honour must be reckoned.
Twelve wounds! 'Twas half [2] great Caesar's number,
That made his corpse the ground encumber.
How many men, for heroes nursed,
Had left their colours at the first.
  'Twas thought Achilles' greatest glory
That Homer was to sing his story;
And Alexander mourned his lot
That no such bard could then be got—
But Hannah's praise no Homer needs;
She lives to sing her proper deeds.

Who the author was of the preceding composition is not any-ways material to our readers; but thus far we can venture to assert of our own knowledge, that he is a poet of no indifferent ability, and one who wrote it purely to gratify his own humour, without any favour or affection to the subject of it, whom he had never seen or heard of any otherwise than by the first edition of this our narrative.

We shall now return to the Wells, and amuse the reader with a succinct account of her several nightly performances there, which she performs with the general approbation of a vast crowd of spectators.

---

[1] A cant word for breeches.
[2] Plutarch tells us that Caesar had twenty-three wounds.

Such of our readers, then, as never indulged themselves so far as to be eye-witness of the various operations of that house must know that there is a stated method of proceeding in their entertainments, viz., rope-dancing, tumbling, ladder-dancing, surprising exploits on the slack-rope, and singing (which is one branch of our heroine's province) are all exhibited with great decency and decorum at their proper times, and all the entertainments in general, which are too tedious here to repeat, are accompanied with a very agreeable concert of music.

All our business is to confine ourselves to our young tar's and marine's operations, which we may venture to pronounce very extraordinary as an actor, since she never received any instructions from those that have made the practice of that art their peculiar study and employment, nor ever appeared in her lifetime upon any stage whatever but where she now is and where she gives as general satisfaction to her audiences as those who have been regularly trained up from their very infancy to such public exhibitions.

The first character, then, which she assumes at her stated times is that of a tar, in which she is very decently dressed in her men's clothes, and entertains the company with a variety of songs, the first of which, for the generality, is this that follows:

Tune: "Come and listen to my ditty."

All ye noble British spirits
    That midst dangers glory sought,
Let it lessen not your merit,
    That a woman bravely fought.
Cupid slyly first curoll'd me,
    Pallas next her force did bring,
Pressed my heart to venture boldly
    For my love and for my king.

Sailor-like, to fear a stranger,
    Straight I ventured on the main,
Facing death and every danger,
    Love and glory to obtain.
Tell me, you who hear my story,
    What could more my courage move,
George's name inspired with glory,
    William was the man I loved.

When from William Susan parted
    She but wept and shook her hand;
I more bold (though tender-hearted),

Left my friends and native land;
Bravely by his side maintaining
    British rights, I shed my blood,
Still to him unknown remaining,
    Watched to serve and do him good.

In the midst of blood and slaughter
    Bravely lighting for my king,
Facing death from every quarter,
    Fame and conquest home to bring.
Sure you'll own 'tis more than common,
    And the world proclaim it too,
Never yet did any woman
    More for love and glory do.

Now in performance of this branch of her province it must be allowed that art and the airs of a player are loss conspicuous in her than in those who have long made singing on the stage their principal profession. But then Nature steps in and amply supplies that deficiency. She puts on no affected, no stupid airs to embellish the words of her poet; neither has she, in reality, as she will readily enough and modestly acknowledge, any acquired judgement in music, to add new graces to the several catches which she exhibits; but then her action is free, easy, and without affectation, and Nature has given her such a voice that renders her services in that way highly acceptable to the public, and that too in such a manner that she is obliged to repeat her operations to gratify the audience.

Though she is furnished with other songs, yet that in regard to the herring fishery, first sung by the anti-Galliciaus, a society who have assumed that title to show their loyalty to their king and sincere wishes to the prosperity and welfare of their country, is her next favourite performance and what is universally admired, and shall be inserted at the end of this work.

As it would not only be endless, but too tedious a task to transcribe all her musical treasures, we shall drop that subject and proceed to her manual operations, in which she acts a marine, and has met with uncommon success.

Herein we think she may be allowed to perform her part as an able and experienced actor.

In this branch of her office she appears regularly dressed in her regimentals from top to toe, with, all the accoutrements requisite for the due performance of her military exercises.

Here she and her attendants fill up the stage in a very agreeable manner. The tabor and drum give a life to her march, and she traverses the stage two or three times over, step by step, in the same manner as our soldiers march on the parade in St. James' Park.

After the spectators have been sufficiently amused with this formal procession she begins her military exercises, and goes through the whole catechism (if I may be allowed the expression) with so much dexterity and address, and with so little hesitation or default, that great numbers even of veteran soldiers, who have resorted to the Wells out of mere curiosity only, have frankly acknowledged that she executes what she undertakes to admiration, and that the universal applause which she meets with is by no means the result of partiality to her in consideration of her sex, but is due to her without favour or affection as the effect of her extraordinary merit.

As our readers may be desirous of being informed in what dress she now appears, we think it proper to inform them that she wears men's clothes, being, as she says, determined to continue so to do, and having bought new clothing for that purpose.

Before we conclude these unparalleled memoirs of our female heroine, we shall be obliged to inform our readers that (pursuant to the gracious promise of his Royal Highness, that her heroic achievements should not be altogether buried in oblivion), our female soldier will have, by the indulgence of his Majesty's letter, the allowance of one shilling per diem for and during the term of her natural life, which amounts in the whole to £18 5s. per annum.

We were in great hopes (before we had closed this account) to have had it in our power to add more substantial rewards to that above mentioned, since we have before hinted that we would do so if possibly we could. What his Royal Highness, however, may possibly do for her hereafter rests still undetermined, and we must content ourselves (since he has not thought fit to exert his bounty and benevolence towards her as yet) with wishing (as we have done before) that it may be some farther annual pension, in order to enable her to spend the remainder of her days in some degree of credit and reputation.

As it is not natural to suppose that the martial exercises of our heroine can continue long to be an entertainment to the town, or that her singing in the manner that she does, which is agreeable enough whilst it is received as a novelty, can stand the test any longer than the present season, our heroine and actress is determined to make hay whilst the sun shines, and, like the laborious ant, to lay up a little stock to support her against a rainy day.

As we have all along commended her for her presence of mind when plunged in the very worst of calamities, so we think her equally commendable for her prudence and good conduct under her success, since she is daily studying how she shall accomplish a comfortable subsistence in some reputable way of business when that of an actress will be no longer regarded, and by consequence will bring in no sufficient grist to her mill.

She is not so vain or so affected as to attribute the applause which she at present meets with to any other cause than the novelty of the thing, and she is very conscious to herself that, had she made her appearance upon the stage in petticoats, she should have made but an awkward figure, and that all her performances would have been lifeless and insipid, for which reason we cannot but think that her notions were very just, and that her resolution to decline the female garb for ever hereafter is not so blameworthy as some may perhaps be apt to imagine; and we think her the more excusable in that particular since she is resolutely bent to be lord and master of herself, and never more to entertain the least thoughts of having a husband to rule and govern her, and make her truckle to his wayward humours.

Since this is the true state of her case, and since (as we have hinted before) she has lately purchased a new suit of decent man's apparel as an incontestable proof of her aversion to the present fashionable hoop, we shall let our readers into the secret of her future intentions, which, as we approve of them ourselves, so we hope our readers will likewise, and encourage her as much in her new station of life as that in which she now makes a tolerable figure.

The scheme, then, or plan, which she has laid down for the improvement of that little money which she has already raised by her uncommon dexterity and address (and such other annual income as may casually be conferred upon her from the indulgence of his Royal Highness the Duke), is to take some noted public-house, either in some conspicuous part of the city or else within the Bills of Mortality, where she proposes to assume a new character—I mean that of a jovial publican; in which, it is our opinion, she will be as able to shine as in that of a tarpaulin or a marine. And we hope, as she proposes to sell the very best of liquors at the lowest prices, those gentlemen and ladies who have favoured her so far as to have been frequent spectators of her dexterity and address in the art military, will hereafter visit her house, and be not only eye-witnesses but partakers of her culinary operations, to which she is no more a stranger than to the former, as she was allowed by her officers to understand the art of cookery, and was often employed by them as an artful hand in their kapelion.

As she has entertained some thoughts of this nature she has already determined (amongst other preliminaries) to hang up a whimsical sign to draw in her customers and to distinguish herself from the rest of her brother publicans.

She has already, for that purpose, agreed with a very able painter to delineate her in her regimentals on one side of her intended sign, and in her jacket and trousers on the other, and underneath each it will be proper to be written in large capitals:

"THE WOMAN IN MASQUERADE."

Now, should our female soldier but once be able to carry this well-concerted project into execution, we may with justice allow her to be an able and experienced pilot—one who has steered a leaky and shattered vessel into harbour. All's well (we say) that ends well, and that would doubtless be her case could she but once procure such an happy establishment.

* * * * * *

If, therefore, we will but reflect on the long series of misfortunes which this our female soldier ran through with amazing intrepidity and resolution and with almost unexampled presence of mind and then again reflect how by her art and industry she has, to the wonder of all mankind, proved her own physician, and extricated herself out of all her difficulties, when death itself has stared her in the face, we think we may very well recommend her to all our readers as a grand pattern of patience and perseverance under the worst of afflictions. From her prudent deportment and presence of mind we may learn to bear our misfortunes whenever they befall us with a good grace, to be always diligent and industrious in using the natural means to extricate ourselves out of the unavoidable distresses which we labour under, and never to murmur or repine at our hard lot, but leave the event to Providence, who is always ready and willing to assist those who put their whole trust and confidence in Him. From the numerous incidents in the preceding narrative we may learn never to despair or sink under the weight of any oppression whatever, but to be manfully cheerful, though the clouds over our heads look ever so black and lowering, and to live in hopes that after the heaviest storm there may come a calm, and the sun, though for the present obscured, may once more shine out in its meridian glory.

The revolution of a day may bring such turns as Heaven itself could scarce have promised. That thought should make us always cheerful, and induce to submit with patience and resignation to the Divine Will when He sees fit to afflict us. As this, doubtless, is the best and most natural application that possibly can be made of the preceding memoirs, we shall take the liberty to close this important lesson of instruction with the following extract from one of our brightest poets (though at present we are not able to recollect his name), which we hope the generality of our readers will allow to be very pertinent to the present occasion, and an agreeable conclusion to this our little undertaking:

> Though plunged in isles, and exercised in care,
> Yet never let the noble mind despair;
> When pressed by dangers and beset with foes,
> The gods their timely succour interpose;
> And when our virtue sinks, o'erwhelmed with grief,
> By unforeseen expedients bring relief.

Mary Lacy

THE
HISTORY
OF THE
FEMALE SHIPWRIGHT

TO WHOM

The GOVERNMENT has granted a Superannuated Pension of TWENTY POUNDS per
Annum, during her Life.

WRITTEN BY HERSELF

LONDON

Printed and sold by M. LEWIS, No. 1; S. Bladon,
No. 28, in Pater-noiter Row; and by the Author
in King Street, Deptford

MDCCLXXIII
[1773]

PREFACE

THE reality of the facts contained in the following History will, it is presumed, conduce in a great measure to recommend the perusal of it to the Public and it will, I doubt not with every candid and considerate reader, prove a sufficient apology for the inaccuracies of style and sentiment which I may be justly chargeable with as the author, that I laboured under many inconveniences in collecting the various materials which compose it. The great number of incidents related therein are presented to public inspection in a plain and simple garb, that being judged the most suitable dress for a narrative of this kind.

The reader will find herein, 1. A circumstantial account of what happened to me during my childhood, wherein will appear many evident tokens of that restless and untractable disposition in an early period of life, which gave rise to all my succeeding adventures and misfortunes.

2. The method made use for leaving my parents by disguising myself in man's apparel, principally for the sake of withdrawing myself from the company of a young man, for whom I found I had conceived too great an attachment, and who was the primary, though involuntary cause of my departure. The uncommon embarrassments and difficulties I struggled with during the first four years of my service, in order to conceal my sex when at sea, where I was almost continually in company, with 700 men for that time, without incurring the least suspicion of being a woman; for which, and the many narrow escapes I afterwards had, I cannot but acknowledge myself indebted to the goodness of Divine Providence, who imbued me with prudence and discretion to conduct myself under every circumstance, and carried, me through all.

3. Of my serving seven years as an apprentice to a shipwright, with the numerous sufferings I endured from ill treatment under different masters, and the various scenes of immorality and profaneness my situation amongst sea-faring people made me a constant, though disgusted, witness to. And,

4. The hardships I went through in being forced to cross the water at Gosport in the most inclement seasons for the space of

five years and a half; the severe labour I was employed in since that time, attended with illness, amidst the dreadful apprehensions of a discovery of my sex through the baseness of the woman who betrayed me.

It will not be amiss to conclude this address by explaining my motives for endeavouring to be as frequently as possible in the company of women, in the way of courtship which were, in the first place, to avoid the conversation of the men, which I need not observe, was, amongst those of this class especially, in many respects very offensive to a delicate ear and, 2dly, for the sake of affording me a more agreeable repast amongst persons of my own sex, many of whom, I am sorry to say were too much addicted to evil practices by their unlawful commerce with the other, as will on many occasions appear in the course of the story.

Deptford, July 1, 1773

M. SLADE

The History of the Female Shipwright

AFTER mentioning my maiden name, which was MARY LACY, it will be proper to inform the reader, that I was born at Wickham, in the county of Kent, on the 12th of January, 1740; but had not been long in the world before my father and mother agreed to live at Ash, so that I knew little more of Wickham than I had learned from my parents, on which account Ash might almost be reckoned my native place. My father and mother were poor, and forced to work very hard for their bread. They had one son and two daughters, of whom I was the eldest. At a proper time, my mother put me to school, to give me what learning she could, which kept me out of their way whilst they were at work; for being young, I was always in mischief and my mother not having spare time sufficient to look after me, I had so much my own will, that when I came to have some knowledge, it was a difficult matter for them to keep me within proper bounds.

After I had learned my letters, I was admitted into a charity school, which was kept by one Mrs. R _____ n; and she, knowing my parents, took great pains to instruct me in reading. As I took my learning very fast, my mistress was the more careful of me; for she was indeed as a mother to me and in these respects was more serviceable than my parents could possibly be. When I was old enough to learn to work my mistress taught me to knit; which she perceiving me very fond of learning, employed me in knitting gloves, stockings, night-caps, and such sort of work, so

59

that I soon perfected myself in it; which I was the more encouraged to, as my mistress rewarded me for every piece of knitting and all the money I earned she reserved in a little box; so that when I wanted any thing, she would buy it for me. Thus, by the help of God and good friends, I was no great charge to my parents; for being always at school, my mistress set me about all manner of work in the house; so that, though young, I was very handy, and in a way of improvement.

About this time I used to go on errands for my neighbours, and help them what I could; but that practice, by occasioning me to go pretty much abroad in the streets, became very prejudicial to me; for I was thereby addicted to all manner of mischief, as will appear by the following instance: There was one C__h__e Cipp__r, about my age, that lived in Ash, with whom, when I could get out, I always kept company, and, when together, did many unjustifiable actions; for one day we took it into our heads to purloin a bridle and saddle out of the stable of one Mr. John R_____ n, butcher of Ash who kept a little horse in a field about a mile from the town. This horse we caught, put the saddle and bridle on, and rode about the field till we were tired, and afterwards restored then to the place from whence we took them; I liked riding so well, that I never was easy but when among the horses; for I used to go to Mr. R__h__rd__n, and say, Master, shall I fetch your sheep up out of the field? And if he wanted them, I immediately took the little horse, without saddle or bridle, and mounting on his back set off as fast as the horse could go, thus running all hazards of my life; and was so wild and heedless, that if any body took notice of my riding so fast, and told me l should fall off, and break my neck, my answer was, "Neck or nothing!" If I happened to fall, I did not care, for I was no sooner off than on again.

I then thought my mother was my greatest enemy, for she being a very passionate woman, used to beat me in such a manner, that the neighbours thought she would kill me. But after my crying was over, I was out of the doors again at my old tricks with my play fellows, and frequently stayed out all day long, and never went home at all for which I was afterwards sure to be corrected.

There was one Mrs. Bax that lived the next door to my mother who every now and then wanted me to bring her something, and often caused me to be beat, so that I did not like her at all. But one morning she asked my mother to let me fetch her a halfpenny loaf for her breakfast, which my mother ordered me to do. I went to bring the loaf but thought within myself I would be even with her and knowing she could not eat the crust, as I came home with it I ate out all the crumb, and putting the two crusts together again, carried it into her house, and laid it down, and then set off for the whole day; for I knew that if I went home I should be beat. When she had sound out that I had eat the crumb of the loaf, she told my mother what I had done; but not finding me, my mother told her that when I came home at night she would chastise me for it, which she accordingly did, and made me go to bed without any supper.

After this, my mother was determined to make me go to service, as soon as she could get a place for me, as she thought I grew worst by running about the streets; and my mistress where I went to school having seven children, the first place I had was with one of her daughters, whose name was Mary Richardson. I staid with her about a year and half, and then returned home to my mother; soon after which I went to school to learn to write.

After I had been at home about a year, I went to live with an elder sister of my former mistress. She was married, to one Mr. Goodson, a shoemaker who was set up in his business, and employed men to work for him. They both lived very happy together and she had three children by him. But as it pleased God to take my master out of the World, his widow settled herself in a milliner's shop, she being capable of making every thing she sold: by this prudent conduct my mistress did very well and used me kindly, but I was at that time too insensible of the good treatment I met with. She learned me to work with my needle, which if I had but applied myself to with proper care and industry, I should, in all probability, have escaped many of the unknown sorrows I afterwards suffered. But, as is commonly the case, when young and inexperienced of the world we are not aware of the calamities that may befall us as we advance in life. I was so very thoughtless and discontented that I was always ill, or had some complaint or other to make; but what, I did not know; and would often go and tell my mother my grievances; and she, having a tender heart, believed all I said, and took my part, which contributed, to make me idle; and if my mistress said anything I did not like, though it was for my good, I used to go and represent it in an unfavourable light to my mother; for which behaviour if she had reprimanded or even beat me, I should have left off so childish a practice; and should rather have minded what my mistress said to me, and obeyed her. But being of a roving disposition, I never liked to be within doors; and if I could get out with the young child, I thought myself happy; for if I staid within doors, I was idle and studying what mischief I should do; so that my thoughts were never inclined to any good for myself.

My mistress married a second time to one Mr. Daniel Deverson, a shoemaker, and they lived very happy together; which I might have experienced the good effects of had I not been of such an untowardly turn of mind; for I had now acquired such a fondness for dancing that I used to get out of the house in the evening, and be dancing all the night long, which was the beginning of all my sorrow; for by this means I contracted an acquaintance with a new sweetheart, so that I never was contented but when in his company. But happening to be out one night at this pastime, the child cried that used to lie with me, and waked my mistress. She hearing the child cry, called to me, but receiving no answer, got up, and came into my room; but not finding me there, she thought I was gone to a house where a young man used to play on the violin; for she knew the young men and maids met at this house. When my mistress came to the house where I was, she found me very merry and happy but when I saw her, I was very much surprised, and seemed very sorry for what I had done, because as it was the first time I was discovered, she thought I had never served her so before; but I had been out time after time, though this was the first occasion of its being known.

The next morning, my mistress told me that I should do myself no good by going on in this course of life and gave me seasonable advice, if I had been but wise enough to think so; but I took it quite the contrary way, and thought I was not well used; whereupon we agreed to part. I was now about sixteen years of age; and have often since reflected that my mistress bore my misbehaviour and cross temper purely with a view to my advantage, and kept me so long with her for no other purpose, if I could but have thought so; for it is certain she wished me as well as if I had been one of her own children.

After leaving my mistress, I went home as usual, to my father and mother. I now embraced all opportunities of going out to dance with my sweetheart; for when I was with him I imagined myself happy. But this young man did not perceive that I loved him so much and it happened very unfortunately I did not tell any of my friends of it, which if I had done, it would probably have been better for me; for my mother would no doubt have persuaded me for my good. But I afterwards felt the bad effects of concealing this warm affection. I could not blame the young man, since he had never given me any reason so to do. Hereupon I was very unsettled in my mind and unable to fix myself in any place; nevertheless, I carried it off as well as I could.

I had not been long at home, before one Mr. Daniel Stoaders at Ash wanted me to come and live with him; accordingly I went and liked the place very well; and, had I been but contented, I might have lived there very comfortably. But my mind became continually disturbed and uneasy about this young man, who was the involuntary cause of all my trouble, which was aggravated by my happening to see him one day talk to a young woman: the thoughts of this made me so very unhappy, that I was from that time more unsettled than ever.

A short time after, a thought came into my head to dress myself in men's apparel, and set off by myself; but where to go, I did not know, nor what I was to do when I was gone. I had no thought what was to become of me, or what sorrow and anxiety I should bring upon my aged father and mother by losing me; but my inclinations were still bent on leaving home. In order to this, I went one day into my master's brother's room, and there found an old frock, an old pair of breeches, an old pair of pumps, and an old pair of stockings; all which did very well but still was at a great loss for a hat; but then I recollected that my father had got one at home, if I could but procure it unknown to my parents; I therefore intended to get it without their knowledge: whereupon I went to my mother's house to ask her for a gown which I had given her the day before to mend for me. She answered, I should have it tomorrow; But little did my poor mother know what I wanted; for I went immediately into my father's room, took the hat, put it under my apron, and came down stairs; but I never said good-bye, or anything else to my mother; but went home to my place, and packed up the things that I had got; and now only waited an opportunity to decamp.

On the first day of May, 1759, about-six o'clock in the morning, I set off; and when I had got out of town into the fields, I pulled off my cloaths and put on men's, leaving my own in a hedge; some in one place and some in another. Having thus dressed myself in men's habit, I went on to a place called Wingham, where a fair was held that day. Here I wandered about til evening; then went to a public house, and asked them to let me have a lodging that night, for which I agreed to give two-pence: now all the money I had when I came away was no more than five-pence. Accordingly I went to bed, and slept very well till morning, when I got up, and began to think which way I should go, as my money was so short; however, I proceeded towards Canterbury. But as I was coming along upon the road, a post-chaise overtook me: I got up behind it, and rode to Canterbury and then the post-chaise stopping, I quitted it, and walked on before, that they might not take any notice of me. After perceiving they did not take the horses out of the chaise I concluded they were going farther, but did not know where; nor indeed did I care what became of me. When they came on the road to Chatham, I got up behind; not knowing whither I was going never having been so far from home in my life.

When the chaise had reached Chatham, I got down, but was an utter stranger to the place; only I remembered to have heard my father and mother talk about a man's being hung in chains at Chatham; and, when I saw him, I thought this must be the place. I immediately began to think what I must do for a lodging; having no more than one penny, with which I went and bought some bread and cheese. Here I was quite at a loss what step to take: to go home again was death to me; and to ask for a lodging, I was ashamed: so I walked up and down the streets, as it was the fair time, and sauntered about till it was dark.

As I stood considering what I should do, I looked about me, and saw a farm house on the left hand of Chatham, as you go down the hill; I thought within myself I would go to it, and ask them to let me lie there; but when I came down to the house I was ashamed to make the request. In this distressed situation I continued some time, not knowing how to proceed; for money I had none, and to lie in the streets I never was used to, and what to do I did not know: but at last I resolved to lie in the straw, concluding that to be somewhat better than lying in the street; accordingly I went and got in among the straw, and laid myself down, but was so greatly terrified that I was afraid to move; for when the pigs stirred a little, I thought somebody was coming to frighten me; therefore I did not dare open my eyes, lest I should see something frightful. I had but very little sleep; and when it was morning, I got up and shook my cloaths, and looked about to see if any body perceived me get out, then came down to the town, and went up to some men that belonged to a collier, who gave me some victuals and drink with them.

While I was standing there a gentleman came up to me, and asked me if I would go to sea? For, said he, it is fine weather now at sea; and if you will go, I will get you a good master on board the Sandwich. I replied, Yes, Sir. He then shewed me the nearest way on board but instead of going to St. Princess' bridge (as the gentleman had directed me) I went over where the tide came up, being half up my legs in mud, but at length I got up to the bridge, and seeing a boat there, I asked the men belonging to it if they were going on board the Sandwich? They told me they were; and asked me if I wanted to go on board? I told them, Yes. They enquired , who I wanted there? I told them, the gunner. They laughed, said I was a brave boy, and that I would do very well for him. But I did not know who was to be my master, or what I was to do, or whether I had strength to perform it: They then carried me on board.

When I came alongside the Sandwich, there were lighters with rigging or something belonging to her that appeared all strange to me, as I never had seen such a large ship before; having often seen the hoys at Sandwich haven. When getting out of the lighter into the Sandwich I thought it was impossible for such a great ship to go to sea. But what the men most took notice of, was my observing how many windows the ship had got; she not yet having got her guns on board, for her ports were open.

When I found that the men laughed at me, I was angry with myself for saying any thing before I was acquainted with it. The sailors asked if me if I would go to the gunner, who was in his cabin in the gun room. Accordingly I went down; but it was re-markable I did not know the head of the ship from the stern; for when I was down I could not find the way up again. When the gunner saw me, he asked where I come from, and how I came there? I told him I had left my friends. He inquired if I had been 'prentice to any body, and run away? I told him, No. Well, said he, should you like to go to sea? I replied, Yes, Sir. He then asked if I was hungry? I answered in the affirmative; having had but very little all the day. Upon this, he ordered his servant to serve me some biscuit and cheese. The boy went and brought me some, and said, Here countryman, eat heartily; which I accordingly did for the bisquit being new, I liked it well, or else my being hungry made it go down very sweet and savoury. After I had eat sufficiently, the gunner came and asked my name. I told him my name was Wil-liam Chandler: but God knows how that came into my head; though it is true, my mother's maiden name was Chandler, and my father's name William Lacy; therefore I took the name of Chan-dler. Then, the gunner told his boy to give me some victuals with him; and that when he went on shore, I was to go with him, (Jeremiah Pane, for that was his name) and we agreed very well: for he used to carry the people over the river, which sometimes put a few pence in his pocket; so that he always had some money, and was very good to me, and often gave me some, with which we sometimes tossed up for pies: therefore I lived very happy, considering the condition and situation I was in at that time.

There was another circumstance that attended me; for though I could not play the rogue much at first, yet in a little time afterwards I learned to do it very completely; But not knowing all this time who was my master made me dissatisfied; for I had no linen to clean myself with, having only the shirt that I had when I came from Ash; and I was very much afraid my fellow servant should see my shirt had no collar; and besides; I had no other cloaths to wear but those I had on which gave me such concern, that I often wished I was at home again. But the thoughts of seeing the young man again when I went home, diverted me entirely from that resolution, and made me conclude that I had rather live upon bread and water, and go through all the trouble that I had brought, or might hereafter bring upon myself, than go home again.

I had been on board the Sandwich about two days when the carpenter came on board; and he only had one servant, who was at work in Chatham Yard; so at that time he had none on board. Now the gunner, whose name was Rd. Russel, liked me very well: he lived in lodgings at a place called Brompton, near Chatham; and the landlady of the house where he lodged had a son, who wanted to go to sea; and this woman was willing, if the gunner would take him, that he should go: whereupon the gunner and she agreed that he should go to sea with him as his servant. He told me, the carpenter would be glad to have me as his servant; for he was not willing I should be the captain's servant, that being the worst place in the ship; but at that time I did not know which was the best or worst: Mr. Russel, the gunner, therefore spoke to Mr. Richard Baker, the carpenter, for me. I was then sent for to the carpenter's cabbin. He asked me whether I had been an apprentice to anybody, and was run away? I told him, No. Well, said he, are you a Kentish boy, or a boy of Kent? For my part, I did not then know the difference between a Kentish boy and a boy of Kent; but I answered, A boy of Kent, which happened to be right. This made him laugh at me; for he was a merry man; but when out of humour, it was trouble enough to please him.

I shall here take occasion to relate what my master said to me concerning being his servant. There were two gentlemen with him. He first of all ordered me to fetch him a can of beer: I accordingly went, and brought it to him. Now; said he, you must learn to make a can of flip, and to broil me a beef steak, and to make my bed against I come to live on board. Come, said he, and I will shew you how to make my bed. So we went to his cabin, in which there was a bed that turned up, and he began to take the bed-cloaths off one by one. Now, said he, you must shake, them one by one, you must tumble and shake the bed about, then you must lay the sheets on one at a time, and lastly the blankets. I replied, Yes, Sir; Well said he, you will soon learn to make a bed, that I see already. But he little knew who he had got to make his bed and he not having any suspicion of my being a woman, I affected to appear as ignorant of the matter as if I had known nothing about it. He then provided for me a bed and bedding of a boatswain who came on board to see him and then directed his mate to sling it up for me. When I attempted to get into bed at night, I got in at one side and fell out on the other; which made all the seamen laugh at me; but, as it happened, there were not a great many on board, for being a new ship, not many had entered on board of her; so that my hammock was hung up in the sun-deck: but when the whole ship's company was on-board, it was then taken down, and placed below in the wing, where the carpenter and the yeomen both were; now it was better for me to lay there than any where else. But I was very uneasy by lying there, on account of a quarter-master that lay in that place, whom I did not much like: and when I came to lie in the blankets, I did not know what to do, for I thought I was eat up with vermin, having been on board ten days, and had no cloaths to shift myself with; so that I looked ;black enough to frighten any body.

One day my master came on board, which was on a Saturday, and called me to go along with him; he had me up on the gangway, and shewed me three hay slacks, and asked me if I saw them. I told him, Yes, sir. Well, said he, I would have you come on shore to-morrow morning, in the first boat that you can get: walk till you have lost sight of those hay stacks, and then enquire for one Mr. Baker, at St. Margaret's Bank, Chatham; and when you come to my house, you shall clean yourself: after which, my master went on shore; and immediately thought that I had a great many particulars to remember; for fear therefore I should forget them, (as ;I could write well enough for myself to understand) I went to my pantry door, and there I set it down. When the morning was come, I got up, and took the direction off the door, set it down on my hat, got on shore as soon as I could; and made all possible haste to find out my master's house, and walked till I had lost sight of the hay stacks. Seeing a woman stand at the door, I asked her where one Mr. Baker, carpenter of the Sandwich lived? She shewed me the house: and when I was got there, how glad was I! For I longed to see my mistress, and what fort of a house they lived in. I went and knocked, and there came a woman to the door, of whom I enquired, if one Mr. Baker lived there. Whereupon she fell a laughing, and said, What do you want with him? I told her, my master had ordered me to come to him. Then she laughed again, and asked me if I knew my master when I saw him. I answered, Yes. She then bid me come in. I went into the kitchen where my .master was sitting. My mistress asked me if that was my master? I replied, Yes, ma'am. My master next enquired if I was hungry? Indeed I thought I could gladly eat a bit of bread and butter, and drink a bason of tea, for I even longed for some, having had none since I came away from Ash. But I told him, I was not hungry; notwithstanding which, he being a merry man, said to me, You can eat a little bit? I answered, Yes, Sir. On my saying this, my mistress gave me a bason of tea and a bit of bread and butter, more than I could eat but I quickly found out a way to dispose of the remainder, for what could not eat, I put in my pocket.

When I had eat my breakfast, my master called me out backwards; where there was some soap and water to wash myself with. How glad was I! hardly being able to contain myself for joy. But there was something that gave me greater pleasure; for after I had washed myself, my mistress gave me a clean shirt, a pair of stockings, a pair of shoes, a coat and waistcoat, a checked handkerchief, and a red night-cap for me to wear at sea: I was also to have my hair cut off when I went on board; but this operation I did not, like at all, yet was afraid to say anything to my master about it. However, I was very glad to find I had got clean cloaths to dress myself in, not having, had that refreshment since I left Ash.

I must next inform you what trouble I was in; for I was afraid that my master would want to see my shirt; but my fears were soon over; for he only ordered me to put up all my cloaths together, and carry them on board with me. Now if I had changed my linen at his house, he would have seen my chest, and then he would have easily discovered my Sex. Accordingly I took my things, went on board, and cleaned myself from top to toe. My master told me that I must wash my things every Monday; and that he would look them over every week; and, said he, if I don't find them clean, I shall flog you. Still I was in great trouble, lest he should ask me for my white shirt, for I had never a one to screen me from telling a lie: but I new that Jeremiah Pane had got one; so I went and asked him if he would sell me his shirt; for it was not worth a great deal. Well, said he, you shall have it for nine-pence. I replied, I will give you nine-pence for it. He agreed; I paid him the money, and got the shirt, to my no small joy. I then went and washed it, and carried it to my locker, for fear my master would ask me about it.

The ship had now orders to sail to Black Stakes, to take in her guns; consequently we proceeded to get them in; When I came to see the guns, I thought it was impossible for the ship to carry them, they being so large; for I had never seen a man of war before; so that it seemed very strange to me. But we had not lain long at Black Stakes before we went to the Nore and there we lay till farther orders. We had now got a great number of men on board; some we had from the Polly Green, some from one ship, and some from another. These men were paid off from their several ships to come on board of us. But while we lay at the Nore there came a bomb boat woman on board us, to sell all sorts of goods; this woman being an acquaintance of my master's, she had the use of his cabbin; therefore I was desired to boil the tea kettle for her; and to do anything she ordered me; and I was glad of it, for she was very good to me, and gave me a new purse to put my money in. Now my master kept the key to the round-house; therefore the women had no convenient place of easing the necessity of nature; and he told me not to let them have the key, unless they gave me something; by this means I got several pence from them. My master then told me that my mistress was coming on board, and intended to stay all night; and desired me not to go from the cabin door, lest he should want me. Agreeable to my instructions, I sat down by the cabin door, and ran and fetched every thing that she had occasion for; but when I carried her any thing, instead of pulling off my hat, I was ready to make a curtsy; however, they did not take any notice of me. In general, I pleased her very well, never having any disagreement with one another.

It being now the last time that my mistress was to be on board, my master asked permission to go on shore, to take leave of all his friends and acquaintance; for we did not know how soon we might sail; and when we were out at sea, none of us knew that we might live to return again. My master and mistress therefore went on shore, and determined to take me with them; and I was very proud to think that I was to go with them to Chatham. We went all on shore; and had a supper at the sign of the Sun: and when we broke up, my master and mistress went home, and I went along with them, and lay at their house. In the morning, I got up, eat my breakfast and did what my mistress desired me: after she had breakfasted, we went and bought two check shirts, and a pair of shoes, for me to carry to sea, which occasioned me to think that I was well furnished, had four shirts and other necessaries; therefore I thought that I was a sailor every inch of me. When my mistress and I came home, we shewed my master what we had bought; he told me I should have a box made to put my cloaths in, and gave me a strict charge to take care of them; for he said, when I came on board, they would steal the teeth out of my head if they could. I promised I would be as careful as possible of them. Well, said he, I hope you will; then told me we must go on board that evening; and added, I shall look at your cloaths, to see how clean you have kept them; which last expression gave me a great deal of uneasiness, through fear of a discovery. My master and mistress parted after this, and we went on board; for we could not tell how soon the ship might sail.

After I was got on board, I began to think where I was going; for neither my father or mother knew where I was all this while, nor what was become of me; therefore my thoughts began to trouble me exceedingly, as I did not know whether I should live to come home again or should ever see my disconsolate father and mother any more. These considerations occasioned me to reflect what sorrow and grief I had brought on my aged parents, who no doubt were very unhappy in having lost me so long. But seeing I had brought this misfortune on myself, I formed a resolution to go through with it, and suffer the consequences: for my mind suggested to me, that when I was out at sea, I could not run away; and if they discovered that I was a woman, I concluded it would be utterly impossible for me to escape. The serious reflection of these circumstances so aggravated the disquietude of my mind, that I did not know what to do: but I was the sole cause of all this perplexity myself.

I shall here take an opportunity of advising all maidens, never to give their mind to frequent the company of young men, or to seem fond of them: and I would also caution them, not to addict themselves to dancing with the male sex, as I wantonly did. But had I been in bed and asleep which I ought to have been, the unknown sorrows which I have since felt and experienced, would not have befallen me: but then I was young and foolish, and had not the thought or care of an older person. I would likewise admonish all young men, to beware how they marry; for I have seen so much of my own sex, that it is enough for a man to hate them; however, there are good and bad of both sexes.

I shall now proceed to relate some farther instances of my folly: In the first place I thought, were I at home, I would be very happy if I could only see the young man again that I came away for; but a little recollection convinced me, it was in vain to think about that, as I could not run away; so by degrees this notion wore off, and I became quite contented: but when my master spoke angry, I used to sit down and cry for hours together. One day he told me I must go on shore with him at Sheerness, and take the little hand-basket with, me, to bring spinage on board: so we went on shore, and the wind blew fresh. We did not stay long, but soon came on board again; which I was very desirous, it being more agreeable to me to be on board than elsewhere.

After this, my master began to teach me the nature of the ship, and how to cook for him which gave me an opportunity of discovering his natural temper. Sometimes, on mere trifling occasions, he was very hot when things were not done according to his mind; on that account I was always afraid of him, and generally (when he was in a passion) stood with the cabin door in my hand, in order to make an escape which when I did, he always beat me. This usage I could hardly brook, especially as I knew that I was as real a woman as his mother. Besides, when at home, I could not bear to be spoke to, much less to have my faults told me. But now I found it was come to blows; and thought it was very hard to be struck by a man; which occasioned me to reflect, that there was a wide difference between being at home, and in my present situation.

About this time, orders came for us to sail immediately to join the fleet at Brest, which put me under the most terrible apprehensions of coming to anchor in the Downs lest I should see someone there that knew me being so near home. But it happened according to my wish since we did not anchor there; for, having a fair wind, we sailed through the channel, and soon found the ship was too light for want of ballast: However, we quickly joined the fleet at Brest; and the captain of the Sandwich, with admiral Geary, came on board us, and took the command of her, who hoisted his flag at the mizzen. With the admiral came all his followers, both men and boys; and our hands were all turned over to the Resolution. We had now our full complement, which was 100. But among the admiral's servants, there were a great number of stout boys, very wicked and mischievous; and quite different in temper and behaviour from those of ours, who were sent from the Marine Society by Justice Fielding. I never was under the least apprehension of these marine boys offering to molest or fight me; but those sturdy boys belonging to the admiral, were every now-and-then trying to pick a quarrel with me, nor was it long before they found means to put their design in execution; for one day being sent down in the galley to broil a beef steak, one of these audacious boys, whose name was William Severy, came and gave me such a slap in the face, that made me reel. This insult bought a little choler on me which by repeated affronts almost grew into fury; I considered it would only make me sick if I could not beat him; and also reflected that my cause was just; for I never had attempted to anger him though he was perpetually using me ill. From these considerations, on his next abuse, I was determined to try the event. Lieutenant Cook, knowing me better than any of them, and at the same time being sensible that I had given no just cause for these proceedings, told me I should fight him, and if conqueror would have a plum pudding, and that he would in the mean time mind the steak. Upon which, I went aft to the main hatch-way, and pulled off my jacket; but they wanted me to pull off my shirt, which I would not suffer for fear of being discovered that I was a woman, and it was with much difficulty that I could keep it on. Hereupon we instantly engaged, and fought a great while; but, during the combat, he threw me such violent cross buttocks, that were almost enough to dash my brains out; but I never gave out, for I knew if I did, I should have one or another of them continually upon me: therefore we kept to it with great obstinacy on both sides; and I soon began to get the advantage of my antagonist, which all the people who knew me perceiving, seemed greatly pleased; especially when he declined fighting any more; and the more so, as he was looked upon as the best fighter among them.

This contest ending so favourably for me, I reigned thereafter over the rest, they being all afraid of me and, it was a most lucky circumstance that I had spirit and vigour to conquer him who was my greatest adversary; for if I had not, I should have been so harassed and ill-treated amongst them, that my very life would have been a burthen. However, all the time I was fighting, my master knew nothing of the matter but, when over, somebody told him. As soon as I had put myself in some tolerable order, I went for the steak, and carried it to his cabin, being a little afraid that I should be chastised. Well, said he, you have been a long while about the steak, I hope it is well done now? Yes, Sir, said I. Why, says he, looking very attentively, I suppose you have been fighting? I answered, Yes, Sir, I was forced to fight, or else be drubbed. But, said he, I hope you have not been beat? I replied; No, Sir. Well, said he, when you fight again let me know, and I will be bound you shall beat them; so that, upon the whole, I came off with flying colours; from this time, the boy and I who fought, became as well reconciled to one another as if we had been brothers; and he always let me share part of what he had.

It was now more-than two months since I had left my father and mother, who had never heard of me; about which time, we received orders for the Resolution to sail for England, to be repaired. I observed the people now on board were employing themselves in writings letters to their friends; which put a thought into my head to write to my mother, to inform her where I was; which I knew would be a great satisfaction to my parents; I could write but very indifferently; and to entrust any person with my thoughts on this occasion I imagined would be very improper. At last; I resolved to write myself; but, after having wrote my letter, I had nothing to seal it with; and, thinking a bit of pitch would do, I went to the pitch-tub for some, which, when I thought I had got, it proved to be tar; so that with using it I soiled the letter very much. I was now greatly perplexed to contrive a method to seal it up. At length, one of the men, who observed I had been writing, gave me a wafer, which did completely. Soon after this, the boat came on board, and took away all the letters, and mine with the rest; the contents of which I now present you with, and are as follow:

Honoured Father and Mother,　　　July 3, 1759.

　　THIS comes with my duty to you, and hope that you are both in good health, as I am at present, thanks be to God for it. I would have you make yourselves as easy as you can, for I have got a very good master, who is carpenter on board the Sandwich; and am now upon the French coast; right over Brest: shall be glad to hear from you as soon as you can. So no more at present, from

　　Your undutiful Daughter,

　　MARY LACY.

　　P. S. Please to direct thus, for William Chandler, on board the Sandwich, at Brest.

These were the contents of the Letter I sent to my father and mother, to acquaint them where I was; and give occasion to the reflection, that children too often grieve and distress their parents by rash and disobedient behaviour; and many, alas! bring sorrow and trouble upon their heads, at the very period of life it behoves them rather to add to their comfort and joy by all the means in their power.

　　In about six weeks after, while we lay at Brest, I received a Letter from my father and mother. When the men called and told me there was a Letter for me, I immediately ran for joy to think that I got an answer sent me; but, nevertheless, was afraid to open it, lest I should find therein a severe rebuke for running away; however, at last, (with some reluctance) I broke it open, and, to my great pleasure and satisfaction, found it contained as follows:

My dear Child,   Ash, Aug. 16, 1759

I RECEIVED your's safe, and was glad to hear that you are in good health; but I have been at deaths door almost with grief for you. Your cloaths, after your departure, were found in a hedge, which occasioned me to think you were murdered; therefore I have had no rest day or night; for thought, that if you had been alive, you would have writ to me before: However, as you have writ to me now, I shall make myself as easy as I can; but shall still have hopes of seeing you again. And I hope you will put your trust in God, and beg that he will help you in all your difficulties and trials. When you have an opportunity to write to me, don't be neglectful; and may the blessing of God be with you! So no more at present, from

Your afflicted father and Mother

WM. and MARY LACY

After I had read the letter I could not help crying, to think what trouble and sorrow I had brought on my parents; and on considering that I should be the cause of bringing aged hairs with sorrow to the grave, perhaps much sooner than might otherwise have happened. I must therefore here address myself to all undutiful children, hoping they will mind what I say, and be attentive to the instructions and advice of their parents in their youthful days, whereby they may escape many dangers and miseries that a froward and stubborn conduct will bring upon them.

Whilst I was reading my letter, one of the boys went and told my master that I was crying; on his observing which, he asked me what I cried for, and if any body had abused me? I answered, No, Sir. What is the cause then, said he? I beg you will tell me. I then gave him to understand I had received a Letter from my father and mother. Well, said he, are they dead or alive? I told him, they were alive and well; but that I was afraid they would chide me for running away. He observed, I like you the better for remembering your parents; and God will love all them who love their parents. On hearing him express himself thus, I thought God was very merciful to me, in directing me to such a good master: for if he beat me himself, he would not suffer any body else to do so: besides, I knew his temper so well, that nobody else could please him like myself, which indeed, I sometimes found it very difficult to do; for if any thing went contrary to his mind, and made him angry, he would be sure to vent it on somebody or other. Upon the whole, it was a hard matter to please him; for he would on some occasions fall into such violent passions, that he neither knew what he said or did. He frequently accustomed himself to sit up late, either with the gunner or boatswain; who when they all met together, would continue in each other's company during the whole night which obliged me to be up very late on my master's account, and have frequently been kept so long from my rest till I have been stiff and almost dead with cold. When in liquor, he used to make me many fair promises; and, amongst others, that he would put me 'prentice, and find me with all my cloaths during the time and that I should have my money to send home to my parents. After talking to me in this manner, he would add, William, you are a good boy; and though I scold you sometimes it is only because you don't do as I desire you: however you are a good boy in the main too. I must also tell you, William, that your mistress is a very good woman. But, do you hear me? Don't tell her that I say so, or that I sit up late at night. She will ask you a great many questions about me, and what company I keep, but be sure not to inform her.

It may not be improper to observe here, that of all the officers' boys in the ship, the boatswain's was the least serviceable of any, inasmuch as he could not even boil the kettle for his master's breakfast; so that I used to do that and other things for him. The boatswain I must own was very good to me for it; as he gave me a pair of stockings, and several other necessaries, which made me take delight to wait on him: and my master told me, that I might go to his cabin when I pleased. But this good fortune did not last long; for he, being ordered away from our ship, I lost a good friend; after which, I had reason to apply the proverb to my own case, which says, "when the old one is gone there seldom comes a better;" as he was, through his obliging behaviour, beloved by the whole ship's company. He was succeeded by a boatswain taken from the Somerset man of war.

A few days after, as the gunner and boatswain's boy were sitting down to dinner, and myself standing (being always in a hurry, and indifferent whether I stood or sat) my master observing from his cabin that the boatswain's boy was sitting while I was standing near him, immediately ordered me to make him rise, and take his seat. For my part, I did not desire to do any such thing, as I imagined it would have been looked upon as a very great breach of good manners to disturb any person so roughly.

Another time the lieutenant told me to put a hand to the staysail braces, and help to hale them up; My master seeing this, called to me, and asked what I was doing? I told him the lieutenant ordered me to do it. He replied, You have no business to do any such work; nor, added he, shall a servant of mine do any thing of that nature; and cautioned me to remember that I did not come to be their servant, but his.

As we lay still at Brest, some men were drafted from the Temple to come on board us: amongst them was a young man that I knew at Ash whose name was Henry Hambrook; and I was much afraid he would know me. However, having been on board for some time, he one day came and asked, if I did not come from Ash? Not being willing to know him, I enquired what reason he had for asking such question? O, said he I thought I knew you. However, I took no farther notice of what he said concerning me: nor did he mention the matter again to any other person, to my knowledge, though he well knew who I was.

Soon after this, I was taken with the rheumatism in my fingers, which occasioned them to swell very much: not knowing the cause, I went and shewed them to my master. Let me see your fingers, said he, and fell a laughing at me adding, hang me if William is not growing rich. You dog, you have got the gout in your fingers. This passed on a day or two, when I was seized with it in my legs, and was so bad I could not walk. My master was then at a loss what to do with me; but thought proper to send down for the doctor to come and look at me. He told me, that I must go down into the bay in the sick birth. Well knowing what a nasty unwholesome place it was, the very thoughts of going thither made me very uneasy; nevertheless, I did not choose to say any thing to my master about it. I was accordingly carried down; but he sent me thither every day some tea and biscuit buttered for breakfast. This I received from the hands of an old man, who was of so uncleanly a disposition, that had I been ever so well, I could not have relished it from him. I remained in this disagreeable place for several weeks; but, growing worse and worse, was much altered.

While in this disagreeable situation, the young man above mentioned frequently came down to see me; but never took any notice that he knew me. Thinking therefore, that he came out of friendship, I desired him to tell my master that I should be gad he would move me to some other part of the ship, for if he did not, it would soon be the death of me. He immediately went and related all I had said to him. Whereupon my master came down to see me: when I told him as before, that I should soon die if not removed from thence. Well, said he, you shall come up and sit in my cabbin. And indeed very glad I was to think I should be taken out of that

loathsome place. He then sent two men to bring me into his cabbin; and ordered, the yeoman to warm some water to wash my
hands and face, which he cleaned and wiped himself; and took as
much care of me as is I had been one of his own, which he evidenced by many instances of his goodness towards me.

I was unable to sit up in the cabin the whole day, and at night
was carried down. Next morning, when the doctor called to visit
the sick, he asked me how I did? I answered, very bad. He then
began to be very angry that I went up to my master's cabbin; and
told me, I should not go there any more till I was better. Upon
which, I fell a crying, which I could not help, on thinking I must be
confined below. In order to prevent, if possible, this disagreeable
circumstance, I desired the man to acquaint my master what the
doctor had said. In consequence of which, my master went down
to the doctor, and told him roundly, that I should come up every
day to his cabin; for my staying there was the readiest way to kill
me. Accordingly, I was allowed to come up every day as before; by
which means I soon became better. But being still very weak, my
master got me crutches, with a spike at each end, for my safety to
walk about on the deck; and, then when any body affronted me in
an ill-natured way, I used to throw my crutch at them. The care I
was constantly taken of by the person under whom Providence had
placed me was such, that he would not suffer me to wait on him,
lest I should catch cold again; so that by this precaution I soon recovered my health and strength.

In a short time after, we received orders to sail to Plymouth, to
take in ballast and more provision, and afterwards to join the fleet
again at Brest. When we were returned, admiral Hawke made a
signal for all the fleet to clear ship, which we did for three or four
days; expecting the French fleet out every hour. But finding they
made no preparation to leave the harbour, we put up all the officers' cabbins; and, on the 10th of November 1759, being his majesty's birth-day, the admiral made a signal for all the ships, to fire
the same number of guns as in England on this occasion. We ran
in as near the French coast as we could, after which the admiral
began to fire: and after having fired all round, we all tack'd about,
and stood off from the land; yet did not stand far off, but lay to, to
see if the enemy would venture out. It seemed as if they thought
we were going to land at Brest, or some other place; for in the
night they made bonfires all round the country, to alarm and give
notice to their people, that we were about to land. But when the
wind was fair for us to stand off from the shore, it was favourable
for them to sail. Soon after, it blowing hard, and from a proper

point for us to quit the French coast, the admiral made a signal for all the fleet to anchor in Torbay; which we accordingly did.

During the time the Sandwich lay in the foresaid bay, orders came for us to sail to Plymouth. But while we were under way, there came a ship acquainting the admiral that the French fleet had got out, and were directing their course towards the West Indies. Immediately, upon this intelligence, some of our ships cut their cables, others weighed their anchors; and we soon came up with them at Quiberon bay, where we began the engagement, and soon forced them to surrender; for some sheered off, others were taken, and several of them threw their guns overboard: So after dispersing and destroying the best fleet they had, we imagined the war would soon be at an end. However, our ship had no share in the battle, for we were at that time in Plymouth; but soon received orders to go to Quiberon bay, to watch the motions of the French there. Here upon we sailed, and anchored in the bay and had a great deal of pleasure in viewing the country, as we were stationed there for some time.

My master now asked how I liked the sea. I replied, I liked it very well. But, said he, should you not be afraid if you were to come to an engagement? I answered, No; for I should have work enough to fetch powder to the gun I was quartered at, therefore should have no time to think of that. He then told me, I should not be able to bring the powder fast enough. I replied, I'll take it from the little boys, and cause them to fetch more, before the gun shall want powder; at which he laughed heartily to hear me talk so, as he well might.

We continued here for some time; and were afterwards ordered to the Bay of Biscay. I must here observe, that a person, who is a stranger to these great and boisterous seas, would think it impossible for a large ship to ride in them: but I slept many months on the ocean, where I have been tossed up and down at an amazing rate. As we were stationed off Cape Finisterre and the wind blowing so hard that we could not lie there, we afterwards went and anchored in Quiberon bay, and when there, the officers went on shore; which our master perceiving, obtained leave for me to go with the admiral's boys when an opportunity offered.

About this time, the princess' boat went on shore, accompanied by all the band of music; and we had a great deal of pleasure in walking about the island in the day time; but there were very few people on it. When they saw our boat coming on shore, they send the young women out of the island, for fear of our officers; and there were left remaining only two or three old men, and one old woman. We here found very fine grapes and other sorts of fruits; but our officers would not allow us to take any of their fruits, except grapes; and if we had an inclination for any others, we were obliged to pay for them. I saw no other habitations than two or three old huts which they lived in.

In the evening, we went on board; when my master asked me how I liked the island? I told him, I liked it very well, and that I thought it was a very pleasant place; but imagined it must be extremely cold in winter. Notwithstanding this agreeableness of his temper at intervals, it was in general a difficult matter to please him; for sometimes, after providing one thing for his breakfast, he would require another; for instance, when I had made sage tea, he would have gruel; and, after green, he would order bohea to be made with biscuit split, toasted and buttered; and if either of these things were prepared in any respect displeasing to him, he would sling it at me, though not with any real intention of hurting me; nay, the very cups and saucers would not escape his violent passion: so that I was afraid of getting ready his breakfast lest he should flog me, and then I should run the utmost risque of being discovered. On this account I was always upon my guard as much as possible. One time, when I did not get his breakfast to please him, he told me I should be flogged at the gun for my neglect and being afraid he would do it, I sat down and cried all the time the gunner and he were at breakfast. My master afterwards said to the gunner, Don't you think now that William ought to be flogged for not getting the breakfast better. But the gunner, being always a good friend to me, said, I will be bound for William this time that he will do so no more. What! returned my master, will you, who have been bound so often for him, be answerable again for his good behaviour? If so, for this time, I'll take your word; but remember, the next time he does any thing amiss, I will send for you and then you shall be flogged for him. By this means I got off scot free. He would sometimes kick me with such violence, as if he would force me through the cabbin; and when he had the gout, would be so peevish and passionate, that I found it extremely troublesome and difficult to please him, insomuch that I often wished him dead.

My master once told me, he should come and look in my locker again, to see what things I had there. Accordingly he came; and on examining it, he missed the blacking bottle, in which I used to make his blacking. Knowing it was broke I stood off for fear, as I know I should expose myself to his resentment. He asked me, Where is the blacking bottle? I answered, Sir, it is broke. He then fell into a great passion. You dog, said he I will have you flogged for it; I thought my shoes did not shine as they used to do. However I happily escaped the flogging at this time. He always caused me to clean my own shoes as well as those that belonged to him; and if they were not done to his mind, he would kick me with great violence. Whereupon he peremptorily expressed himself thus, You dog, I will make you go neat and clean for you are a carpenter's servant; and you shall appear as such.

Not long after this circumstance, my master was seized with another severe fit of the gout, which increased to such a degree that I was obliged to sew some flannel upon his legs; and if I did not do it to please him, I was sure to be severely reprimanded; and he was withal so troublesome, that if I was but just lain down in my hammock, he would send somebody to fetch me up; therefore I had but little rest at a time; as he was always wanting something. If I was gone only a minute from the cabin door, he would pass the word fore and aft for boy William as he called me; so that I was forced to run, lest I should be chastized; But when everything went agreeable with him he would then be apt to make me many fair promises and among others, that he would bind me out 'prentice, and clothe me during the time, though I could never believe it would come to any thing.

At this time, there were the Ramillies, the Royal William, and five other ships with us but on January 12 1760, a dreadful hurricane arose which lasted two days; by reason of this storm we lost sight of each other, not knowing where we were; and the sea running mountains high, all of us expected to perish. We had seven men drowned, had sprung our main and foremast, and were very nigh the land but as it pleased God to give us a sight of the danger we were in, we very happily kept clear of the land, and next day went into Plymouth Sound, when my master went into the yard to report the damage of the ship. I went with him; and we were greatly affected on seeing that only twenty-five men were saved out of 700 that were in the Ramillies, which was lost on the 14th of January 1760. On this melancholy occasion, I thought God was very good and merciful to us, that we escaped in that terrible tempest; notwithstanding which, we were no sooner delivered from the danger of the seas than we forgot it, and neglected to give God thanks for so great a mercy; but on the contrary, were still from one day to another running on in a greater course of wickedness than before.

I now thought that if I could but get clear of the ship; I should esteem myself very happy, but recollected I had no money; for my master had never paid me any; and my cloaths were made out of old canvas. When I was served with wine, I sold it for two shillings a bottle, and that helped to provide me some shirts; for I had very little money of my master.

At this time we received orders to go into the Hamoaze, to have our ship repaired, which I was glad of, as I always went on shore with my master, who frequented the sign of the Cross Keys at North Conner, kept by one Mr. P _____ s. He obtained leave to stay on shore, and gave me the like permission till we went on board. An unfortunate circumstance attended me here which was, that I had a bedfellow allotted me, being obliged to lie with the post-chaise boy, which gave me great concern; however, it was the will of God I should not be discovered at that time, though I continued in this situation while the ship lay at Plymouth.

When my master was sober, he would sit down and reckon what money he had spent, the thoughts of which ruffled his temper greatly, and at such times I was always the chief object of his resentment; therefore I was sorry when he was not in liquor.

In a short time our ship was ready, to go to sea, again; then my master and the gunner went into the country to buy some fowls, pigs, ducks, and a great quantity of garden stuff, which were all carried on board. Being ready for sea, we were ordered to proceed to Rochelle and Basque Roads and keep our station there till farther orders. We had not been long at sea before my master was seized with such a severe fit of the gout, that I thought he would have died before we could get home; therefore I heartily wished we were in England again. Besides I had no peace day after day; and as he still grew worse and worse, I was quite tired of my life, having a great number of different kinds of messes continually to make for him.

One day as he was sitting in his cabin, he told me he heard we were going for England; and he seemed greatly pleased, as well as I, that the ship had received orders to sail for Portsmouth; because I thought he would then have liberty to go into sick quarters as soon as he could. When we came in sight of the Isle of Wight, my master began to pack up all his things to be ready to go on shore at Portsmouth; and on his arrival there, he wrote a letter to Chatham for my mistress to come down to him. It was not long before she came on board the Sandwich, where she lay all night, but was soon tired of the ship. Next day my mistress was conducted all over the cabin, when she asked my master several trivial questions concerning the time how long he had had this and the other convenience. To all which, he told her, it was as his master pleased; for when he was in a good humour he would call me so. She did not find fault with any thing, but was soon tired of being on board, which I was not sorry for because I thought I should then have a little time to myself.

My master having liberty to go on shore, took lodgings at one Mr. Allen's, a shipwright, where I accompanied him; and as a favourable opportunity offered itself, by the leisure time afforded me here, I resolved to embrace it, in order to write to my parents, which I did in the following terms:

Portsmouth Oct. 27, 1760

Honoured Father and Mother

This comes with my duty to you, and, I hope these lines will find you in good health, as I am at present. I am very sorry that I ran away from you, and that I have been so neglectful in writing; but I beg leave to tell you, that I have no thoughts of coming to Ash again, but should be very glad to see you; however, in that I must trust to the will of God. Last January, in a storm of wind, we lost seven men. The Ramillies was lost at the same time, and only 25 men saved; but by the blessing of God it was not my lot. I am in some hopes I shall have a little money to send you, when my master pays me; for I have received none yet. He talks of paying soon; so that you need not expect to hear from me till such time as I am able to send you what money I can spare. My kind love to my brother and sister, and all friends that know me. Shall be glad to hear from you as soon as you can conveniently write. So no more at present, from

Your Undutiful Daughter,

MARY LACY

N.B. Please to direct thus, for William Chandler, on board the Sandwich, in Portsmouth harbour

I shall now return to my master and mistress. Being on shore one day he told me I must go on board with him next morning. We staid in the ship that night and in the morning he packed up some wine for me to carry on shore. But the wind blowing fresh, he would go in a cutter that was there; and not being able to reach the harbour, we were obliged to land at the south beach. Just upon our reaching the shore the cutter filled with water, which made us very wet; and from this unfortunate accident I had the basket of wine to carry full two miles to Portsmouth Common after having narrowly escaped with our lives; However, we got home in good time, though I was obliged to lie at a public house, the sign of the Ship and Castle.

In the morning I went down to my master's lodgings, and did the usual business; such as cleaning his room and getting his breakfast ready. My mistress then began to enquire what condition my cloaths were and whether they wanted repair. My master told her he had bought me a purse. Whereupon she ordered me to bring my things onshore when I went on board again, and she would teach me how to mend them. Accordingly I went on board, and brought them with me: and my mistress and I being alone, she began to ask how my master and I agreed, what time he went to bed, and what company he kept? I told her, the gunner and he, who both messed together, were very agreeable; that my master kept very regular hours, and went to bed in good time: for I took great care not to say anything that might cause a disagreement betwixt them. Nevertheless, she would often shift me from one thing to another; yet I still kept upon my guard: And telling her at last I knew nothing of the things she questioned me about, she left off importuning me.

Next day my mistress told me I must go to the town market with her, to buy something for Sunday's dinner. Taking the hand-basket with me, we went together; but had not gone far before we met with one or two of the sailors companions who knew me. They asked me how I did; and a little conversation passed, betwixt us. My mistress did not stop to observe who they were, or what they said: but when I came up to her again, she asked me who they were? I told her what I knew of them. When we came to the market, my mistress was always upon the wing, going from one place to another, asking the price of several things, and at length she bought of those whose provisions she cheapened at first; and after having bought a duck, we went home to our lodgings.

As soon as my master came home, his wife began to tell him how many women had been enquiring after me. Well, said my master, I suppose you have boiled the tea kettle for them? Yes, Sir, said I, I have, for I don't like to be ill-natured; if I had, I should have been beaten unmercifully ere now; but thank God I never had the ill will of any of them; and I believe if any of them had seen me ill used, they would have taken my part. My master replied, I

83

would have you learn to be good natured to everybody and not to practice any bad tricks.

I still continued on shore, and lay at the Ship and Castle; but went every day to wait on my mistress. At last the ship was ordered into dock, where my master set me to work, which was to saw some wood up, and bring it home to his lodgings: however, I was ordered to lie on board, and come on shore every morning, which I was very glad of, because I thought in that case nobody would interrupt me.

One day wanting to put on a clean shirt before I came from aboard, I found my shirts were all wet; notwithstanding which, I did not stop to dry the one used, but very unadvisedly put it on as it was, and went on shore. I had not been long there till I was seized with the rheumatism to such a degree that I was carried on board; and next day grew so very ill that the doctor told me I must go to the hospital.

At this time my master had procured a boat to carry his things from the ship to his lodgings; whereupon the doctor's mate asked my master if he would let him have the boat, with two or three hands to carry me to the hospital? to which he consented, and sent one J_____n B_____n, the carpenter's mate, and the doctor's mate, whose name was Mr. L_____e. I was then carried up to the agent in the hospital, and he ordered me to be taken into the fifth ward south, where I was put to bed very bad, and grew worse and worse every day; and at length became so delirious, that I neither knew what I said, or to whom I spoke. In this condition I remained till they thought it necessary to bleed me, by which received great relief.

Being now grown a little better, I got up, but was not able to walk much; however, I recovered the use of my hands, and mended by degrees. When I was able to walk about the room, it came into my head, that I would try to go down stairs; and having got as far as the staircase, the wind blew so cold, that I thought it would cut me asunder; therefore I was obliged to go back again into my ward. The nurse asked me how far I had been? I told her, as far as the staircase; but felt it so very cold, that I could venture no farther. She then told me the danger I was in of catching cold again, which determined me not to attempt going again till the weather was finer.

While I continued here, the Sandwich sailed from Spithead to the Nore, with orders to go to Rochelle; but being sick, my master went and left me behind.

The weather now proving warmer, I endeavoured a second time to go down stairs: But when I came to the stair case, I found I was not able; for I could not bend my knees. I therefore sat down on the stairs, and slid from one step to the other till I got to the foot, which was very troublesome to me before I could effect it. I then went under one of the arches where the sun shone warmest.

Being now pretty well recovered, they sent me on board the Royal Sovereign a guard ship at Spithead, as a supernumerary man, which I was glad of; for soon after admiral Geary and all his servants came on board, whom I knew; and they were glad to see me. There was one John Grant who had a woman on board with him, and one George Robinson, a quarter-master, both of whom invited me to mess with them. I was very glad of the offer; because I then thought I should have some tea, as there would be a woman in the company. The quarter-master was like-wise very kind to me; for he always kept some tea and sugar partly on my account; and we often drank tea together!

I shall now return to my former relation concerning my being admitted into the mess which I continued in for some time. The young woman and I were very intimate, and she was exceeding fond of me; so that we used to play together like young children; insomuch that our messmates believed we were too familiar to-gether; but neither of us regarded their surmises; and if they said anything to her, she told them that if anything like what they sus-pected had passed between us, the same should be practised in future. However when John Grant became acquainted that she and I were so fond of each other's company, he began to be some-what displeased; nevertheless, he was afraid to take any notice of it, lest his messmates should laugh at him; yet though he seemed to wink at it, he shewed her several tokens of his resentment, by beating her, and otherwise using her very ill, threatening to send her on shore.

Soon after this I received a letter from my parents, which gave me great pleasure, the contents of which are as follows:

Dear Child,   Ash, May 22, 1761
I RECEIVED your letter very safe, and hope these few lines will find you in good health, as we are at present, thanks be to God for it. I would not have you believe that I thought it was too much trouble to write to you, since I am very glad to find you are in good health. But still, my dear child, when I think about you, it makes me almost distracted to

reflect on your present situation, and the hardships you must needs go through. These thoughts, I say, make my heart ready to burst. However, I hope you will study to put your trust in God, who will help you in all your distresses; and also flatter myself, that I shall have the pleasure of seeing you some time or other! All friends send their kind love to you, wish you well out of all your troubles, and desire you will write as soon as convenient. Your brother and sister send their kind love to you. I shall now conclude with our parental affection and blessing, from

Your afflicted Father and Mother,

WM and MARY LACY.

When I had read the above letter, I again condemned myself for the sorrow I had brought on my parents, by running away from them, which I was the sole cause of; for if I had made them acquainted with my design, they in all probability would have prevented it. May these bad effects of my rash conduct serve as a caution to froward children to mind their parents in their youthful days, which may prove to them a means of escaping many dangers they may be exposed to; and thus, by an obedient behaviour, they will bring comfort on their aged parents heads, instead of grief and affliction as I did.

I proceed now to further instances of my folly. While I was standing one day on the deck, the boatswain's mate desired me to go down to the yeoman for a bucket. As I was going to the storeroom, the men were scraping the side of the ship the ports being open on one side and shut on the other, and the men drawing water out of the hold, I perceived I could not go down there; however, the gratings being open I thought I would jump over the cable, the consequence of which imprudence was, I fell down the fore hold with my head upon the chime of a cask, and cut a terrible wound in it, which laid it quite open. When my messmates came down and beheld me, they were so frightened that they knew not what to do; however, they carried me into the cockpit to the doctor's mate, who bled and dressed my head, but was forced to sew it up with three stitches. During the time he did this, I was senseless; and when I came to myself, I was very apprehensive lest the doctor, in searching for bruises about my body, should discover that I was a woman; but it fortunately happened, he being a middle aged gentleman, was not very inquisitive; and my messmates being advanced in years, and not so active as young people, did not tumble me about to undress me.

As it was next to a miracle my sex was not discovered on the above occasion, I esteemed it a singular mercy God had prevented it at that time. The pain in my head, in consequence of the fall, was so exceeding bad, that I was almost deprived of my senses; yet, not withstanding my pain and illness, I had a continual fear upon me of being found out: and as I lay in my hammock, I was always listening to hear what they said, or whether they had made any discovery. My apprehensions were soon afterwards removed, on finding they were as ignorant as before, with respect to that particular; so that I continued in my hammock very easy and satisfied.

When one Mr. P__g__e, the doctor, came on board, he ordered my hammock to be lowered; and after dressing my head, he left me to the care of my messmates, who accordingly attended upon me.

There was at that time a bumboat woman on board, who gave me some tea and cake, and was otherwise very good to me. Her kindness was the more acceptable, as my teeth were grown so loose in my head, that I could not eat anything; but by the care of this woman, I wanted for nothing; and in a short time found myself so much recovered, that I could go to the doctor: and have my head dressed every day. He often told me that he should give me the St. Andrew's Cross which made afraid to go afterwards, lest he should cut me. However, as he perceived I was in a fair way of being cured I escaped the operation.

Once on the doctor's mate dressing my head, he bound it so very tight, that it ached prodigiously; and I was not able to bear it. For this reason I went to him myself, desired he would look at my head, and told him it pained me so much that I scarcely knew how to sustain it. His answer was, he could not open it. Whereupon I went away as I came: but in a little time after, I found myself obliged to go to the doctor again, and tell him, that if he would not open it, I must endeavour to find somebody else that would. After hearing me express myself in this peremptory manner, he began to look at my head, and by loosening the bandage, gave me great ease, and removed the excruciating pain which the tightness had occasioned.

I then went to bed; and was taken so ill of a fever, that I became senseless for three or four days. The doctor perceiving this, told my messmates he would have me conveyed to the hospital in the morning, if I grew no better. They replied, he should not send me there, alleging, it would be the only way to put a final period to my existence, if I was carried into the cold. But it pleased God to remove the fever in a short time so next day when the doctor came, and found it had left me, he thought I should soon recover my wonted health and strength. During the time of the fever, the doctor's mate let me blood, as found afterwards, by my garter upon the orifice; which put me in great fear, lest he had discovered my sex. But when he came next to see me he did not mention a word concerning that, which I am sure he would, had he known I had been a woman.

I now grew better every day; and if I had had a friend, I could have procured a smart ticket for Chatham, and should have received four pounds a year, or something more. But I was at that time utterly ignorant of such a provision and had nobody to advise or direct me about it, my master being gone to sea. But by the blessing of God I was at last better provided for.

As soon as I was pretty well recovered, I went to work again; and in a short time was as well as ever. I was very sorry to find my messmate George Robinson had left the ship, as I knew not what was become of him, nor have I heard of him since. This occasioned me to get a new messmate, which was the captain of the forecastle, whose name was Philip M__t__n, who had a notable woman to his wife. They were worth money, and lived very happy together on board the ship; and indeed few in our circumstances lived so comfortably as we did. This woman used to wash for me, and also for impressed men as they came on board; and if I did any work for these pressed men, my messmates would tell them they must pay me for it, because I had no friend in the world to help me: so that when I had done any thing for them, one would give me a pair of stockings, another breeches, and the rest would supply me in return with other necessaries; therefore I wanted for nothing of that sort.

The boatswain observing me so very tractable, by which I gained the good-will of every body, seemed desirous I should come and mess with him which appeared very strange to me, because he never knew me before: however, I soon found out the cause, which was as follows: There being a quarter-master's wife on board that came from the Isle of Wight, who sold all manner of things and being a particular acquaintance of the boatswain's, she urged him to ask me to mess with him, in order to look after her things. But at that time I had an opportunity of doing something more serviceable for myself, than barely looking after their matters, which was to go down into the school to learn to write and cast accounts.

Some time after this, having gone through a great deal of trouble, by serving different persons on board, my whole endeavour being always employed to please and assist every body as well as I could; at length, being induced by the boatswain's repeated acts of kindness to me, I came to a resolution of messing with him whenever he should hint the matter again, which he soon did: and indeed I afterwards found I had exchanged messmates to my own ease and advantage. He being very kind to me, I lived extremely happy; for as he did not come on board above once or twice a week, I had little else to do than make his bed, and dress him a bit of victuals; so that I had time enough to wait upon the woman. The boatswain's wife, who was a handsome woman, coming on board with her father and mother, I was ordered to dress some fish for them, which they were pleased to say were very well served up, and gave me sixpence as a gratuity for my trouble and care. He told me at the same time, that he would procure leave for me to, go on shore from time to time; but I never had the good fortune to find that be performed his promise.

I had now been on board the Royal Sovereign one year and near seven months, when I received a letter from my master, which I here present to you, and is as follows:

From on board the Sandwich, Basque Road

William,   Oct. 2, 1762.
I HAVE taken this opportunity to write to you, to let you know that very shortly we expect to come to Spithead, and then hope to hear a good account of you; which if I do, will perform my promise, to put you 'prentice in Chatham Yard, if you like it. Give my compliments to Mr. Jennings, the carpenter on board your ship; and you may shew him this letter if you please. I would have you be good; and take great care of yourself. The last time I heard from your mistress, she was very well.

   Take no cloaths from the captain; if you do, I shall not get your wages. So no more at present, from
               Your's, &c.
               RICH. BAKER.

This letter, according to my master's instructions, I shewed the carpenter and boatswain, who said my master promised very fair; and observed I had no reason to be afraid of having a bad name, for every body that knew my behaviour and conduct, would speak well of me. It gave me great pleasure to hear from my master; and when the Sandwich came, that the peace would be concluded.

Soon after this, the boatswain told me that all the ships were going into harbour to be paid off, and that the Sovereign would be the first; which induced me to think of engaging as an apprentice to my master at Chatham, though it did not entirely suit my inclination, because I knew there would be many persons at that place who were acquainted with me and by that means I might soon be discovered: therefore I did not choose to go to Chatham with him, but was rather willing to take my chance at Portsmouth.

It was not long before the Royal Sovereign was ordered into harbour to be paid off, but the St. George was the first ship, and ours the next. The boatswain told me to make myself easy, for I should stay with him till the Sandwich came in, and if she went to Plymouth, he would send me down in her. In a little time after, the ship was paid off; and it was not long before I went on shore, which I was very glad of; and my joy was so great on this occasion that I ran up and down, scarcely knowing how to contain myself.

I had now been on board the Royal Sovereign one year, and almost nine months, without being ashore all the time; nor was I in the least suspected of being a woman. On December 21st, 1762, I went to the boatswain's house, and eat and drank there; this being much about Christmas time, the weather was very cold. As I was going down the town, I met the cockswain of the cutter to the Sandwich, which very much surprised me. I immediately asked him whether he belonged at that time to the Sandwich? Why yes, I do; and your master ordered me to tell you to come on board to see him. I told him, I could not come till tomorrow After I parted from him, I went and informed the boatswain that the Sandwich was arrived, and that my master had sent for me to come on board; and also mentioned to him that I would go in the morning.

Being determined to write to my father and mother that day, it being nine months since they had heard from me: accordingly I sent them a letter, the purport of which is as follows:

Portsmouth Harbour   Dec. 25, 1762

Hon Father and Mother

THIS comes with my kind duty to you, and hope these few lines will find you in good health as I am at present, thanks be to God for it. I am sorry to trouble you so much with writing; but your not answering my last letter, in acquainting me how you both are, makes me very uneasy. My master is just come home; and I shall go on board to him very soon. I am lately come on shore from the Royal Sovereign; and long very much to see you both, but must wait with patience. Pray give my kind love to my brother and sister, and all friends, together with my duty and prayers for your preservation.

Your most undutiful daughter,
MARY LACY

N.B. Please to direct to me as follows, For William Chandler, on board the Royal Sovereign, in Portsmouth Harbour

These were the contents of the letter which I sent to my father and mother on this occasion; and, as I intimated before, that I should go on board to my master in the morning, accordingly I went down to the point, and seeing a barge I thought was the captain's, but it proved to be his clerk's, I asked the favour to let me go on board, with him, which he readily complied with. This was immediately after Christmas day. Having got safe on board, I went directly to my master's cabin, where I found both him and the gunner, who were very glad to see me. As soon as my old friend Jeremiah Paine came, who was formerly my fellow servant, my master gave him a bottle of wine to make ourselves both merry, in telling our adventures concerning what had passed and happened to each other since our last parting.

Soon afterwards my master sent for me, and asked me whether we had drank out the wine, and eat the plum pudding he ordered? I told him, we had. He then renewed his old story of telling the gunner that he would put me apprentice in the yard, with such other specious promises as he had often made me before. I thanked him heartily for his good will, and endeavours to serve me. Having ended this story, he began with another, which was an account of the loss he had met with since he had been at sea: but this will more properly appear in another place.

After this I went onshore to Mr. Dawkins the boatswain and told him what my master had said to me, which he approved of, and observed, that he hoped my master would not take me up to Chatham, and there leave me, without binding me 'prentice; for, says he, if he does, he will be very unjust to you.

I next went onboard the Royal Sovereign to see after my box, and other things, which I brought on shore, and after went to my master, who told me that my mistress was come thither in order to go to Plymouth; for his son was arrived there as carpenter of the Bienfaisant, and lay in sick quarters, and at the point of death; but before she could get an opportunity of seeing him he died, which was a melancholy circumstance to his father and mother, he being their only son.

When my mistress had taken an account of her deceased son's effects, she returned to Portsmouth. But the afflicted parents were so overwhelmed with grief and sorrow for the loss of their child, that their case excited compassion in every one present. Having settled their affairs here, my master and mistress went to lodge at the sign of the Ship and Castle. But I was kept constantly employed in going backwards and forwards, sometimes on board, and at others on shore to light his fire besides doing the other common business of a lodging.

My masler still continued talking to me about placing me out as an apprentice as soon as we got to Chatham; whereupon my mistress remarked, that such an action as that, could it be accomplished, would be greatly to my advantage; though by the way, she seemed very far from approving of it in general. Perceiving her inclination with respect to the matter, I thought it was a very fit opportunity for me to get clear of the apprenticeship. So when my master asked me if I would go to Chatham with him, I bluntly told him I would not; for I thought myself too old to go 'prentice. Well, said he, William, I will send your money, down to one Mr. John Lucas, when I get up to Chatham. However, this promise he never performed; for he only wrote to Mr. Lucas, concerning the money, due to me whilst on board the Royal Sovereign, which he had no manner of business with. But the captain kept me upon the books, and paid me; which the former never did to this day.

My master and mistress being gone to Chatham, I went on board the Royal Sovereign again, was entered as purser's servant, and had liberty to leave the ship when I pleased. I continued here a month employed by men and officers in going on shore for their necessaries; so that by frequently rowing in the boat, I became perfectly acquainted with the nature and management of it.

One day as I was going on shore with the boatswain of the Sandwich, he very seriously asked me if I would go 'prentice to the carpenter of the Royal William, whose name was Mr. M'Clean? I told him, I would let him know tomorrow; for I did not know how to deny him, being afraid they would mistrust me if I evaded it. Accordingly I went to Mr. Dawkins, the boatswain of the Royal Sovereign, and told him what Mr. Summers, the boatswain of the

Sandwich, had said to me: whereupon he advised me to agree to the proposal; for that it was better to have some trade, than none at all; and added, I know him to be a good tempered man; and seven years is not for ever, so I would have you go. But the dread of being discovered that I was a woman before the expiration of my apprenticeship, was a great obstacle to this proposal.

The next day according to my promise I went on shore, and saw Mr. M'Clean waiting for Mr. Seamer to introduce me to him; for we were unacquainted with each other. In a short time after he came to me, and asked if I would go 'prentice? I told him I would. While we were thus talking, Mr. M'Clean came up to me, and asked if I would be his apprentice? I answered, Yes, Sir. Well, young man said he, will you go on board with me? I told him I would, provided he would let me have a boat to go on board the Royal Sovereign. Young man, returned he, you shall have a boat, and the boys shall go thither to assist you. Accordingly I went; and brought my chest, bed, and bedding, on board the Royal William.

My master had another boy out at sea, who was not big enough to work as an apprentice in the yard, nor would the builder agree to take him; however, his own parents being dead, and his father-in-law taking no proper care of him, my master very generously maintained him.

I thought till about this time that my master was a married man for he had a woman on board with him and a girl that was her daughter. But I soon had reason to believe they were not married, from her impudent behaviour, having had frequent opportunities of making particular observations on the conduct of loose women, and could discern their vicious inclinations immediately.

I had now been on board some time before I was bound apprentice: but the woman who cohabited with my master, began in a little time to be so familiar with me, that I thought it very extraordinary a woman who was an entire stranger to me, should become so suddenly enamoured.

Soon after this my master ordered me to clean myself and be ready to go ashore with him, as he designed to bind me 'prentice that very day, which was the 4th of March, 1763. A boat (though it was not the proper harbour boat) being now along side the ship to receive us, according to my master's directions, I immediately made myself ready, and prepared to go; but as this boat of ours was very old, and not capable of carrying much sail, especially when it blew a little fresh; and there being moreover a pretty brisk gale of wind, we had a great deal of trouble to reach the shore. My master then stood for the Sandwich, and went onboard, as the boat was going on shore. We left our boat at the stern of the Sandwich, and went in theirs: but the wind blew so hard that we could not reach the hulk, but were forced to go to the north jett, where some caulkers stages lay alongside, at which place they had driven some nails into, the piles (to climb up by) instead of ropes which were at least sixteen feet high.

My master and the gunner had got safely up, and were walking on; but when I had almost climbed to the top, letting go the rope to take hold of the ring-bolt, my foot slipped, and I fell down into the sea; but as soon as I appeared again, the boys upon the stage soon pulled me up, though I was wet from head to foot: however, I recovered myself as well as I could.

Presently after this sad disaster my master and the gunner began to miss me; and coming back to see where I was (observing me on the stage) asked the reason why I had been so long in coming? I then told them that I had fell overboard. On which my master laughed, and sent me to a blacksmith's shop, where I immediately pulled off my coat and waistcoat to dry myself; after which he brought me out of the yards and gave me something hot to drink, to wet the inside, for the outside was sufficiently soaked before.

My master and I went together to wait on the builder, to know if he approved of me for an apprentice; but he not being in the office, we went to his house. On asking if he was at home the servant told us he was, and called him to us. My master then asked him, how he liked me for an apprentice? Why, said the builder, I like him very well; for I think that he is a stout lad. So my master had me entered; but not as a yard servant, as he was not allowed two, being only carpenter of the Deptford, a fourth-rate man of war. At this time he did duty on board the Royal William, the carpenter of which was dead, and he had some hopes of procuring the place for himself.

I shall now proceed to relate in what manner I went to work in the yard. My master began to enquire for a quarterman for me to work under; accordingly he went to one Mr. Dunn and found him in his cabin. After paying his compliments, he told him he had brought him a new hand; and that he hoped I should be a good boy. (And indeed I must confess, he gave me a good character): and at the same time told Mr. Dunn that he hoped he would put me under a skilful workman to learn my trade; which Mr. Dunn engaged his word and honour to do: For you must know that I was a cadet, to work one week in the yard, and another on board a new ship, the Britannia, just launched. There being an overflowing in the harbour, all the carpenters and servants were ordered to open the men of war, to let air in, and keep the ships from rotting: But this did not last long, for; we only went in the morning and evening; so that we were in the yard the greatest part of the day.

Mr. Dunn put me under one Mr. Cote to learn my business, who was a very good tempered man, and took great pains to instruct me; he liked me very well, and seemed to be greatly delighted to hear me talk.

This affair being thus far concluded, my master went and bought me a saw, an ax and chizzel which made me very proud to think I had got some new tools to work with. On shewing them to the man I served under, he told me he would put some new hafts to-them; which pleased me very well, thinking that would be very serviceable to me in beginning to learn my trade.

The first work I began upon was, to bore holes in the bottom of the ship called the Thunderer, which, as I was at first unacquainted with the method of doing it, proved hard work for me. This occasioned me to think I should not be able to serve out my time without being discovered.

My masiler and mistress living at this time on board the Royal William, I had no house on shore to reside in, and was therefore obliged to go on board every night; so that the boys on board our ship had a great deal of trouble to fetch me backwards and forwards: however, I soon began to lessen their trouble, by taking an opportunity to go back again in the shipwright's boat. But when it was my week to be on board, my master frequently sent me to fetch beer and other necessaries, Sometimes with and sometimes without money, just as it suited his humour. However, as it happened, the ship did not lie a great way from shore, and the place where we landed was called the Hardway.

I must here observe, that the boatswain had a canoe, which I was very fond of making use of, though if I slept ever so little on one side she would overset. I continued for some time to pass and re-pass in her; and having learned by frequent practice the right method of rowing, could make her run with surprising expedition.

One day my master came to the yard in a four-oared boat and said he wanted me on board, bidding me get my ship ready. Accordingly I got into my canoe, and my master into his four-oared boat, when he told me he would row with me for sixpence. I replied, I would; but if I got on board first I would insist on having the money. He promised I should. I then went alongside their boat with my canoe, that is to say over-against them; after which we started and plied our oars as fast as we could. To enable me to proceed with greater ease and expedition, I pulled off my waistcoat, quickly overtook them, and got first on board; which when I had done; I fell a laughing at them, and called out, Where's my money, where's my money! He told me I should have it. But instead of giving it me, in the evening he took us all on shore and spent it among us. From this time my master every now-and-then challenged me to row with him; which I told him I was very willing to do whenever he was disposed for it, provided he would pay me the money when he lost. My mistress observed at the same time, that he did not do well in refusing to pay me, as he had engaged to do it.

At this time there were, on board our ship a deputy purser's wife with one Mr. Robinson and. his wife, all acquaintances of my mistress, who were brought up together at Gosport. As I was then on board, they sent me for some liquor, and would often get as drunk together as David's sow: and in the height of these frolics they would often say, Ay, he is, ay he is, the best boy on board. In regard to mother Robinson, I must acknowledge, she would do any kind office for me. Indeed I was in general well beloved by the women, if by nobody else; and, thank God, greatly respected by my master: so that I lived a quite happy life; and went to work, at the yard every day.

When we went to work on board the Niger frigate, I had a tool-chest made; and the quarterman, a person that I worked with, was very kind to me. I had my provisions of the king; so we made one allowance serve us, and sold the other to the purser for a guinea a quarter, as we both often dined at my master's house.

When I worked in the dock-yard, I tried to sell my chips at the gate; and sometimes would carry a bundle to Mr. Dawson, the boatswain, and was always welcome to his house whenever I pleased. Besides, my master frequently asked me to dine with him on Sunday, if they had any company on board, and I then got a sufficiency; for he would always have me to wait at table. While I was laying the cloth my mistress would stroke me down the face, and say, I was a clever fellow. Which expression made me blush.

Frequently after supper my master would ask me to favour them with a song, adding, that if I condescended to this, it would oblige them very much. Wherefore to divert them, I commonly sung them two or three songs, which often made them merry, till about twelve o'clock; when my master would order me with three more boys to row them to the Hard at Portsmouth Common; after which they made us a present to buy a little beer; but we made all the haste back we could.

I continued working in the dock; and my master and mistress were very fond of my company, because I could sing to please them. When I came home in the evening, I generally sat down by them, and sung a merry song, with which they were greatly delighted; so that I thought it no manner of trouble to serve them either by day or night. And thus having the good will of all, I lived very happy.

One evening my master had some company came on board to see him, and I was appointed to wait at table. When my mistress kept calling so repeatedly, I concluded my master was not married to her. This suspicion occasioned me to observe to my fellow-servant, (whose name was Jonathan Lyons) that I thought they were not man and wife; at which he fell a laughing: however, I did not care to speak much about it, lest I should not say right. So it passed on for some time.

A little while afterwards, coming on board in the evening my master and mistress had same words; and the woman that was acquainted with my mistress, let me into the secret of their intimacy. You must know, said she, your mistress, as you call her, was never married to your master, nor ever will, for he is at present married to another; her lawful husband lives at this time at Greenwich Hospital, and his name is Mr._____.

To proceed with the rest of my adventures. My master having no other ship, we lived on board; though he often talked of taking a house on shore, which (by the way) my fellow servants and myself heartily wished he would do. But he now began to take more and more notice of me every day; yet he was very kind to us; and would not allow me to clean his shoes; nor the knives and and forks, or do anything when I came home from the dockyard, except when there were company on board, and I waited at table.

It appeared my master formed a strong suspicion that I had got a sweetheart who lived upon the Common, and was often talking about it, advising me to be cautious, and not to marry til I was was out of my time; and then he would give me a wedding dinner. Indeed I often laughed to myself, when I considered that my master imagined I went a courting; for I was acquainted with several young women, which occasioned him to think that I was rather too familiar with them: and truly very glad I was he thought so; for in that case he could have no mistrust of my sex.

One day when I was on board, and my master on shore, my mistress and Mr. Robinson were disposed to make themselves merry: accordingly they sent me on shore to fetch some liquor, which they repeated so often that I was quite tired and kept it up till they had spent all their money, but did not know where to get more: and I remember, that I once mentioned in their hearing, my going to one Mr. Penny to bring liquor for my master on credit. This opportunity they thought was a specious pretext to get more liquor. My mistress therefore sent me for a pint of rum, and desired me to tell them my master would pay for it when he came on shore. Accordingly I went, and brought the rum; imagining, that as my master allowed me to call her mistress, he would not blame me for fetching it, having given me no orders to the contrary. So that, according to the proverb, with this liquor they got as drunk as pipers.

On my master's coming on board in the evening, he soon perceived what they had been at, but took no notice, only sat and laughed at them, he being very well acquainted with their frolics. But they were so pleased with me for bringing this liquor, that my fellow servants seemed almost to envy me; and said, they believed my mistress and I were too intimate, and that they wished she was so fond of them; for they observed, she was always giving me something or other, and that it was enough to spoil the most sober man in the world, because she would never go on shore but I must go with her, and then went in all sorts of company, both good and bad. But, thank God, it happened very well for me, as I never went to these licentious places but it occasioned me to be very much on my guard, and to be extremely cautious what sort of company I kept.

I must here reflect with gratitude, that if some sort of people had been witness to the variety of scenes of life that have passed under my observation, the sight would have made their very hair stand on end: Some were quarreling and fighting; others had their eyes knocked out, and afterwards kicked out of the doors and sometimes even driven from their warm beds, and had no person of reputation or humanity to receive them. Therefore all these disagreeable prospects should teach us to amend in ourselves what we see amiss in others. These considerations occasioned me often to think with great sorrow, that I had done mischief enough in leaving my parents, without their knowledge or consent; and hope this will be an example to all others not to be guilty of the like imprudence.

I shall now proceed (according to my journal) to relate what passed concerning the pint of rum I brought to my mistress; for my master had been on shore to pay the beer, but not the rum: Mr, Penny, it appears, had then given him to understand, that there was a pint of rum to pay; A pint of rum, said my master! I have had hone. Do you know who came for it? Yes, replied Mr. Penny, I know the boy when I see him. Upon that my master came on board, and asked if we had fetched any rum on board for anybody from Mr. Penny's? They all answered, No. He then said, I shall find it out; therefore you had better let me know before I go on shore. Hearing this, I went and told my mistress what had passed on the occasion; but she would hot suffer me to tell him till we went on shore.

My master soon after ordered us all to go on shore along with him. He going first into the house where we had the beer and rum, found there the carpenter of the Thunderer, who was present when I fetched the rum; but he would say nothing to my master, lest he should affront my mistress because she was a very good customer. Upon this we were all called in, when my master asked Mr. Penny which of us all it was that brought the rum? Mr. Penny began at top, and narrowly examining the physiognomy and habit of everyone till he came to me, then said, This is the boy who fetched it. My master then said, William, did you fetch it? Yes, sir, returned I; but I shall be glad to speak with you. Hereupon we both went out. Well, said he, did your mistress send you for any rum? I told him, Yes. Why, says he, did you not tell me before you came on shore. Because, I replied, my mistress would not let me; though I was sure you would soon find it out. Well, says my master, go in and get some beer. Accordingly we went in, and got two or three pots of beer, and then went on board again.

After this my mistress came to me, and asked if my master had found it out? Found it out? said I, yes, to be sure he has; and you had better have let me told him before I went on shore, and then, no one would have known any thing of the matter; but now every body knows it. Soon after my master came on board, but took no notice of the above mentioned affair.

He began now to think of taking a house on the Hardway, for he heard there was one to let; which we were glad of. I still went to the yard to work; but was forced to go round to Gosport, which was two full miles; walk twice every day. And after I got home in the evening was forced to hail the ship: and when the wind was in the east they could not hear me; therefore I was often obliged to stand in the wind and cold till I was almost froze to death which made me think how happy I should be if my master had but a house; for then I should have a good fire to sit by, and victuals to eat till the boat came for me.

I used every now-and-then to go on board with my canoe; and here were three apprentices that were very idle, who would take my canoe to go a perrywinkling; having therefore all got into her, with a bucket to hold the perrywinkles; they set off, and got a great many, with which they returned, and came alongside the ship; but beginning to play their pranks, they overset her, lost all the perrywinkles, and narrowly escaped being drowned, though two of them could swim, who getting at last alongside the ship, with our assistance got on board. It was with much difficulty we saved poor Abraham Mills, who was very near drowned; and my canoe left bottom upwards. These boys were continually plaguing me to go with them; but I was always afraid, lest they should overset her; for the least thing would do it: so that I never had the courage to venture with them; and whenever they got in first to go on shore, I would go in the harbour boat; and on our return, would get in my canoe, and go on board.

It came now to my turn to keep watch at night, when my master ordered me to watch four hours, and then, call somebody else. Mine being the middle watch, I was ordered to strike the bell every half hour. Accordingly I went forwards, and struck as I was directed. However, being but a cadet in the yard, my master ordered me to go a fishing with him in Stock Bay, when he caused to me sit down all the way backwards and forwards to sing. One day it being very wet, the fish began to bite very fast, and my master would not leave off till the tide obliged him to retire. We then weighed, set our sails, got safe into the harbour, and safe on board, though in a very wet condition.

Sunday following, my master had given an invitation to an old landlord and his family where he once lodged to come and take a dinner with him on board; therefore he ordered me and my fellow servant to go and fetch them from the shore. I immediately cleaned-myself, put on my blue jacket, went for them and rowed them to the ship; and while they were at dinner, I waited at table. My mistress asked them how they liked me? Why I think, said they, that he is a very handy lad. To which my mistress answered, Ay, and he is a sweet tempered lad too: for she was then in a good humour; and made me eat and drink of all that was prepared for the guests.

When the evening was come, we prepared to row the visitors on shore again: and as the wind, began to blow pretty fresh, I haled the boat alongside the ship, put the masts and sails, up, and set sail. We had a fair wind to the shore, and landed them at the place where we took them from in the morning: we afterwards tried to work out from the shore, and tack about backwards and forward's, but could make no way, which obliged us to lower the sails, and pull the boat out to the stern of the Essex and, and then hoist sail again; but the wind being northwest, was right against us and blew so hard that we could not carry sail enough to work on the other shore. However, we ventured to sail; but when we got over against the hulk, there came a squall of wind, which almost overset us. I had got the main sheet in one hand, and the tiller in the other but I let them go, and luffed her up as she was almost full of water; being very old, and not having ballast enough to carry much sail. In this distress; I struck sail, and let her drive where she would. We then drove down Palchester Lake where fortunately for us a lighter lay moored, on board of which was a man, who seeing us coming, hove out a rope, which I caught hold of, took a turn with it, and moored her to the lighter. We then went on board, and staid all night; for we were as wet as we possibly could be, not having so much as a dry thread about us. As there was no fire, we were forced to sit up all night in our cloaths; and thanks be to God, we were so well off, seeing it was a great mercy we were not drowned.

My master rose in the morning, and looked about the harbour to try if he could see or hear any thing of us. Getting no intelligence of us, he began to be frightened, and at length concluded we were drowned. But I had ample reason to be thankful to Divine Providence, which had preserved me in all my extremity and trouble, and continued to help me; for we bailed the water out of the boat, and then rowed up to the ship. Before we came on board, we saw our master looking out of the stern gallery; who perceiving us coming, made, up a large fire for us as soon as we came on board, and gave me a pair of dry stockings to put on.

Having got some dry cloaths, my master and I went to the dock-yard but too late for my call: whereupon I went to the clerk, who taking my checque off, I went to work till night. When I came on board in the evening, I was very glad to sit down by the fire; but did not sit there long before I turned into my hammock; for being greatly fatigued, I found I wanted rest most, and could sleep without rocking, having been up all night before.

It unfortunately happened that I could not continue to work in the yard, as I wanted to do, being obliged to go to work with my master every other week on board the ships, which in a great measure hindered me from learning my trade. I therefore asked my master to let me go into the yard to work. He told me the yard was so far off, that it was not worth my while to go down to work. I observed to him, that as I met with so many interruptions, I should never be able to learn my trade. Well, said he, if you don't learn to build, you will learn to pull to pieces: for it seems my master expected to be carpenter of the Royal William, having done duty on board her for some time: in that case he was to have to boys allowed him in the yard; this, however, never happened; one Mr. Williams being appointed for her. I afterwards learned he was to have a third rate, which has as many boys as a second-rate, tho' there is ten shillings difference.

My master had now obtained a warrant for a new ship that was building at Lippe, called the Europa; and coming home one night, I happened to be on shore, when he said to me, Well, Master Chandler, what news now! Sir, I replied, I don't hear of any. Why, said he, have not you heard that you and I are to go to plough, and that I am to hold the plough, and you drive the horses? I found he was only joking; because he had got a new ship building in the country at Lippe.

Next time I had occasion to go to the dock, wanting to come on board sooner than usual, I went in my canoe and got alongside the shore; but the wind blowing pretty fresh, I could not keep her off the shore nor get a head. Mr. Dawkins of the Royal Sovereign seeing me in distress, sent his four-oared boat to fetch me on board, otherwise I should certainly have been drowned. As I came by the ship, he said to me; Your canoe will be your coffin one day or other; and kindly added, if your boys are so lazy that they will not carry you down to the dock in their duty-weeks, I will send my boy to fetch you. I returned him thanks for his kindness.

I shall next proceed to relate what passed concerning, the young woman who lived at Mr. Dawkins' house, which place I often went to. Being there one evening, he asked me to stay till morning, as he himself was to remain on board all night; and moreover, the maid insisted on my promising to stay there. Having consented, we sat at cards till twelve o'clock; when some young women who spent the evening with us went home. I then asked the maid where I was to lie? She answered, there was no place but with her or her mistress. I told her I would lie in her bed. Accordingly she lighted me up to her chamber. Perceiving her forwardness, I thought it was no wonder the young men took such liberties with the other sex, when they gave them such encouragement; and I am compelled, for the sake of truth, to say this much of the women; but am far from condemning all for the faults of one or two: however, when a young woman allows too much freedom, it induces the men to think they are all alike.

I must confess, that if I had been a young man, I could not have withstood the temptations which this young person laid in my way: for she was so fond of me, that I was ever at her tongue's end; which was the reason her master and mistress watched her so narrowly. In short there was nothing I could ask that she would refuse; and, to make me the more sensible of it, my shirts were washed and prepared for me in the very best manner she was able.

One day my master took me to task about keeping this young woman company; adding, that he was afraid she would be a means of corrupting my morals, since her brothers were given to dancing, and night-revelling. But when she asked me to go amongst them, I gave a flay denial on that head. She then inquired the reason why I would not go? I answered, that it generally brought young people into bad habits and company of loose behaviour, destroyed their constitution, and rendered them incapable (by being up all night) to do their business the following day. Finding me determined not to comply with her solicitation, she never after that time asked to go with them.

I was now a yard servant; and lived at my masters' house on shore, who told me that I should have a new suit of cloaths, and not go so shabby as I was. To this end he went to Mr. ____ ge, a taylor in Gosport, and ordered him to come on Sunday morning to take measure of me for a new suit of cloaths. The taylor came as he was directed; and my master gave me my choice of the color, for which he seemed well pleased with: and I was not a little proud to think that I should have good and decent apparel to appear in, as I could then walk out on Sundays with their young women.

When I had got my new cloaths, one Edward Turner, who messed with me when I was on board, and between whom and myself there had always subsisted a very intimate friendship, came on shore, and invited me to walk out with him. Having first asked leave of my master, which he readily granted, we accordingly set out; and when in each other's company, we were always talking about the young women, or of working in the yard; for Wednesday and Saturday being the women's chip days, I soon made myself acquainted with some of them; and found them at all opportunities as well pleased in procuring the acquaintance of the men as in any place in England.

One day the above mentioned Edward Turner invited two young women to come and take a dinner with him and his messmate on board the Royal William; for on my coming to live on shore, he got another messmate to dine with him. On this occasion, my trusty friend Edward, asked me if I would come and dine with him at the same time and place? and then, says he, I will help you to a sweetheart. I told him, if my master would permit me to come, I certainly would. He accordingly gave me leave; and I immediately went down to Gosport on board the Royal William, that was brought into dock to have a thorough repair. But the young women not being come, I was very impatient till they arrived, for I wanted much to see them.

We had a leg of mutton and turn-ups, and a fine plume-pudding provided; with plenty of gin and strong beer, which I considered as a grand entertainment for me and the young ladies. I had not been long on board before they came; on the sight of whom, I went immediately and paid my compliments to them; and soon became acquainted together, they not forgetting to ask where I lived, which I as readily told them. We were very merry with our new acquaintance; and I soon found that Vobbleton Street was the place of their residence. This street in Portsmouth town in inhabited with diverse classes of people; so that I soon found what sort of company I was with.

Having spent the day on board with a good deal of mirth and humour, we agreed to escort the young women home; and indeed it was very proper we should. Having therefore trudged to town with them, we were prevailed upon by their importunities, to stay supper with them. To that, with one thing or another, we tarried there so late that we could not get a boat to carry us over the water; at which I began to fret lest my master should severely reprimand me for as I had my new cloaths on, and knew that I must go to the yard to work in the morning, it really made me very uneasy. However, to remove this difficulty, the young women insisted on our lying together at their house.

I knew not what to do in this case: but recollecting that this young man had no suspicion of my being a woman, we went to bed together; and lay till four o'clock in the morning, when we got up and went to dock. As we were walking along, he asked me what I thought of those girls, and how I liked them? I told him, I thought they were a couple of merry girls.

As. soon as I came up to the place of call, the people began to stare at me, which brought scarlet in my face; and asked me where I had been all night? I made them no answer; only went to the clerk, to desire leave to go home and pull off my cloaths, and put others on to work with; which he readily agreed.

After this, lest I should meet my master, I crossed the water: but I was no sooner got home than I found he was gone round to look for me, thinking he would meet me coming round that way. I went up stairs, pulled off my cloaths, and put others on; and desired my master's nephew to take no notice to his uncle that I was come home; which he promised not to do. But my mistress neither hearing or seeing any thing of me and being more inquisitive than usual, as soon as she got up in the morning, went up stairs, and looked in my chest; on seeing my cloaths there, she came down, and severely reproved the boy for not telling her of it.

In the evening when work was over, my fellow servant and I went home; and the first word my master said to me was, How do you do, master Chandler? I hope you and she lay very close together last night? No, Sir, I did not lie with any woman last night; for I lay with Edward Turner. I have only your bare word for that, said he. Sir, I replied, you may believe me if you please. My master, it is true, believed I was very fond of some young woman or other; and so I was; but not in the manner he thought I was guilty of. However, he was not angry with me for lying out all night; and I took pretty good care not to stay out again. As for my fellow servant, he was always asleep as soon as he came home from dock; and though we lay together six months, I was in no danger of his finding me out, as he was no sooner abed but asleep.

It now happened that my master's young nephew lay along with us; and I was more afraid of him than of the other, because he was not so sleepy; though I considered, that being so young, there could be no apprehension of danger from him.

My master asked me sometimes on a Sunday, whether I would go along with him, or meet my sweetheart? I often chose rather to accompany my master to Blocks fort, where we often staid some time; and I might eat or drink any thing I pleased; for he was a very good-natured man to me: notwithstanding which, there was one thing in him that I disliked, which was, that he would swear very much. This unjustifiable practice I was very averse to; and could not help thinking he quite blameable in living with a woman as a wife, that was every day contributing to ruin him; for I often heard it reported that he might have married with a woman of fortune, who in all likelihood would have made him a very happy man.

The pernicious effects of his criminal cohabitation with this person appeared in several instances, and particularly in the following one: In a short time after we came to live on shore, she used to fetch so much liquor in his name that he could scarcely discharge debts she had contracted which very frequently soured his temper, and occasioned him with some heat to tell her he would turn her out of doors; which made me think I should soon lave a new mistress.

Some time after this, my master had some business at Blocks fort, and she determined to follow him; but with no other intention than to scandalise him in the worst manner she could, which produced a great many reproachful words betwixt them.

When my fellow servant and I came home from work at night, we found the doors fast, which occasioned us to go to the next house to inquire if the key was there. The people told us my mistress had left it. Having got the key, we both went in, supped, and retired to bed; but had not been there long before our mistress came, and brought a waterman along with her for he had been at Gosport amongst her old acquaintances. She soon called for me. I told her I was coming down which I did without the knowledge of my bedfellow, who never heard me either get out of bed or in again; so that I could never have had a more agreeable bedfellow in my life: for if I had lain abed a week, and ever so earnestly wished for such a one, I could scarce have had such another.

When I came down, I found the waterman along with my mistress, who began haleing and pulling me about in such a manner, that I could not tell what was the matter with her, or the reason of her doing so. Afterwards I found that she wanted some beer; for she said she was thirsty. Accordingly I went and brought a pot of ringwood: and it being summer time, she sat at the door to drink it; over against which there being a wheelbarrow, I went and sat down upon it. My mistress observing me, came and placed herself in my lap, stroking me down the face, telling the waterman what she would do for me: so that the few people present could not forbear laughing to see her sit in such a young boy's lap as she thought I was. However, she had not been long in this situation before my master came home, and passed by her as she sat there; but taking no notice that he saw us, went in doors. And indeed, I was very much frightened lest he should beat me; but I thought he could not justly be angry with me, as it was all her own fault.

I went then to try the door, to discover if my master had locked it, which he had done; therefore I told her the door was locked, and that we must both lie in the street. Upon which, she said, She would go to Gosport, and that I should go along with her.

As we were thus talking together under the window, my master overhearing her say, She would set off for Gosport, was resolved to give us something, if it was only a good wetting, to remember him before we went; and accordingly in a moment he threw up the window, and soused us all over with a chamber-pot of water; which made me fall into such a fit of laughter, that my sides were ready to burst. In short, I could, not restrain from laughing to see what a pickle she was in.

After this a thought came into my head that I would again try whether the door was locked before we set off for Gosport, and as I wished, found it open. I did not stop to tell her of it, but immediately took off my shoes and stockings, ran up stairs, pulled my bedfellow out of his place, and got into it myself; for I supposed if my master came up to thresh me, he would lay hold of him first, and then I should have time to get away. However, as good luck would have it, he did not concern himself with me; but vented his anger on my mistress when she came in, telling her she might go to the waterman again, and would not let her come to bed.

In the morning my bedfellow John Lyons wondered how he came into my place; for he had heard nothing about the matter, being such a sound sleeper. We both went as usual to work at the dock. But when we came home I was under most terrible apprehensions that my master would chastize me; but to my great comfort he did not seem to take the least notice of what had passed on the occasion. Having now given you some account of the behaviour and disposition of my mistress I shall leave her for a while, and proceed to other occurrences.

My master found out at length that I had a sweetheart who lived at Portsmouth Common, but in what part he could not tell, though he imagined he should find it out some time or other; but after all, he was mistaken in the person; for he thought of a young woman that lived in Hanover Row, which was the very house I went to and therefore resolved one day or other to go at dinner time to enquire for me, imagining that to be the best time to find me there. Accordingly my master took an opportunity to go to the place where he believed I frequently resorted to; but when he went there, the people happened to be out.

When I came home at night from the dock, the first word he said to me was, Your servant, Mr. Chandler, pray how does your wife do, that is to be? For I have been at the house today, but the people were not home; however, I suppose you know where they are gone to. At first I could not tell what he meant by it, not knowing he had been at the house, or who had told him that I went there. I made answer, A wife, Sir! that is more than I think of yet. He then said, You can't make me believe so. Sir, said I, I don't know who you are talking about. No! replied he, don't you know; the house that has steps to go up at the door? Steps to the door! said I, I don't know what you mean. Immediately upon that I recollected the house in Hanover Yard upon the Common; and asked him (describing such a house) if it was that he meant? O! said he, with a little raillery, you have thought of it at last. Which in fact was so far true: but I did not care who knew that I went there; for the woman was most certainly a very good friend to me, though she knew not what I was.

At last, my master said to me, Well, William: I would have you stay till you are out of your time before you marry; and if she be a sober girl I'll give you a wedding dinner. Indeed I could not help laughing at what he had said to me about going a courting; and I was very glad to find he thought so.

I now began frequently to talk to the young women, and soon became a tolerable proficient in the art of courtship, but was very cautious of what I said to them; for our sex are so weak as to think, that if a young man does but once speak to them, he must become a sweetheart at once. In this respect we are greatly deceived; but they who know as much of both sexes as I do, would be of a different opinion; therefore would not have you trust too far, lest you should be disappointed. But true it is, my master would ever be pestering me with something or other about the young women; and my mistress was so evil inclined, that she thought every body, as bad as herself.

One night when I came home from work from the dock, I found myself pretty much indisposed and seeming somewhat uneasy, I sat down to rest myself, which my mistress took the opportunity of making a ground of invective; for thinking I was fast asleep, she began to question my fellow servant about the cause of my indisposition. He said he knew nothing farther then he heard me say, I was not well. Ay, said he, I am sure he is ill indeed, for he has no life in him; he never used to sit down sleeping in this manner before; little thinking I heard every word, she uttered. When I began to move, she thus addressed me: Well, Bill, what is the matter? I told her, Nothing more ailed me than being a little sick, and out of order. She said, I am sorry for it; and declined making any more mention of her suspicions at this time: and for my part I took no farther notice of what passed. She, nevertheless, told my master a strange pack of stuff; but he had too much good sense to take notice of it.

When we sat down to supper, he would often say to me, Well, master Chandler how do you find yourself now? I hope you are something better. Nor would my mistress be behind-hand in her questions, and insinuations; and frequently gave me very great liberty to be free with her, even more than I could wish to subscribe to, or acknowledge; but I took it from whence it came.

Thus much is certain, that she did not know what to think of me; but verily believed I kept company with the above mentioned young woman in Hanover Row on the Common, though she was greatly deceived; for I seldom went out with any young woman except Elizabeth Cook, who being very fond of my company, would not leave me, which gave me some cause to believe the intimacy would bring trouble upon me one day or other. I thought therefore, the best way to put an end to this matter would be, to frame some cause of dislike in her conduct: to effect, which, a very favourable opportunity soon offered for going on board the Royal Sovereign to see her where her master and mistress then were, I observed a man to be very familiar with her: and in truth, her master himself, who was frequently giving me the most wholesome instructions, seemed very glad of the occasion to mention to me a hint of their too great familiarity.

One evening I went to the house of the young woman's father and asked for Miss Betsy. Her mother answered, She was gone out; but she expected her home very soon. I therefore waited till her return, when we took a walk together.

After a little conversation, by way of prelude to my design I told her, I thought it would be best for us to break off acquaintance; because it plainly appeared to me I was not the only person she gave her company to, mentioning at the same time what I saw pass on board the Royal Sovereign. On this, she seemed greatly confused; and asked what I could mean by questioning her constancy; adding, that she never once entertained so much as a single thought about any person besides myself, and that if I would promise her marriage she would not grudge to stay twelve years for me. To which I made no other reply than that from what I had already seen, I ran the risk of buying a bad bargain, and then I would be in an unhappy situation indeed. Notwithstanding all this, she was determined not to quarrel with me on any pretense: so that not knowing what to do with her, it passed off for that time; and we still continued our walks as opportunity served.

Soon after this, some misunderstanding happened betwixt her parents and herself; the consequence of which was, she took a room by the Common, to follow the business of a mantua-maker, to which she had served an apprenticeship, and could get a good livelihood by it. She gave me an invitation thither to see her as often as I pleased which happened but seldom, on-account of my great distance from it; though this was sufficient to keep our courtship alive.

But my watchful guardian, Mr. Dawkins, for so I may call him, discovered that we continued our intimacy; at which he seemed much displeased; and was astonished that I could not penetrate into her real character nor see my own folly (as he thought) in perserving in such an inconsiderate proceeding; for it must be confessed, he wished me as well as if I had been a child of his own: so that he could not forbear speaking, when he plainly saw (as he imagined) the trouble I was bringing on myself. But I knew myself to be clear of these things; nevertheless, I ought to return Mr. Dawkins thanks for his care over me, since he always supposed me to be a man.

I shall now return to my master and mistress. This pretended or nominal wife had greatly run him in debt for liquor. At a certain time, my master had occasion to go to Gosport; and she resolved to follow him thither. When they both got there, they began to quarrel, and had high words with one another whereupon he left her and came home.

As soon as he returned to his house, he shut the front windows, fastened the doors; took the little boy into the room, and caused him to pull-off his cloaths, which induced the poor boy to think he was going to flog him: he then ordered the boy to put his two thumbs upon the table, which when he had done, my master put his two thumbs upon the boy's, and compelled him to declare truly, Who had been to see his aunt, and what liquor she had had; for, said he, if you don't tell me truth, I will flog you as long as I am able. The poor boy dreading the worst, confessed there had been a gentleman to see his aunt, who had a bowl of punch; that she had some beer and brandy for herself; and that whenever any person came to see her, she would send him for such sorts of liquor as best suited their palate. On which confession he was very well pleased; and directed the boy, with, some visible marks of satisfaction, to put on his cloaths.

My master had no sooner opened the door and windows than his wife came in; but he took no notice of any thing at that time. A day or two afterwards, he went to pay Mr. Lambeth for the liquor then went home and called her to account, enquiring what she had done with so much liquor.

A short time after this, a more disagreeable circumstance than the above happened, which put us all to a stand, and is as follows: My master having occasion to go upon some business to Gosport market, was arrested, carried to a spunging-house, and confined there the whole night. As soon as I was acquainted with the affair, I was determined (in company with my fellow-servant) to go and see him. When we found the house, I enquired if Mr. M'Clean was there? and was answered, Yes. After telling them my business, and who I was, the officer's servant took us up stairs, where we found him in a lock-up room. But on seeing him in such a place, I could not forbear crying. Whereupon he asked what I cried for? Telling him my reasons, he bid us make ourselves easy, for that he believed tomorrow he should be out; and then caused us both to sit down and refresh ourselves.

After this we returned home, went to bed; and in the morning got up to our work when we found by the discourse of one of our company that he had seen my master going to Winchester jail that morning in a post-chaise.

Next morning I set off for Winchester; but did not know one step of the road beyond Farnham; at which place, I was obliged to enquire what road to take. And indeed I thought I never should get there, the passengers being so few to that place; and so much up and down hill, that I could not see Winchester till I came into it. It is fifty miles there and back, which I walked in one day.

I soon found out the jail and having made my errand known, with the reasons for my coming, and a multiplicity of other questions that were asked me, at length the turnkey let me in. But when I saw the felons with their chains on, it much grieved me, to think that my master should stay in such a place. However, I followed the turnkey, who led me from one room to another, till at last he brought me to my master but could scarce believe his own eyes: nor could I restrain from crying the very instant I saw him; who to moderate my grief, he assured me he should be out again in a little time. But why, says he, do you keep crying? Sir, returned I, to see you in such a place as this. He replied, There are a great many more in this place. Yes, Sir; but you are not like them. Why not like them? said he. Because, Sir, they are put in ;for robbing but you are not.

When I came home, I found my fellow-servant and the little boy together. After I had related to them what I thought proper, we went to bed; and in the morning went to work as usual. However, very fortunately for my fellow-servant and myself, there was one Mr. Colman in the dock-yard, who kept a cabin for the shipwrights. He being very lame, always carried his chips home in his boat; and if his boys did not come down to carry them, which sometimes they neglected to do, he used to prevail on me to carry them to his house, and would often make me stay supper; and sometimes, ordered my fellow-servant to go along with me, where we were sure of being well satisfied and sent home, contentedly; for Mr. Lambeth at this time had refused to let us have any farther credit which in truth put us often into great straights.

At length my mistress came home and immediately began stripping the house, and carrying the furniture to the pawnbroker which indeed was the only method that could be taken to procure us some victuals: and I am sure we had little enough from her; but our neighbours kindness supplied the deficiency. My master was so much in debt that we could not expect any money from him; therefore we were obliged to shift, and live as well as we could. My mistress seldom lay at home above a night in the week, and went abroad in the morning: so that for the remaining part of the week, when I came home from work at night, was obliged to go from house to house as it were in my master's name, or rather on his account, which was upon the whole a very fatiguing situation to me.

It happened once when my mistress was not at home, that I lay in her bed; and Mr. Colman, who was obliged to pass by our door to the water-side, always gave me a call, upon which I jumped out of bed, and told him from the window that I was coming; which occasioned him to spread a report all over the yard, that I was abed with my mistress, because I had looked out of her window; and this they believed was true, (though they did not blame me for it) and the more so because she would frequently come into the yard, and take me with her over to Gosport into those lewd houses in South Street, where I was obliged to be very free with the girls, and where I was promised first to have the daughter of one, and then of another for my wife; so that I had plenty of sweethearts in a little time; and got myself a fine name among them. As I was frequently walking out with some of them, the men of the yard concluded that I was a very amorous spark when in the company of the women.

My master still continued in jail; and I did not know when he would be able to get out. It happened however, that the Africa was ordered to sea, the carpenter of which keeping a pawnbroker's shop at Gosport, did not care to go with her; and well knowing what unhappy circumstances my master was in and that both their ships were of the same rate, thought he would be glad to go in his room, rather then be in a jail: he therefore wrote a letter, which I was appointed to carry. This office I undertook very readily.

When my master had read the letter he objected to the proposal in it; as he chiefly wanted all his creditors to agree to a composition in order for his enlargement. But this the plaintiff refused to consent to, insisting on the whole of the debt being paid, which it was not in his power to do; and he could have willingly turned me over to him as a satisfaction for the debt. But the creditor wanted somebody to pay the money down at once, or to receive my wages till the whole was paid. My master, however, would not consent to this, unless he would take me altogether, and receive my money from one pay-day to another, as he could think of no other way of discharging the debt. But this Mr. _____ not agreeing to, I let out for home again.

Soon after this, my mistress, as I used to call her, came to me in the yard, and desired I would come to her at the sign of the Coach and Horses. Accordingly at night, when I left off work, I went and enquired for her at the place where she had directed me; and after meeting with her there, she asked me if I would go to the play with her, and a young woman called Sarah How, who indeed was a very handsome girl. If you will go with us, said she, I will give you a ticket. I promised to her I would go; and from that time the above Sarah Howe became very free and intimate with me; nor did I ever go to town without calling to see her, when we walked out together; and my mistress believed she had helped me to very agreeable company.

However, the night I went to the play, my mistress took care to be there; and when I came, back I was to lie at Mrs. Cook's; but how, and in what manner, I did not yet know. On asking them therefore, where I was to lie? they answered, that I must lie along with them; for they had but one bed, and there were no less than four to lie in it; but it happened to be a very large one. They made me get into the bed first, which I did with my breeches on: but indeed I never had such an uneasy night's lodging before in my life. So they pinched me black and blue; and glad was I at the appearance of morning, when I got up and went to work. But if any body had assured me there were such women existing, I could not have believed it: but God-forbid there should be many such!

About this time Mr. Simmons sent for me to come to him directly; for the purport of whose message was that he had agreed to pay the jail fees to set my master at liberty. My mistress being returned, and present at this time, when she saw Mrs. Simmons give me half a guinea to hire a horse and set off, took it out of my hand, and went to the Dolphin in North Street, Gosport, and there procured a horse to carry us both, though it was not intended she should go, yet being determined upon it, the horse was got ready, and away we set off Jehu-Dobbin-like.

I drove on pretty fast all the way, which occasioned all my mistress's cloaths to become quite loose about her; and going through Waltham, the people took me to be a sailor, and that I had got my Moll (as they term them) with me; for her cloaths were almost off.

At last we reached Winchester, about nine o'clock at night; but too late to be admitted into the jail. Next morning being Sunday, my master could get no business done; I was therefore obliged to return back; and in the afternoon about seven o'clock, set off from Winchester, and rode very easy home; but had not gone far before I overtook a young woman whom I invited to ride, (well knowing what fatigue there was in walking). She at first refused my offer. I then asked her how far she had to go? She replied, As far as Waltham. I told her she had better get up and ride. A gate being near, accordingly she got up, and we rode on very gently.

She began to ask me where I came from? I replied, from Gosport. At which she laughed, and, said, What! you come from Gosport! Whereupon I repeated to her, that I really did; and added, that if I might be so bold, should be glad to know her reason for asking me such a question? Her answer was, that she had heard great talk of Portsmouth and Gosport, and of the young men and maids there. I said, I hoped she had heard nothing bad of them. Why, returned she, I can't say that I have heard any thing bad of them; but have often heard that the young women are too apt to be seduced. Supposing they are, said I, I hope you will not condemn all for a few. No, says she, I dare affirm there is a mixture of good and bad; for God forbid they should be all alike! In this manner we kept talking till we came to Waltham, where she alighted thanking me for the obliging favour I had done her in giving her a lift.

I soon got safe home; and went to the dockyard to my work as usual. At length the man that arrested my master agreed to have me turned over to him; and Mr. Simmons obtained a board order from my master and him to exchange warrants. This being done, my master made over all his goods to Mr. Simmons; and after they were appraised, he went over to Winchester, paid all the jail fees, and brought my master home with him to Gosport, who soon after went on board the Africa at Spithead, where I went to see him; and he was, I believe, very well pleased with my visit.

Here he began to recount to me what measures he had taken to procure his enlargement; and that as he was under an absolute necessity of going to sea upon those conditions he hoped that I would use and comply with every reasonable measure for the satisfaction of us both, till it should please God to give a more favourable turn to his affairs: and, proceeded he, you are now to understand, that I have turned you over to Mr. Aulquier; and as soon as I am gone to sea, you must go to him for board wages, which if he does not think proper to allow, you must then board and lodge with him.

Addressing himself next to Mr. Simmons who was then present, he said, I hope Sir, that if William should not like to live with Mr. Aulquier, you will be so good as to take him away, and get him board wages. To which Mr. Simmons replied, Yes, Mr. M'Clean, you may depend upon it I will.

Matters being thus agreed upon, Mr. Simmons and I went on shore but I was to return on board the same evening with my master's watch, and some sea stores: however, there being some difficulty, in procuring them that night, I was obliged to defer it till next day; and I lay for that time with his boy, who belonged to the same company as I did. His name was John L_____y. He was a very sober youth; and well respected by his master and mistress.

I must now return and proceed to relate how matters went with myself. My master was now gone to sea; and I scarce knew what steps to take; however, one Mr. B_____t, cook of the Royal William, told me in a very friendly manner, that he would go along with me to Mr. Aulquier's house. I had never seen him but once before in my life and that was when he kept the Sign of the Bell, before he lived at Kingston, about a mile and a half from the Common, where my master had treated my mistress with a pint of wine. I thought, upon the whole I liked him very well. He was, with respect to his person, a handsome man; and was bred a shipwright in Portsmouth yard.

It was now in the year 1765 when this Mr. Bout went along with me to Mr. Aulquier's house. We enquired whether he was at home? To which they answered, No but that he was expected in a short time. However, we went in; and soon after, Mr. Aulquier's wife came from the garden. I really thought she was the handsomest woman I ever saw; but her looking so much younger than he, occasioned me to think that it was impossible she could be his wife.

But to come nearer to the purpose. When Mr. Aulquier came in, I told him my master was gone to sea, and that I had no place to reside in, where I might be maintained; and that it was impossible to work without the convenient necessaries of life. He replied; I am very sensible of that; adding withal, that he did not agree to board me, because my master was to do it; To which I answered, Sir, it is by Mr. Simmons' order I come to you. Well, says he, I shall not give you any board wages; but you may come and board here. Accordingly at night I went to his house and had not been there long before supper was ordered, which was pork and apple pudding. When he sat down to his meal, I found I had enough to do to look at him: for he eat in such a voracious manner, that I though he was going to disgorge it back again upon his plate. He had a brother that lived with him as a servant, to look after his horse, work in the garden, and go on errands, who supped with me when they had done, and whom I was to lay with. In the morning I went to work in the dock as usual; and was put to the inconvenience of walking a mile backwards and forwards to and from dinner, being only allowed an hour-and half for that purpose, which was very disagreeable to me.

Having thus agreed with my new master, the first thing he set me to do was to clean his shoes, knives, and forks, every night, which being a slavish and dirty employment, wore out everything I had on my back. This sort of business I had to do after my work in. the yard, before I went to .bed.

It may with great truth be said that Mr. A_____'s house entertained a very bad set of people: I had not been long with him before he turned me over to another man to pay his debts; and when I had worked that out, was again turned over to a third: so that being shifted from one to another, I had neither cloaths to my back, nor shoes or stockings to my feet notwithstanding which, I was frequently (even in the dead of winter) obliged to go to the dock-yard bare-footed.

But my hardships did not end here for the little provision I sometimes had, would scarce enable me to go through the work of the yard; and sometimes I had none at all. And to add to my farther miseries, as though I had not enough already, they compelled me to lay with the most vile and abandoned wretches of all denominations, who were in all respects the greatest blackguards that ever could be seen: so that for five years and a half of my apprenticeship I went through as great a variety of hardships as any person in my station could possibly experience.

One evening after my work at the dockyard, though in very rainy weather, I was sent with the cart to the Common to fetch grains, which made me very wet. But as they seemed to pay very little regard to my condition, I took a candle, and went up stairs to bed; and was scarce there before I heard all the house in an uproar, the cause of which I could not immediately learn. Soon after this, I heard my mailer calling his wife Lewis' whore, and her mother a bitch, which caused me to make some reflection on what the young man had told me before.

At this time there was a young woman that had been a servant there three years, and knew their temper very well. This person, as soon as the noise and quarrel was over, began to think of me. She accordingly came up, and brought with her a pint of beer, and some bread and cheese, telling me not to mind their quarrels; for it was no new thing, as it very often happened. I thought within myself, they may quarrel, as often as they please, for I should never quarrel with them. Next day when I came home, and the storm was over there was nothing heard but my dear; and they appeared as loving as if no quarrel had ever happened.

Not long after this, on my coming home to dinner, I found my mistress throwing all the maid's cloaths out of the chamber window, at the same time calling her all the abusive names she could think of, which set the poor maid a crying, almost ready to break her heart; all which gave me great concern; the poor woman making no other request than only desiring her wages might be paid; that she might go about her business. But when I came home at night, I found things bore a different face; for all was made up, and every thing appeared quite calm: and she promised, that as soon as they removed to Gosport, she should be their chambermaid.

It being now brought to my mind, that I continued very undutiful in not having writ to my father and mother for some considerable time, I therefore took this opportunity of so doing; and shall here present the reader with the letter, which is as follows:

Kingston, Dec 5, 1765

Honoured Father and Mother.

This comes with my duty to you both hoping these few lines will find you in good health, as I am at present, though I live but very poorly. My master, after having been in jail some time for debt, in order to regain his liberty, was obliged to go to sea, before which he turned me over to Mr. Aulquier. He is not so kind to me as my old master was, whose return home I will endeavour to wait for with patience, though that will not be these three years; nevertheless, I still hope I shall see him again: for he behaved towards me more like a father than a master. I hope my brother and sisters are well, and all friends that know me; and I beg you will write as soon as it suits you, to let me know how you both are. I conclude with praying for the blessing of God to attend you both, from

Your most undutiful daughter,

Mary Lacy

These were contents of the letter that I sent to my father and mother. I must now return to my former narrative; and inform you, that as the maid was to stay again, she and I one day began to talk about sweethearts. I told her there was a young woman I kept company with; who lived upon the Common but that Mr. Dawkins had persuaded me to break off my acquaintance with her. I then observed, that she was a very pretty girl; and, when lived at Kingston, she would often come to the dock-yard to see me, and we sometimes walked over the Common together, and one of us afterwards accompanied the other home alternately. It happened when we had been a pretty long time in each other's company, that I had scarce reached home, and taken care of the horse, before it was time to go to bed; so that I thought myself in a critical situation, because she often declared, as I have before observed, that she would stay twelve years for me if I would promise to marry her.

Christmas day being now come, we all went to live at Gosport, which was the more agreeable to me, as I had some time to eat my dinner and, being made boatswain of the dock boat, I had a shilling a week for the locking up and care of her, which was a great benefit to me though the money was earned with great labour and fatigue; for let the weather be ever so unfavourable, I was obliged to be with her.

My master and I now agreed very well; but I did not like my new bedfellow as he was a young man that attended the billiard table, yet of an exceeding good temper, but one that loved the women, though a little inconstant which made me very uneasy in any mind, for fear he should find me out.

One night when I came, home there were many, compliments passed betwixt us; for as I observed before, he was thoroughly good natured: so that if I wanted anything that he could get, I was sure to have it. But there was one thing I greatly disliked in him; and that was, when he came to bed he was extremely talkative, and made a very great noise, which broke my rest. However, notwithstanding this, nobody could come into my room but I heard them; and therefore thought myself obliged to pass over this circumstance as well as I could; though the best of it was disagreeable enough.

I must take occasion to mention here, that being now pretty well settled in our house, my master bought a four-oar'd boat, which we put in one of the coach houses, and shoar'd her up; so that when I left the yard at night I went to work upon her.

I shall now leave my master and bedfellow, and return to my old sweetheart, who still lived on the Common. On Shrove-Tuesday, in the year 1766, one of her brothers came and asked me if I would go to his sister's house, as there was to be dancing there. I went accordingly the same day; but though I was ignorant of dancing, yet I thought my going might induce her to think more of me. When we came to the place, she asked me why I did not care to dance? I told her the reason (the same which I formerly mentioned) that is I once began to revel and dance, I should not easily leave it off; that it would inevitably lead me into bad company, and render me incapable of doing my duty in the yard; all which I supposed would be sufficient to make her desist from importuning me any more on that head; and that my not going near her, would be a sure means of making her forget me. However, I found myself mistaken; for one day, as I was going down the Common in Union Street, she happened to stand at a door; and seeing me, said, Will, I thought you was dead. Why so? returned I; did you send any body to kill me? No replied she; but I thought I should never see you any more. What made you think so? You know the reason well enough. Well, said I, you are welcome to think so still, if you please; but I must be going. What! said she, you are in a great hurry now to be gone; if you was along with that Gosport girl you would not be in such haste to leave her. I said, I am not in such a hurry to be gone from your company, Betsy; what makes you think so? After this little chat, though with some seeming reserve on both sides, she asked if I would come in? I went in and sat down, and then asked her if she would come next Sunday to Gosport, and drink tea? She told me she would. Thus it was all made up again!

When Sunday came, I went down to wait the boat's coming, to help her out, which was just before my master's house, where all the servants were looking at me, and at my girl; but I paid no regard to that. From this place we went to my old mistress, who was to make tea for us. The old gentlewoman was highly pleased to think she had met with one who was formerly her man, in company with his sweetheart, to drink tea with her. She told the young woman, I was a clever little man, and that I would make a very good husband. After tea, miss and I walked out; and then I went over the water to see her safe home.

On my coming home in the evening, all the servants asked me how my spouse did? I told them she was in good health. This occasioned Sarah to be a little jocose on me about it; however, it passed on. But, by some means or other, Mr. Dawkins had heard we kept company again; on which he was very angry with me. In order to pacify him, I went down to his house, when he immediately asked me how Miss Betsy did? How does Miss Betsy do! said I; upon my word, Sir, I don't know. Not know! said he: when you go on the Common, and call in to see her! when you are so great, and walk out together! William, I am sorry you will walk out with her, when I have told you what she is. Well, Sir, said I, I am much obliged to you for your advice; but as for keeping her company, I do not; nor do I know that I shall ever speak to her again.

This matter passed over for some time; and by giving attention to my work, I thought little or nothing about things of this kind. However, one evening my fellow servant, Sarah Chase, began talking as we were sitting together about sweethearts, and said to me in a joking manner, I think you have lost your intended. Well, I replied, I must be content. She said, There are more in the world to be had. Ay, replied I, when one is gone, another will come. For my part, added she, I have got never a one. Why, returned I, I think, Sarah, you are joking with me now are you not? No, said she, I am not; observing at the same time, that she thought we were both in one condition. Well, said I, suppose you and I were to keep company together? You and I, answered she, will consider of it.

I had not yet served quite three years of my time; nevertheless, it was agreed upon to keep company together; and that neither of us should walk out with any other person, without the mutual consent of the other. Notwithstanding this agreement, if she saw me talking to any young woman, she was immediately fired with jealousy, and could scarce command her temper. This I did sometimes to try her. However, we were very intimate together. And to give me a farther proof of her affection, she would frequently come down to the place where the boat landed, to see me, which made the people believe we should soon be married. One observed to me, Well done, Chandler, you come on very well: another, that she and I do it very well: and then a third would add, that I should be a cuckold before I had long been married, for that she was too large for me, as I should make but a little man; and many such like ridiculous remarks.

This young woman was always very fond of walking out with me, where we were sure of meeting with some of the shipwrights, which I well knew I should hear of the next day I went to work; when they began rallying afresh. Ay, ay, Chandler thinks himself as fine a man as any of them, now he has got a sweetheart; let him go on, he will soon have a child, sworn to him. Ay, ay, says another, this is not the first he has had, for he had one on the Common; but I heard that a sailor ran away with her; however, Chandler has found a comely one in her room: and when they saw us together, remarked, Ay, ay, there goes a woman and her husband.

Notwithstanding these things, it soon came to pass that Sarah began to have a very suspicious opinion of me, on observing I spoke to another girl; for one evening when I went in doors to ask her for some supper, she looked at me with a countenance that bespoke a mixture of jealousy and anger. It then came into my mind, that there would soon be terrible work. Whereupon I asked what was-the matter with her? She told me to go to the squint-ey'd girl, and enquire the matter there. Very well said I, so I can: from hence I soon knew what was the ground of all.

It seems the tap-house woman had been telling her more of this affair at large, which brought me into a great difficulty; and indeed I lived a very disagreeable life at home especially; since I could not get my victuals as before. On which account, I went and asked the cook what was the matter with Sarah? She said; I knew very well what ailed her. Well, replied I, she will come again very soon; during which time, when I was at home there was nothing but grumbling. Sarah declared at the same time, that she would never speak to me again; pretending too that she did not want for a companion, which she thought would vex me, though I well knew she had none. However, to make some amends for this, the young woman sent me a letter the contents of which are as follow.

SIR,   April, 26, 1766.
THIS comes with my kind love to you hoping these few lines will find you in good health, as I am at present; and shall take it as a favour, if, dear Mr. Chandler, you will give me the pleasure of your company this evening; for you are so agreeable, that I don't know how to be without you: and if you can't come, I shall be very uneasy about you; for without you I am quite unhappy. So no more at present, from;
From your sincere Lover,
E. W.

When I had read this letter, I could not help laughing heartily. But I was apprehensive that the woman of the tap-house would come and tell Sarah that the letter was from this young woman; therefore I did not answer it, because I could pretend it was on account of Sarah's using me so ill for she thought she could do with me as she pleased. Knowing therefore her attachment to me, I used to place myself at a window where I saw this young woman pass and re-pass in quest of me: for she could not think where I was; which induced her to watch my bedfellow, and ask him if I was not well? But he thought I was deeply in love with Sarah.

These circumstances made me seriously reflect what troubles I had brought on myself: so that by running over one thing after another, and nobody to relate my tale to, of the trouble and sorrow I had brought upon my parents, and the hardship I was like to endure myself; I say these things crowding in upon me at once, worked on my spirits at particular times to such a degree, that they robbed me of all my peace: and if at any time I endeavoured to give vent to these melancholy reflections, my expressions of grief were immediately ridiculed as the effects of love. And they would sometimes tell Sarah, that I had been crying all night for her; adding, How can you slight him so! Not I indeed, said she; it is all his own fault; for if he had not refused me, I should not him. And glad I was that she appeared so indifferent; for they little knew the cause of my troubles.

In this and such like manner things went on for four or five weeks, during which time I had not seen the young woman. For as I had kept myself close within doors, she had no opportunity of seeing me. She therefore determined to write me another letter, and leave it with the woman of the tap-house, which she accordingly did; and at night the Woman brought it to me; of which the following is a copy for the perusal of the reader.

DEAR SIR,

THIS comes with my kind love to you, hoping these few lines will find you in good health; but I cannot say the same because I am full of trouble; to think you slight my company. But I don't wonder at it; as I find you have so much love for Sarah. I know you can't love us both; and since it is your choice, I hope you will marry her, and spend your days together in pleasure. But though it is not my lot to have you, yet I hope you will be kind enough to answer this letter; or, if you will come and speak to me, I shall take it as a great favour, and that is all I can desire of you. So no more at present, from

Your sincere Lover,
E.W.

When I had read the above letter, I was resolved to go and hear what she had to say. Accordingly I went: but as soon as she saw me, she fell a laughing. Upon which I told her, I should be glad to know what she wanted with me? Here-upon she said, She thought I slighted her, by keeping company with Sarah; but now, added that those thoughts all vanish for I knew your intimacy with her would not continue long. How came you to think so? said I: was it that I might keep you company? Why, said she, when I sent you the first letter, desiring to see you, you came; which was very sufficient reason for me to think you would comply with my request. To this I replied, I am sensible that I came at your desire, but was wholly ignorant of your intentions, or that your inclinations extended to me; for I urged, you must consider how long I have to serve of my time. She answered, I don't want to be married yet, if you will only consent to keep me company. Pray, returned I, what good will that do you, since you are not over hasty to be married? Well, says she, to put an end to this matter, since you seem to slight me, I will go and live in the country. To which I answered I did not slight her at all; and so bid her a good night; and home I went.

As soon as I came into the house I was set upon by Sarah; and in short, there was not any place I could go to but I was pointed at some way or other, whether at work or elsewhere; for was looked upon as a smart fellow among the women; all which only increased Sarah's pain, by reason of my keeping this girl's company.

When I went to bed, my bedfellow said to me, Chandler, if ever you speak to Sarah again, you deserve to have your head cut off. On which I told him, that I should not speak to her again for some time. Indeed he was frequently speaking to me about her; and frankly told me it would be my ruin, if I did not take care of myself: for, says he, you look dull very often, tho I knew it was not upon her account but merely owing to my own foolishness.

It was now the year 1767, when I came to a resolution to see my father and mother; and obtained leave for that purpose, as the navy had orders at that time to sail for the Downs the first fair wind; They sailed on the Sunday and we got thither on Monday, then went on shore, and afterwards passed on to Deal where I breakfasted. After dinner I set off for Sandwich, where I had some letters to deliver; which having done, I set forward for Ash. When I came there, I went thro' the church-yard, and read the headstones, and saw several people I knew, though, they did not recollect me. However, having a letter to deliver from a young woman to her aunt, who once knew me very well, though she had now almost forgot me, she read it: and looking at me with a mixture of surprise and joy, said I will be whipped if you are not Mary Lacy. This expression of hers forced a flood of tears from me; for indeed she was very glad to see me.

I had not yet seen my mother; and the above woman was extremely solicitous as well as myself to manage, our interview with a suitable precaution; lest from too great transport of joy some bad consequence might happen, which very often does, in such extraordinary cases. However, it was agreed, that I should stay in another room till she had opened the matter, and prepared my mother to receive me. In a short time after, she came and told me not to be uneasy. But I could not forbear crying, being under apprehensions of my mother's fainting. She came in a little time afterwards, and ran to embrace me with all the transport and affection of a tender mother, saying, O, my dear child, where have you been all this time from me, that I could not see you before! After mutual and affectionate salutations, we went home, where I soon found all the family very well; and took this opportunity of satisfying their earnest expectations, by recounting the various turns of fortune I had met with and gone thro', during my absence for almost eight years.

Before I quit this matter, it should be observed, the young man on whose account I at first left my parents, had frequently caused enquiry to be made when I was to come home, expressing a great desire to see me: but I had no inclination to receive any visits from him. And having now been at home nine days, I signified my desire of leaving them, which caused them to shed many tears. It was now Thursday; and my time expired on the Sunday following, when pursuant to my leave of absence, I was to be at Portsmouth.

At length, after parting from my friends I set off and came first to Canterbury, and soon afterwards reached Chatham by the help of a coach, where I expected to lie that night; but learning that another coach was going to London, I watched an opportunity of getting a lift in it; thinking that if I could get there at night, I should be able to reach Portsmouth in good time, on Sunday. But I had not gone far behind the coach before the guide's light went out: however, he went and lighted it again; and when he returned with it, seeing me behind, he made me get down, though I told him I would pay him for it.

It now rained hard, which made me very wet; and the night being quite dark, I did not know where I was: so that in this dreary condition I had no prospect of a house to shelter myself from the inclemency of the weather. But being still inclinable to trudge on, I at length, though unexpectedly, found myself at Gravesend, where I had some refreshment. The people of the house where I had a little repast, on hearing me say that I wanted to go to London in the morning, told me I might go in one of the boats at six o'clock. I paid for my lodging and supper before I went to bed, and desired them to call me up in the morning. Accordingly I went on board; but the wind being unfavourable, we were much longer than usual getting up to London.

Among the passengers on board this boat; there was one old lady, who took me to be sea-faring man, and enquired, where I came from. I told her, from Gosport. From Gosport! said she; who do you live with there, pray? I answered her, with one Mr. Aulquier. She replied, I don't know him; but asked me if I was acquainted with one Mrs. _____. Yes, ma'am, returned I; I know her well; for my mistress and she are very intimate. Why, turned this old procuress, she is my daughter. At which I gave a dry look, and thought to myself she was a dextrous hand at a watch. She then asked me to take a glass of wine, and a bit of cake, which I accepted, as I knew it would do me good; and at the same time asked if I would (when they got to London) carry a little box to her daughter that lived just at hand, telling me at the same time; she would shew me London; and put me in the road to Kingston; all which I did: and when I came to the door which her supposed daughter opened, there immediately came down stairs and addressed me as fine a girl as ever my eyes beheld, who at first sight I knew must be a kept mistress. To say the truth, this old Duenna regaled me very handsomely, and afterwards set out for the Royal Exchange and to see other curiosities.

In this walk (which was a very extensive one) I luckily met with a carpenter of a ship, who knew me very well, and asked me where I was going? I told him to Portsmouth. Why says he, this is the wrong way; I am going down, and you may as well go with me. Accordingly we set off: but he stopping to speak to a person, I left him, and travelled on by myself. Soon afterwards he overtook me at Leephook, where hearing me talk, he knew my voice, called to me, and said, What, Chandler are you got so far already! Yes, Sir said I; but I am almost tired, and don't care to go any farther to-night. No more will I, said he: but where did you lie last night? Why, Sir, I lay at Kingston. So did I, replied he, and endeavoured to find you out, but could not; and what did you pay for your lodging? Sixpence Sir, returned I. If you had been along with me, said he, you might have had one for twopence. We then went to a house and got a beef steak for supper, and lay there; and the whole expense amounted only to sixteen pence. On asking him what I had to pay, he said, Nothing. But before we went to bed, the landlady asked if we lay together? Yes, said he, my friend Chandler is a clean lad; He little knew who he had got to lie with him; I am sure if he had, I should have been otherwise disposed in this respect; for he was always too free among the women.

In the morning we set off, and some time afterwards stopt to refresh ourselves; but he would not suffer me to pay any thing so that I thought I lived very cheap. Though I was lame, and greatly fatigued by this journey, nevertheless I made shift to get to Portsmouth punctually at the time appointed, and soon crossed the water to Gosport.

As soon as I was come to my master's house, my mistress, being in a good humour, gave me some refreshment immediately; and I then told her I had seen Mrs. Cureall's mother at London; and, of the civility she shewed me at home and abroad. Whereupon my mistress sent for her and we had a great deal of conversation together. At night I went to bed, and slept very sound.

In the morning I went to work as usual. But on my return home at night, my mistress was standing at the bar, and Mrs. Cureall with her. Seeing me come in, she said to Mrs. Cureall, Here comes my little curl-pou'd dog; he is ashamed to come and kiss me; and I can't say but what I was. Upon this I went backwards to consider how I should act, provided she should say so again. After having considered how I should behave myself on this occasion, I went in; and the very moment she saw me return, said, Why I told you he was ashamed to come and kiss me. No, that I am not, said I. Accordingly I went to her; and she stooped down to let me kiss her, when I perceived she was very much in liquor; so that I was obliged to put her to bed, our maid being abed with a young man, who swore next morning that I had been in bed with my mistress. Indeed as I was willing to do any thing for a quiet life, it was no wonder that such reports prevailed among the people; though they all agreed that I acted quite right.

But I must here acknowledge with truth, that the frequent quarrels and fighting between my master and mistress made my life very uncomfortable. Their differences and skirmishes were so often repeated, that I was obliged to take a tinder-box in my room, to strike a light upon occasion, and go down to part-them, if I could. One night it happened that I forgot the box; but was obliged to leave my bed on their account, though without light. In groping my way without cloaths on in the street, I stumbled upon a door that was ajar, where I perceived the glimmering of a candle upon the mantle-piece, which I was going to take, not thinking any person was near; when on a sudden a woman entered the room, and cried out, What the devil do you do here naked! I begged of her not to stop me, because I was in a hurry: and, have often since thought it was a great mercy I was not found out, that being a very bad house: and it was still a greater wonder that the woman did not take hold of me.

I had no sooner got within doors than I found my mistress with her head out of the window, crying Murder, as loud as she could bawl, with the children all in tears about her; which frightened me very much, my master appealing to me as a witness if he was beating her; for he lay at the same time in his bed laughing at her. When she was grown tired of this howling fit, I asked her if she would go to bed, and not alarm the people by these uproars? On which, she said, O the dog! I'll pull out his guts! Come, said I, will you go to some other-bed, and take no farther notice of him to-night? But it was all to no purpose; since the more I talked to her the worse she was, and the greater noise she made. At length, I got her up stairs, and put her into another bed, where she lay pretty quiet till the morning.

I was indeed very glad when the morning came that I might go to the dock to my work, because there I was free from noise. However the men used to tell me, out of a sort of waggery, that they would have my mistress and me taken up for common disturbers. I wish you would, said I, for then I should have some peace.

Some time after this, when I came home at night from the dock-yard, I found the maid was going away; and my master being gone over the water, my mistress, who was pretty much intoxicated, put on her hat and cloak, and would forsooth cross the water to find him which she did at the sign of the Fountain in Portsmouth. The first salute she generally gave him was a great blow with the first thing she could meet with; which put him into such a passion that he rose up and beat her in such a violent manner with a stick, that he left her almost lifeless.

Soon after this fray my mistress came home where she found me reading my book, and rocking the cradle. On observing her countenance I perceived she had two black eyes; so that I concluded she had been after my master for something She then asked me if he was come home? I told her, No. Whereupon she loaded him with the most reproachful names her imagination could suggest and afterwards went abroad again. She had not been gone long before my master came home, and asked is my mistress was come? I told him she had been at home, but was gone. Whereupon be took a candle, hammer, and nails went-up to his bedchamber, and nailed the door up to prevent her coming to bed to him.

He had not been in bed long before she came back; and there I apprehended I should have no sleep that night; for I found the old trade was going on again. She asked, If my master was come in? I answered, Yes. O the dog! said she, I'll pull him out of his bed; for he shall have no rest here this night; and up stairs she flew. But finding the door was shut, she came down immediately in a great fury for something to break it open, but met with nothing; as I had taken care to put everything out of her reach; for she would take the first thing that came to hand. By some means or other she at length got a scrubbing brush, with which she soon broke a piece out of the door, and then sat down looking through it, saying, Now I can see you, I am content. But she had not sat long before she got up and fell to work again, till she had demolished the door so far as to make room enough to go in herself; but was afraid to sit down. Having thus done, she went and brought up the young child; and getting upon her knees, first put the child in at the door, and afterwards entered herself. This being done, she threw the child (which was only about two months old) at him: so that I was very, much afraid she had killed it. I ran down to fetch the cradle to put the child in, and there sat till three o'clock; all which time they continued fighting; sometimes one getting the better, and sometimes the other; during the whole of which encounter I was obliged to see fair play, though murder should be the consequence. These contests frequently happened, till it was time for me to go to work; and, I was very glad to be out of their way; besides, the children were ever crying after me: and it gave me great concern to think the mother should have so little regard for her family as to neglect them in the manner she did. However, I have some reason to believe the fault was equally chargeable on the husband.'

Though I was now turned over to another master, I could not get quite clear of my former; for when I came from the dock, my mistress would make me clean shoes, knives, forks, and do all the drudgery of the house as before. But I had sometimes the courage to tell her, that I was not put 'prentice to be treated in such a manner: with that she catched me by the hair of my head, and turned me out of doors; which the people observing, asked if she was not ashamed to use me in such a rough manner? She said, I should not come there again; though it was excessive cold weather, I had no friend to go to. Upon this, I went to the tap-house at the Red Lyon, and told the women in what manner my mistress had served me, and that I would not go there any more if I could help it, though I had no money to pay for a lodging. The women then told me I should lay there.

On going to work next day, I told the men in the yard in what manner I had been handled by my mistress. They bid me go to the man that I was turned over to, and ask him for my board wages, he being (they said) the only fit person to apply to. Next day I went and told him my case. Whereupon he directed me to come the following day, and he would send his brother over to Mr. Aulquier's, which he did. But Mr. Aulquier would not agree to give me board wages; saying, That if I would not come home and board, he would do nothing more for me. During this time I was obliged to shift as well as I could. But my mistress sent all over the town to find me out, in order to get me back again; however; I took care she should not meet with me.

Soon after-this, I went to the Common, to see one Mrs. Reading, who knew me very well when I was on board the Sandwich; and asked me in a very friendly manner how I did? I began with telling her how my mistress had served me, by turning me out of doors. She immediately said, You shall live with me and that she would engage to get my board wages. Hereupon I went over to Gosport, and related the matter to the woman, telling her where I was going to live, and thanked her for my lodging. She said, I was very welcome for while I lay there I had a sailor for my bedfellow; and I was glad when I parted from him.

After this I returned to the Common, and lay with Mrs. Reading's eldest son, who had no suspicion of my being a woman; and I lived with her as one off her own children; and the man I was turned over to promised me my board wages: on which I thought myself happy.

I shall now present the reader with a letter I sent to my father and mother, as follows:

Gosport, Feb 2, 1768

Honoured Father and Mother,

This comes with my duty to you both, hoping these few lines will find you in good health, as I am at present, thanks be to God for it. Your last letter I received very safe; and am glad to find my mother is so well recovered. Since I wrote to you, I have been turned over to another master, one Mr. Bedworth, who lives upon the Common. My kind love to my brother and sister, and all friends, that know me. So conclude with my duty and prayers for you both, from

Your dutiful daughter,

MARY LACY.

N. B. Please to direct for me thus,

To William Chandler, at the King of Prussia's Head, in Gosport.

To resume my former narrative. My master being returned home from the king's-bench, they were very solicitous for me to come home again; which I would not consent to till my friend Mrs. Reading was satisfied for my board and lodging, which they promised should be paid, as soon as they received some money due to them from a sailor, who at that time was on the other side the water, in Portsmouth town. In order the more speedily to obtain it, they employed an officer to arrest him. But he being well known, they were afraid to go into the houses to look after him; and therefore came home and said he could not be found.

My mistress then asked me if I would go with her in search of him (which was to be the night following)? To this I the more readily consented, as I was very desirous my friend should have her money. Accordingly next night we went over to the Naked Boy at Portsmouth, and there found him playing at bowls. My mistress then went up to him, and asked if he would drink whilst I went to call the bailiff's follower: but before I could return, he decamped. She cried out, Stop thief, with the follower after her; nevertheless he got clear off for that time.

Soon after, we went in search of him again; and among the number of people we saw, I met with the boatswain's mate of the Sandwich,who stared at me, and asked what brought me out at that time of night? I told him I was looking for a particular person; but could not find him; and asked him if there were any other people in the house? To which he answered, There were some up stairs. I then called the bailiff, went up stairs and found him in bed with a girl, with his face very bloody. We pulled him out of bed, and carried him to Gosport. Mr. Aulquier was gone to bed; however, we soon obliged him to get up and secured the person we were in quest of. But, notwithstanding all the pains and fatigued I had been at in this troublesome affair, my poor landlady did not recover any of the money due to her the man being insolvent.

We began now to live at the same poor rate as heretofore, having sometimes had victuals and at other times none; At length my master gave me two-pence a day for a dinner; and indeed I could not well have less. However, by some fortunate means or other, I used to procure a dinner; so I reserved that two-pence for other uses.

My master was now become so poor, that he was not able to buy me a pair of shoes: and tho' at this time it was very cold wet weather, I was obliged to go almost bare-footed. However, to make things a little more comfortable, when I went home at night, I used to wash my stockings, and-dry them before the fire, to be as comfortable as I could the next day. I had no money to purchase second-hand shoes, which if I had had, they would not have lasted long: and as for shirts, I was obliged to go on trust for them, till I could pay. But I always took care to discharge what I owed for one thing before I bought another; and that was the way I got my cloaths.

The next day I went to the dock, it was whispered about that I was a woman; which threw me into a most terrible fright believing that some of the boys were going to search me. It was now much about breakfast-time; when coming; on shore in order to go to my chest for my breakfast, two men of our company called and said, They wanted to speak to me. I went to them. What think you, Chandler, the people will have it that you are a woman! which struck me with such a panic that I knew not what to say. However, I had the presence of mind to laugh it off, as if it was not worth notice.

On going to my chest again, I perceived several apprentices waiting, who wanted to search me: but I took care not to run, lest that should increase their suspicion. Hereupon, one Mr. Penny, of our company, came up, and asked them what they meant by surrounding me in that manner? telling them at the same time that the first person that offered to touch me, he would not only well drub him, but carry him before the builder afterwards, which made them all sheer off; and they were from that time afraid of molesting me any more.

I now sat down, and gave full vent to my tears, which were not few: but the men that I worked with, were gone to breakfast, and knew nothing of the matter till they came back; when my friends thus accosted them. What think you of your man now? Why, 'tis no such thing, said the others and I'll wager you any money upon it; which made me glad to think they gave it such a turn. However, when I had done work the man whose name was Corbin, and his mate that taught me my business, came and told me in a serious manner, I must go with them to be searched; for if you don't, said they, you will be over-haul'd by the boys. Indeed I knew not what do in this case: but I considered they were very sober men, and that it was safer to trust them than expose myself to the rudeness of the boys.

They put the question very seriously, which I as ingenuously answered, though it made me cry so that I could scarce speak; at which declaration of mine, in plainly telling them I was a woman, they seemed greatly surprised; and offered to take their oaths of secrecy.

When they went back the people asked them if it was true what they had heard? No, said they, he is a man and a half to a great many. Ay said one, I thought Chandler could not be so great with his mistress if he was not a man; I am sure she would not have brought him to the point if he was not so: and another said, I am sure he's no girl; if he was, he would not have after so many for nothing, and would have soon been found out. From such talk as this among the men, in a day or two the matter was quite dropt: yet now and then they could say, I wonder how it should come into the heads of the people to think that Chandler was a girl: I am sure there is not the least appearance of it in the make or shape of him. Indeed Mr. Corbin never gave the least hint or token of such a suspicion, any more than if he had not known or thought anything of the matter: nor could I discover or conceive, at that time, what gave rise to this extraordinary affair, or by what means it could take wind about the yard. My girl at Gosport had heard it, but could not believe it. She believed I had received every favour, and taken every freedom that could be practised by the gallants, or she would not have given her company to me, though at this time I was not so very intimate with her as heretofore.

I must now return to my old lady, who was going to remove to another house; so that there was no place for me to lie in, which obliged me to go home to my master's house, who had lately hired a new servant. I was to lie in the fore garret, and she in the back one. Mr. Aulquier lay below; but I had some suspicion they lay together, though I never heard her go up or down stairs. However, when I went down one morning; I overheard them talking, which confirmed me in the opinion that they were bedfellows. It grieved me to know what ruin the girl was bringing upon herself; and therefore thought it my duty to tell her of it, which I did when I came home to dinner, though she denied it: but when I came to tax her with what passed betwixt them, she could not help owning it to me. Whereupon I advised her to leave him. She said, She did not know what to do. And I should have been heartily glad if she had quitted the place; for she used me very ill, by dashing my milk with water at supper, and then charging the fault upon another. And at dinner time, when they had duck, fowl, or any fine roast meat, they would frequently send me away with a piece of bread and cheese, by saying that, dinner would not be dressed time enough for me. But she soon afterwards began to use me better, being afraid I should go and inform her mother of her behaviour. The following Sunday Mr. Aulquier and she fell out, and had a scuffle together; and in the fray she tore off his shirt sleeves, and then went of doors. So that there being nobody to dress the dinner but me, I put on the pot with some pork and greens, which was a good meal for me. But he soon prevailed on her to come back again.

It will be necessary here to make some farther mention of my old mistress, who still lived along with Mr. _____. She took no thought or concern about her children, and was alike neglectful of herself, owing to her turbulent and furious disposition: for after she had lived with Mr. A_____r but a short time, she cut his head and hand with a quart pot, which provoked him to send her to Bridewell for her good behaviour. While she was there, her mother desired me to carry a letter to her, which I said I would do provided she first obtained my master's consent; which he readily granted. Upon bringing her the letter, she said, Bill, what do you think I dreamt of last night? I don't know; said I Why, says she I dreamt that you and I were married. O then replied I, you will have a good husband when you have me. Whereupon she called for a pot of beer to drink with her: she then read the letter, the contents of which gave her a better opinion of herself; and afterwards asked. me if I would go to Mr. Rimes, the man she had lived with and endeavour to prevail upon him to procure her release. I told her I would which accordingly did; when he began with telling in what manner she had used him. Well, said I, you have put her in, and you must take her out again. He replied I know I must and this I know also, that all the people will think me an arrant fool for doing; however, you may let her know, that she shall be discharged to-morrow. I went immediately and told the mother and her what I had done in the matter. The mother was glad to hear of my success in it; but desired (tho' she was her child) that she would not come near her again.

To return to my old sweetheart Sarah. The next day when I was going from work, she came up to the dock-yard, and asked me if I would go along with her to a christening? After a short pause, I told her I did not care to stand for the child. Whereupon she went and gave the people notice of my dislike to the proposal, who took care to provide a godfather in my room. But, notwithstanding my refusal to answer for the child; I could not be excused from going with her to the house; so that when I came from the dock after dinner, I was obliged to lose half a day's work to please her. We were very merry together: every thing was conducted in tolerable order; and we broke up in good time, which gave me an opportunity of seeing her home which caused a report to be spread all over the town, that we were going to be married next day; and there were many that believed it. For my part I was glad that I was so near the expiration of my time, because I should then be my own master; for I still went to Mr. L_____'s, and met with a very good sort of gentlewoman who lived there. She asked me if I went to church? I told her, Yes, when I had an opportunity. She afterwards gave me many useful admonitions, which disposed me to be very thankful to God for his goodness, in protecting me amidst the many dangers I had brought upon myself: and I flattered myself that I should some time or other be enabled to make amends to my parents for all the trouble I had brought upon them. But the worst embarrassment I had involved myself in, was my being so intimate with Sarah. Indeed I had almost taken a resolution to break off correspondence, not only with Sarah, but even, with every one of those with whom I had contracted an acquaintance of that sort for I found it almost impossible to free myself from their importunities any other way.

I considered it as a very surprising event that Mrs. H _____ should pretend to have such a regard for my interest, and at length betray me; She told me, I should be welcome to come and lodge with her, when I was put out of my time: and by continually repeating this profession of her kindness towards me, I thought she was the best friend I had; for I could not form the least idea of her being so deceitful as to discover me, after she had given my mother an absolute promise to the contrary. Indeed I esteemed myself happy in having met with a person I could freely un-bosom myself to, being perfectly satisfied of her fidelity; on which account I really though I could not make her a too grateful return; which consideration often induced me to carry her a bundle of chips.

I shall now proceed to the concluding scenes of my folly. Being but very indifferently accommodated in regarded cloathing, my master aggravated my distress, by not permitting me to receive the three pounds a year; neither would he procure me any apparel though the money was regularly paid him: and, notwithstanding he enjoyed every advantage he could possibly expect, yet was so unkind as to refuse me even a pair of shoes, when I was bare-footed.

On the day before my time expired, being at work upon the Pallas frigate, Sarah came and invited me to breakfast with her the next morning which I did. Having afterwards cleaned myself, I went to the builder's office, and told him, it was the last day of my time, and hoped he had no objection against my certificate's being allowed. On asking to whom I served my time? I told him. He then called his clerk, and ordered him to prepare my certificate; which he accordingly did; after which, I went to each of the proper persons, who readily signed it. I then carried the certificate to the clerk of the cheque's office, where I was entered as a man.

After this I went to reside upon the Common, as I supposed it would be most satisfactory to my mother. I lived there as retired as I could, and kept to my work. Soon after which, the company that I belonged to were ordered to go and break up an old ship that lay in the dock: but we found it very hard to demolish her; and I likewise found the labour much too hard for me, tho' I never gave out; for at the best of times the work was very fatiguing. But the money when earned was acceptable to me, since having owed some during my apprenticeship, I was glad to have it in my power to pay every one as fast as I could: and besides, I was willing, if I could, to make a creditable appearance.

Being now out of my time, I resolved to send down for my mother to come to me, believing it to be best for both, that no time might be lost. So I wrote the following letter, to my parents :

Portsmouth, May 15, 1770

Honoured Father and Mother,

I HOPE these few lines will find you both in perfect health, as I am at present, thanks be to God for it. I have the pleasure to let you know I am out of my time, and live along with Mrs. L_____w, and shall be very glad if you will come down and see me; which if you are inclined to do, pray write me word, and my answer shall contain directions for the best road you are to take. Pray give my kind love to my brother and sister, and all friends that know me. I conclude, with my prayers to God for you both.

Your dutiful daughter,
MARY LACY

P. S. Direct to me as follows:

To William Chandler, at Mrs. Low's, in the
Tree Rope-walk, Portsmouth Common.

Next day as I lay in my bed, I heard the dock-bell ring, on
which I got up, and dressed myself as fast as I could, lest I should
be too late to the call. But, notwithstanding the haste I made, the
bell still kept ringing, which raised my wonder at the reason it
rang so long. As soon as I came up to the dock-wall I met a boatswain running with his coat off, which made me conclude something very extraordinary was the matter. When I came up to the
dock gate, I found that all the yard was in a blaze, and the engines
getting out; for the fire was so great and powerful that its heat
almost-resembled that of a furnace and I think I never in my life
suffered so much for want of drink, as I did during the hurry and
confusion it occasioned; the yard, and tap-house being crowded
with people, there was no getting my liquor.

While the fire was burning, a quarterman was dispatched to
London with an account of it; and I was appointed to guard his
house till he returned. After it was extinguished, we had orders to
work a day and two tides; and were in a very great hurry at Portsmouth. The reason why I left Mrs. L_____w was because, after
taking her for my friend, I at length discovered she had been all
along the greatest enemy I ever had, having done many pitiful
mean actions to me: but the betraying me exceeded all the rest,
and was almost equal to the depriving me of life. It is most certain,
she was an inveterate enemy to me, which she evidenced by endeavouring to do me all the disservice in her power, and that at a
time when I was not possessed of a penny of money in the world,
which I could call my own. However, all other injuries I should
have regarded but little, if she had not discovered me to the men;
for when Mrs. F_____s told me what I was, I fretted myself quite
sick, and thought I should have broke my heart; but could not tell
who she had told: and the apprehensions I felt from persons med-
dling with me, greatly affected me. So that by fretting and hard
working I was reduced very low and thrown into a fit of illness;
which those people who were ignorant of the real cause, construed
to be love.

About this time an order came down for us to leave off working
double-tides, and only to work one day and two tides, which I was
not sorry for, particularly on one account, as I was almost spent
with working so close; for in a little time afterwards, I was seized
with so bad a swelling in my thighs that I was not able to walk, and

was unwilling the doctor should look at it, lest he should find me out: I therefore sent for the quarterman to answer for me that I was sick; which he accordingly did; and I continued a week before I was able to go into the yard again, and was then incapable of doing any work.

In a short time after I became better, and resumed my labour; after which we were ordered to go to Spithead to work, where we were in as bad a situation as before, having no other place to lie on but the softest plank we could find: so that such a wretched accommodation during that time made me catch cold again in my thighs, and occasioned my illness to return; however, I soon mended. But as the people were shifted about from one company to another, on the first of April I became very uneasy, lest something disastrous should happen to me.

A short time after this, I was on account of lameness, forced to go upon the doctor's list for a fortnight: but thank God I got the better of this, and went to work again, though continually apprehensive of being surprised unawares; for I did not know the particular persons my false friend had betrayed me to.

Soon afterwards our company was ordered to tear up an old forty-gun ship, which was so very difficult to take to pieces that I strained my loins in the attempt; the effects of which I felt very sensibly at night when I went home, for I could hardly stand; and had no appetite to my victuals. But, notwithstanding my legs would scarce support me, I continued working till the ship was quite demolished, and then we were ordered on board the Sandwich to bring on her waleing which was very heavy. This increased my weakness to such a degree, that the going to work proved very irksome to me, insomuch that every body wondered what was the matter; however, I still continued my labour, till want of strength obliged me to quit it: and then I went to the doctor's shop, and told him I had strained my loins, which disabled me from working. Whereupon he gave me something which he thought would relieve me. I took it; but had it not been for the infinite mercy of God towards me, I should certainly have been killed by it, the medicine being altogether improper for my complaint; in consequence whereof, instead of growing better, I became every day worse than the former, which made me think I could not live long. However, in process of time my complaint abated, but not so as to enable me to work as I had done before, nor could I carry the same burthens as usual, which, made me very uneasy.

While I continued in this weak condition, I imagined that if I could go down to Kent I might get a friend to help me out of the yard: but growing somewhat better, I went to work as well as I could. The loss of my father and mother like-wise greatly aggravated my concern; and I began to think of endeavouring to obtain liberty of the builder to go into Kent for a fortnight, which he readily granted. I went accordingly in one of the transports to Dover; from thence to Ash, and afterwards to the house of Mrs. Deverson, who was very much surprised at seeing me, and told me she had been up to London last week; and that her brother and sister at Kensingston would be glad to see me.

On hearing this, I took my leave of Ash, and set off for London; and when came to Deptford, I met with William L_____y, who was glad to see me. I told him I had got a letter for him from Betty S_____e. I went home,and lay all night with him; for as I had done so before, I was not afraid of him. Having talked much to him about his girl, the next day he went with me; to London; for I wanted to go to the Navy Office; to get my liberty prolonged, where they told me I must come again some other day.

From the Navy Office my companion went with me to Kensington but when I came there, I was apprehensive Mr. Richardson would betray me to the young man who did not know what I was: to prevent which, I immediately enquired for that gentleman's house; which being directed to the people belonging to it informed me that he lived; but I did not know any of them, as it was seventeen years since I had seen them before.

I told Mrs. Richardson that I had brought her a letter from Ash; and almost as soon as she had looked on it, the recollection who I was: but I desired her to be careful what she said before the young man, other wise it would be the means of betraying me. She strictly complied with my request till he was gone. This was on Thursday; and I staid there till the Sunday night following, and then set off; for I did not know that my liberty was renewed at the Navy Office. I got to Portsmouth on Monday; and immediately informed the builder I was come back. Where upon he told me my liberty was renewed. However, I went to work: but was in a short time after taken as ill as ever.

As soon as I heard that Mrs. L_____w had told every body who I was, I was ready to break my heart; and immediately wrote to Mr. Richardson at Kensington, to desire him, if possible, to assist me. He sent me word he could not do any thing, for me at that time, because all the gentlemen were out of town; but that in a month's time he would write, and let me know farther.

I endeavoured to keep up my spirits under these discouragements as well as I could; but still found the work proved harder and more fatiguing, to me: Now had I been from London a month before I was entered on the doctor's list; for we had been putting the Sandwich in thorough repair, the working on which gave me such a pain in my side, that I was obliged to have a blister applied to it; and though the doctor's mate dressed it every day, he never discovered that I was a woman but often asked me why I did not marry.

In this condition I continued for some time; during which Mrs. L_____w came from Woolwich. The very mention of this traitorous woman's name made me worse (for three or four days) than I was before. She had been but a short time in Portsmouth before Mr. Richardson sent for me to come up to Kensington; for as they knew my father and mother, they were very much concerned about my welfare. This news in a few days gave a happy turn to my disorder, and almost restored me to health: so that I embraced the first opportunity of going over to Gosport, to take leave of them all; and went directly home to make myself ready to go with the coach.

My parting with the young woman occasioned a scene of great perplexity and distress; and indeed one of them was ready to break her heart. This was poor Sarah whose pitiable case affected me very much. However, I set off from Portsmouth the second day of December, 1771, and reached Kensington the next day; when Mr. Richardson advised me that the best step I could take was to present a petition to the lords of the-admiralty; which I accordingly did: and their lordships, in consideration of my extraordinary sufferings and services, circumstances as I was, have been so generous as to settle £20 a year upon me: for which, as in gratitude and duty bound, I shall pray for them as long as I live.

After the lords of the admiralty had granted my superannuated pension, I continued with the above-mentioned Mr. Richardson at Kensington for about the space of ten months, during which time, on going to Deptford to receive my money, I was met by one Mr. Slade, who had removed thither from Portsmouth yard by order of the board. He had not seen me before in women's apparel; yet having heard of my metamorphosis, he enquired kindly after my health, and offered his service to conduct me back to Kensington.

On the road thither, he expressed a great affection for me; and at the same time requested me to give him my hand at the altar, allowing me a proper time to consider of his offer. Though I had repeatedly declared that I would remain single, yet afterwards having the utmost reason to believe that there subsisted a real and mutual affection be: twixt us, and that the hand of Providence was engaged in-bringing about our union, I at length gave my consent; in consequence of which, we were married, and now enjoy the utmost happiness the state affords; which I have the most sanguine hopes of a continuance of, since my husband is not only sober and industrious, but having been convinced, ever since 1762, of the important truths of Christianity, his conduct towards mankind in general, founded oh a love of virtue, is upright and exemplary; at the same time that in his conjugal relation he behaves in the most endearing and indulgent manner. Thus united, I have, by the blessing of God, attained more than a bare chance for happiness in my present state, and have also the most solid grounds to look for the permanent enjoyment of it in future.

Mary Ann Talbot

LIFE AND SURPRISING ADVENTURES

of

MARY ANNE TALBOT

In The Name of
JOHN TAYLOR,

A NATURAL DAUGHTER OF THE LATE EARL
TALBOT;

Comprehending an Account of her extraordinary Adventures in the
Character of Foot-Boy, Drummer, Cabin-Boy, and Sailor. Also
of her many very narrow escapes in different engagements,
while in the land and sea services, and of the hardships
which she suffered while under cure of the
wounds received in the engagement
under Lord Howe, June 1,
1794, &c. &c. &c.

RELATED BY HERSELF

LONDON:
PRINTED FOR R. S. KIRBY, No. 11, LONDON HOUSE YARD,
PATERNOSTER ROW.
Published,June 16, 1809]   [Price One Shilling.
J. G. Barnard, Printer, Skinner Street, London

ADVERTISEMENT

THE Biographical Memoir contained in the following sheets, was originally presented to the Public in the second volumes of Kirby's Wonderful Museum of "Remarkable Characters," &c. for which work the copyright of it was exclusively purchased.

In consequence of the numerous applications which he has received from various quarters, the publisher has been induced to reprint it in a separate form, with the additions and corrections made by the writer herself, during the last months of her life. These were designed to have been more extensive; but extreme ill-health prevented her from bestowing the necessary attention on the subject.

The new portrait expressly engraved to accompany this account, must be allowed by all to whom the author was known, to be an accurate and striking resemblance.

The Life and Adventures of Mary Anne Talbot

I WAS born to experience a large portion of the disagreeable circumstances incident to human nature; and if the reader of the following pages should judge harshly of the circumstances that precipitated me into the early part of the misfortunes which have attended each succeeding year of my life, I have only to supplicate commiseration towards a female, bred in a country village, and thence sent to a boarding-school 180 miles from the metropolis, on leaving which, after nine years careful attention to my education and morals, I have to date the commencement of my subsequent troubles.

I am the youngest of sixteen natural children, whom my mother had by Lord William Talbot, Baron of Hensol, steward of his Majesty's household, and Colonel of the Glamorganshire militia, with whom she maintained a secret correspondence for several years. I never learned that any particular event occurred at my birth, unless it was the circumstance of my being a surviving twin, nor do I know any thing relative to the juvenile part of my life, but from the information of an only sister considerably older than myself, and whom indeed I had taken to be my mother. From her I learnt that I was born in London, on the 2d day of Feb. 1778, in the house in Lincoln's Inn Fields, now in part occupied by Mr. Gosling the banker. The hour which brought me into the world deprived me of the fostering care of a mother, whose loss I can never sufficiently regret. In a short time I was sent to nurse at a small village called Worthen, about twelve miles from Shrewsbury, where I remained until I attained my fifth year, under the care of an excellent woman, without feeling the irreparable loss I had sustained in the death of the only parent who might have been my protector and guide through life.

At the expiration of my fifth year I was removed, (I know not by whose orders, but am inclined to imagine by some friend of Lord Talbot's, who died before I left my nurse) to Mrs. Tapperly's boarding-school, Foregate Street, Chester, in order to receive a liberal education. Here I remained nine years, unacquainted with the vices of the world, and knew no unhappiness but that of seeing children more fortunate than myself receiving the embraces of their parents and friends. During my residence at Mrs. Tapperly's, I found a kind protector in my only surviving sister, who was married to a Mr. Wilson of Trevalyn, in the county of Denbigh, North-Wales.

From this relative I experienced every attention and care expected from a parent; and indeed, as I have before stated, I always looked upon her and addressed her as such. When I was about nine years of age, she took me from Chester to Trevalyn, on a visit. One day while in her own room she opened a kind of cabinet, and took a miniature of a lady from a drawer. I asked her who it was? She burst into tears and told me she was not my mother, but that I owed my existence to the lady represented in the picture, whose daughter she also was, and my only surviving sister; adding, that she would endeavour to discharge the duty of both a sister and a mother towards me. The miniature represented a female of small size and very delicate appearance, with a remarkable blue spot on the forehead between the eyes; though I never saw it afterwards, the physiognomy is so strongly imprinted on my mind, that nothing has been able to erase from my memory. My sister was so much agitated on the occasion, as not to have told me my mother's name and family, of which I remain in ignorance to the present hour; though I have been informed that she belonged to a family whose name I do not think proper to mention, not having as I think sufficient evidence of the fact.

In the society of my sister I enjoyed the only gleam of happiness that I was doomed to experience, from the moment of my coming into the world to the present instant; but even this was of short duration; for alas! in the bloom of her youth and the flower of her age, she unfortunately fell a victim to childbirth, leaving me to regret, by the same visitation of Providence, the loss of a second parent, in that of a sister and friend united. She informed me that the name by which she was known before her marriage, was the

Hon. Miss Dyer, being the name of the family she was brought up in; and that she possessed a fortune of £30,000 besides an income of £1,500 per annum.

Deprived thus of the only relation and friend whom I knew in the world; and at an age too when I stood most in need of her advice and assistance, I felt a vacuity in my heart, which rendered existence irksome. The care of me now devolved solely on a gentleman of the name of Sucker, who resided at Newport in the county of Salop, and who within three months after the decease of my sister, taking on himself the authority of a guardian, removed me from the school at Chester, and placed me in his own family. Here I soon became more sensible than ever of the loss I had sustained in the death of my dear sister, as the severity of Mr. Sucker seldom permitted me to quit the room allotted me but at mealtimes; and he seemed by his general conduct and manners, to wish to inspire me with a dread of his person, and consequently to avoid as much as possible any conversation on my circumstances, or those of my deceased sister. I must confess I was at a loss during the period I resided with him, to assign any reason for his conduct towards me; but have been since perfectly satisfied of its being a premeditated plan to throw me in the way of any person whatever, who would remove from his care a charge, the sight of which, for reasons only known to himself, was intolerable.

I had not long been under the roof of this inhospitable man, before he introduced me to Captain Essex Bowen of the 82d regiment of foot, whom I had once before seen at Chester, in company with Mr. Sucker; and who as I understood from the latter was then on the recruiting service. This was about a week previous to my quitting the house of Mrs. Tapperly, who then appeared to be well acquainted with the particulars of my birth and family.

From the moment of his introduction to me at Mr. Sucker's, Captain Bowen paid me particular attention, which I accounted for in consequence of Mr. Sucker's observing that I was to consider him as my future guardian, he being appointed to superintend my education abroad; and requested me to pay him every possible regard, as the person to whose care I was entrusted.

In a few days I quitted Mr. Sucker's in company with Captain Bowen, who, on our departure, pretended to my late guardian the most inviolable attachment to my family; and assured him in my hearing, that he would, on his arrival in town, place me under the care of a female friend, in order to complete my education, and knowledge of the world; without which, he declared I should be considered as an alien by my own family.

Inexperienced in the ways of a deceitful world, my youthful mind was elated at the thoughts of visiting London, a place of which I had heard so much, and I was highly delighted with the varying scenes which presented themselves to my view on the road, though the season of the year was rather inauspicious, it being in January, 1792. On our arrival in the capital, which we reached without any remarkable circumstance, I was conveyed by Captain Bowen to the Salopian coffee-house, Charing-Cross, kept at that time by a Mrs. Wright, to whom I was introduced as his charge. Here I soon after experienced a visible change in the manners of my pretended protector; who in a very short period put in practice the villainous scheme which he had, no doubt, before our arrival in town, resolved on. Instead of exhibiting the least remorse, or endeavouring to soothe a mind agitated by his proceedings, he threw off the mask which had hitherto concealed the villain, and placed in my view the determined ruffian. Intimidated by his manners, and knowing that I had no friend near me, I became every thing he could desire; and so far aided his purposes as to become a willing instrument to my future misfortunes.

It was not long before I was destined to become the object of still greater degradation. In consequence of an order from the regiment to which Captain Bowen belonged, he was obliged to embark for St. Domingo, and conceiving me properly subjugated to his purpose, and remarking that my figure was extremely well calculated for the situation he had projected for me, he produced a complete suit of male attire; and for the first time made me acquainted with the unmanly design he had formed, of taking me with him to the West-Indies, in the menial capacity of his foot-boy.

I had not much time to deliberate how to act; and by this time knowing his peremptory disposition, in a fit of frenzy and despair, I yielded to the base proposal, and assumed the character he had thought fit to assign me, together with the name of John Taylor, which I ever after retained.

Thus equipped, I travelled with him to Falmouth, where soon after our arrival, we embarked on board the Crown transport, Captain Bishop, and set sail for the West Indies on the 20th day of March, 1792. We had not long been on our voyage before I began to experience the hardships of my situation: A ship even to the most robust and daring of the male sex, is at first a very unpleasant dwelling; and it must naturally be supposed, that to one like myself it was particularly disagreeable; as the novelty of my new attire did not exempt me from being compelled to live and mess with the lowest of the ship's company, for Captain Bowen never suffered me once after I was on board to eat with him, but forced me to put up with what he left at his meals.

Fearful of incurring the raillery which detection would have occasioned, I resolved to endure the hardships which I suffered with patience, rather than discover my sex.

During our voyage we encountered a most tremendous gale, which continued several days with such fury, that we were obliged to throw our guns overboard, in order to lighten the ship, and were reduced to such distress, as to render it necessary for the pumps to be kept at work continually; in consequence of which every person without distinction, (officers excepted) was obliged to assist in the laborious office. It was in this extremity that I first learnt the duty of a sailor; being obliged on some necessary occasion, to go aloft, which frequent use rendered at last familiar, and by no means irksome.

In addition to our affliction, the storm had driven us considerably out of our latitude. Having in our eagerness to lighten the ship, thrown overboard besides the guns, casks of water, bags of biscuit, and many articles of indispensable necessity to our future comfort, which we afterwards severely missed, we were compelled to put ourselves on the short allowance of a biscuit per day; and for water we were so much distressed as to be wholly without it for the space of eight days, during which period we were happy in consequence of some favourable showers, to wring the rain water from our watch coats, which, on such occasions, we never failed to hand out, in order to catch as much as possible of the providential succour. Nay, to such extremity were we reduced for want of this necessary article of life, that I have gladly flown to any little settlement of water on the deck, and eagerly applied my lips to the boards to allay the parching thirst which I experienced.

As if the measure of our troubles were not yet accomplished, our main-top-gallant mast was broken asunder, and swept into the sea four men busily engaged at the windlass for our preservation, whom we never saw more.

Whether in consequence of the agitation I underwent, in the exertion of what I now conceived my duty, or the want of necessary provision, I know not; but the sudden loss of appetite I experienced, threatened to bring on me a fit of illness. After the storm was abated, a strong gale sprung up, and being in favour of our course we proceeded at the rate of thirteen and fourteen knots an hour.

We put in for repairs, up the Windward Passage, on the Musquito shore, and on one of the islands that distinguish this place, I went with the boatswain and five others of the ship's company on shore to forage, and perceiving a bear approaching us in a retrograde position, the boatswain fired at the animal when near us, and killed it. Having been so long kept on scanty allowance, we immediately opened our prize, and took out the heart, for fresh provision: the hams also we conveyed on board, and committed them to the pickle tub for curing. Before quitting the island, we proceeded farther in search of water, and fell in with a party of the barbarous natives, who make a practice of scalping the unfortunate victims that fall into their hands. These people approaching us in a menacing manner, we fired on them, and killed one, on which the remainder fled with precipitation towards the sea. On coming up to the dead man, we found that he was naked, except a wisp round his body, like a hay-band; his hair was long, black, and strong as that of a horse. He was about six feet in height, and proportionably lusty; armed with a tomahawk, or scalping hatchet, with which each of his companions that fled was furnished. They were of a tawny complexion, and had no more clothing than their deceased comrade. Their weapons hung dangling to their hay-bands, resembling girdles.

We arrived early in the month of June, at Port-au-Prince, in the island of St. Domingo, where, after the fatigue and distress I suffered on the voyage, by fortunate opportunities of taking moderate rest, my health and spirits were quickly restored, except a little weakness and debility brought on afterwards by the heat of the climate, and occasional melancholy reflections on my own unfortunate situation; as during my continuance on this island I avoided as much as possible the sight and company of my abandoned betrayer.

Our stay at St. Domingo was but of short duration, owing to the arrival of a packet from England, which had been directed, if possible to overtake us, with orders to countermand our destination, and to join the troops on the Continent, under the command of his Royal Highness the Duke of York, but had missed us in consequence of the gale before described. I was now doomed to undergo another change of character; for Captain Bowen, judging it not convenient to continue me in the situation of his foot-boy, proposed my being enrolled in the regiment as a drummer. On my objecting to this, he threatened to have me conveyed up the country, and sold as a slave. From the dread of his really putting his threat into execution, I reluctantly acquiesced in his desire, and was immediately equipped in the dress of a drummer, and learnt the art of beating the drum from the instructions of drum-major Rickardson. In pursuance of the orders brought by the packet, we immediately embarked on board some transports appointed for that service; and, being favoured with a brisk gale during the greatest part of our voyage, we arrived in safety at the place of our destination, a port on the coast of Flanders, the name of which I cannot remember. Immediately after our debarkation, we were marched off to join the main army at head quarters; previous to reaching which, I found I was to answer the purpose of Capt. Bowen, as before, in the capacity of his drudge and foot-boy, whenever opportunity would allow the dispensing with my duty as drummer. This mode of life was by no means congenial to my feelings; and, indeed, was in my eyes worse than the situation which I was in while foot-boy only, although I was more immediately compelled to endure the sight of a man now become detestable to me.

I perfectly remember one among a multitude of harassing excursions, which had nearly proved fatal to his Royal Highness the Duke of York, and a part of his army, as well as to myself. After a long and heavy march of thirty miles in one day, without halting more than once for refreshment, while pitching our tents and making entrenchments, a part of our troops taking a temporary rest, were surprised and surrounded by the enemy, excepting a small space which led to an adjacent wood, and furnished a means of retreat to a part of the army, with which I was, though without other apparel than my small clothes. The enemy observing our camp at rest, made the attempt in the middle of the night, owing to which circumstances many others, as well as myself, were equally unprepared in point of accoutrements, though the most we suffered on this occasion was the alarm, as a large party of Austrians, who had doubtless watched the motions of our adversaries, came timely to our assistance, and compelled the unwelcome intruders to make a precipitate retreat, by which we regained our former station.

We continued to have frequent skirmishes with the enemy previous to the grand object of our royal commander, namely, the celebrated siege of Valenciennes, at which place I was exposed to greater hardships than any that I had hitherto experienced. Compelled to remain among my comrades wherever duty called, in the various struggles which preceded the surrender of the place, an eye-witness to hundreds of friends and foes indiscriminately falling around me; where the 11th dragoons, conspicuous above the rest, fought with their broad-swords hand to hand, over heaps of dead and dying soldiers, I was shocked to see many a brave fellow at first but slightly wounded, meet his death by the trampling of horses, spurred on by the contending antagonists. During these conflicts, I was obliged to keep a continual roll to drown the cries and confusion on the various scenes of action. The infantry equally distinguished themselves; as, wherever the enemy, howsoever superior in number, opposed their progress, they never failed to meet their fate on the point of the British bayonet.

Towards the end of this memorable siege, I received two wounds, though fortunately neither deep nor dangerous: the first from a musquet ball, which glancing between my breast and collar bone, struck my rib; and the other on the small of my back, from the broad-sword of an Austrian trooper, which, I imagine, rather proceeded from accident than design, the marks of which two wounds I still bear. I carefully concealed them, from the dread of their discovering my sex, and effected a perfect cure, by the assistance of a little basilicon, lint, and a few Dutch drops. These accidents happened on the same day the Hon. Mr. Tollemache was killed by a musquet ball.

Soon afterwards Valenciennes surrendered, and we in consequence marched in and took possession of the town. Most of the women and children had taken refuge in cellars and places underground. I need scarcely observe, that every possible protection was afforded to these unfortunate sufferers. In the place was found a young man who had deserted from the 14th light dragoons. A summary punishment was inflicted; he was immediately elevated on a powder cask and hanged upon a tree. All the troops were drawn out to witness the execution; and General Abercromby wept at the idea that an Englishman could be guilty of so unnatural a crime. The same day this unfortunate man deserted, our powder magazine was accidentally removed, otherwise it would in all probability have been destroyed; for no sooner had he reached the town than the enemy began to fire shells and bombs on the building that had been used for the magazine, which, with three young men who were playing at Casino, was blown to atoms. On our arrival in the town I learnt that my persecutor, Captain Bowen, was no more, having fallen in the attack; this I was informed of by one of my comrades: and though I had every reason rather to rejoice at such an event than grieve, yet it was with the greatest difficulty I could smother the sudden emotion which I experienced on the intelligence, or conceal the hidden character of a woman, in shedding a tear over his fate, however unworthy. I had no great difficulty in discovering his body; nor was it thought strange that I should endeavour to find him out, being always in the habit of attending him at his tent, when I was off duty. I took from his pocket the key of his desk, out of which I took some letters, which on perusing in private, I found chiefly relating to myself; being the correspondence of my former guardian, Mr. Sucker: these I carefully preserved, and sewed up under the shoulder straps of my shirt.

I now felt my situation truly distressing; left in a strange country without a friend to consult, or a place where I could find an asylum, I suffered under the most poignant grief, at the same time labouring under excruciating pain, and my wounds so situated, that I durst not reveal them without a discovery of my sex, which I ever carefully avoided. I hazarded every thing to keep my secret inviolable, and committed the care of my wounds to my own single endeavour and the hand of time. Thus situated, I formed a resolution to desert from a duty at best imposed on me, and endeavour to return to England. This step I might not have thought on, had I not discovered by Mr. Sucker's letters that I had been grossly imposed on, as money had been remitted to Captain Bowen, and my name was mentioned in a way which gave rise to suspicions to which I had hitherto been a stranger. Having formed my plan, little time was necessary to put it in execution. I set out on foot the same morning for the first place that providence might point out. However inexperienced I might be in some respects, I had the precaution to change my drummer's dress for one which I had been accustomed to wear when on board, and which bore evident marks of the service it had seen; and during my journey I carefully avoided any town, or place of considerable appearance; always on such occasions taking a circuitous route, frequently sleeping in a tree, under a hay-stack, and sometimes in places much less convenient.

The diminutive and insignificant figure which I made in my sailor's attire, served me as a passport among the peasantry of the country villages, through which I was under the necessity of passing, to obtain refreshment from any straggling boy I could meet with on the skirts of the place; for no one thought it worth while to question a person of my mean appearance.

In this manner I arrived at Luxemburg in September, without experiencing the least molestation; here I soon found my ignorance had led me into an error of a very auk-ward nature; and that being a town in possession of the French, they would not suffer me to proceed farther on my journey. Had I fortunately taken the contrary route, I should most probably have reached Dunkirk or Calais in one third of the time it occupied me, in traversing that part of the country; as I have since learnt that the distance from Valenciennes to either of the last mentioned parts, is small in comparison to that of the route which I had inadvertently taken to Luxemburg. Finding myself thus situated, destitute of every necessary of life, and in the midst of a country where no one paid me the smallest regard, I was constrained through mere necessity, though sorely against my wish, to engage with a Captain Le Sage, commander of a French lugger, on board which I embarked on the 17th of September, 1793. Soon afterwards we dropped down the Rhine, and sailed on a cruise, when I was put to the most common drudgery of the vessel; but even this I could have borne with patience, had not the painful idea occurred to my mind, that in this new situation, I should be doomed to raise my arm against my countrymen, which I learnt too late was the purpose of Le Sage, whom I had taken for a captain of a merchantman, but found no other than commander of a kind of privateer. Fortune however, in this one instance, proved kinder to me than she had hitherto been accustomed. Instead of falling in with some of the English merchantmen, as it was generally thought we should, and according to the ardent wish of Le Sage, our commander, we cruised about four months without any success, or meeting with any thing worthy of notice, and then fell in with the British fleet, under the command of Admiral Lord Howe, then in the Channel.

On our first sight of the British, Le Sage ordered all hands to their duty; and observing me to be missing, he followed me to the place where I was concealed among the ballast, to which I had contrived to gain access through the cabin, for fear of being obliged to act against my country; and finding that I persisted in an obstinate refusal to come on deck, he beat me on the back and sides with a rope in a most inhuman manner, and drove me before him up the cabin stairs; but when on deck I absolutely refused to assist in defence of his vessel, and he being too much occupied to think only of me, left me to my own meditations. The British now bore down upon us, and, after a trifling resistance from the French, through desperation only, we were captured, and I being considered as an English boy acting against my country, was carried with Le Sage and his companions before Lord Howe, on board the *Queen Charlotte*, to be examined.

Being interrogated by his Lordship respecting the cause of serving on board an enemy ship, I briefly told him, "That being without friends in England, I had accompanied a gentleman to the Continent in the capacity of foot-boy, on whose death, I had in the greatest distress reached Luxemburg, in hopes of obtaining a passage to my native country; but finding it impossible, as the place was at that time in possession of the French, I was constrained, though much against my inclination, to enter into Le Sage's vessel, having experienced during the short stay I made in the town, no attention to my distress, chiefly, as I imagined, from being English; and that my determination from the moment I engaged with Captain Le Sage was to desert the first opportunity that offered to forward my passage to England; but I assured his Lordship, that had I known that the intention of Le Sage was to act offensively against my countrymen, I would rather have perished than have set my foot on board his vessel; having, previous to sailing, taken him to be the commander of a merchantman, and as such engaged with him."

Fortunately, his Lordship did not think of questioning me concerning the place where my late master died; as in such an event I must unquestionably have acknowledged myself a deserter from the British forces at Valenciennes, being totally unprepared for such an enquiry, as my readers will be convinced that the whole of my answers to his Lordship's questions were a true representation of the hardships which I had experienced, and in no shape framed to deceive. This statement joined no doubt to the Frenchman's declaring my unwillingness to act in defence of the lugger, with the beating I had a little before experienced from Le Sage, gained me a favourable dismissal from Lord Howe, and served as a passport to a situation in one of the ships in his Lordship's fleet, on board of which I was immediately sent.

My heart expanded with joy on beholding myself placed once more among my countrymen. The ship to which I was assigned was the *Brunswick*, Captain John Harvey, where the story of my adventures, and of the hardships I had suffered, particularly those which I had undergone while on board the Frenchman, gained me among the seamen as many friends as hearers. Our object in this cruise was to seek the fleet of the enemy, and bring on an engagement. The service allotted to me, was to serve at the second gun on the quarter deck, and hand cartridge to the men; or, to speak in the seamen's phrase, to act in the capacity of powder-monkey. I had not however been long on board before Captain Harvey observing my cleanliness, and that my manner was very different from that of many lads on board, called me to him, and questioned me as to my friends, and whether I had not run away from some school, to try the sea. Finding by my answers that I had been better brought up and educated than most in the like situation, he assured that if I would consider him as a confidential friend, and tell him the whole truth, I should find a protector in him, as he had children of his own, and could not tell what hardships they might encounter if he were dead. On this I told him I had neither father nor mother living; that the oppression of the person to whose care I was entrusted, had first caused me to quit my home; and that in short, I was wholly destitute of any friend in the world. He appeared concerned at my early misfortunes in life, and promoted me immediately to be his principal cabin boy, in which capacity I continued to serve him until our fleet came within sight of the enemy.

Three months after my coming on board the *Brunswick*, our fleet fell in with that of the French, which brought on the ever memorable action of the 1st of June; an event which will ever be remembered with heartfelt satisfaction by the brave fellows who shared the toils of that auspicious day, and indeed by every lover of our glorious constitution and country. I cannot give from my own observation a minute description of the action, being in the beginning so busily engaged, and toward the conclusion so much wounded; and shall, in consequence, introduce an account of the part which our gallant crew took in this exploit, from information obtained when lying under cure of the wounds I received while employed on board the *Brunswick*.

This ship was chosen by Lord Howe for his second on this occasion, and contributed perhaps more than any other to the glorious result of the day. The instant the signal was made for engaging, she bore down in company with the *Queen Charlotte* for the centre of the French line, by the galling fire of which, the *Brunswick* suffered so severely, that her cockpit was filled with wounded before she had fired a single shot.

The *Vengeur* was the ship to which the *Brunswick* was opposed, and the two antagonists were laid alongside each other in such a manner, that the starboard anchors of the latter hooked into the forechains of the *Vengeur*. The master having informed Captain Harvey of this circumstance, and asked whether he should cut the *Vengeur* clear. "No," replied the gallant captain, "we have got her and we will keep her." So closely were they grappled, that the crew of the *Brunswick*, unable to haul up eight of her starboard ports, were obliged to fire through them. Thus hotly engaged they went off to the distance of a mile from the hostile fleets, and in about an hour, the smoke dispersing a little, our people perceived the *Achille*, another French seventy-four, bearing down upon them with her rigging and decks covered with men ready for boarding. Captain Harvey immediately ordered the lower deck to prepare for her reception. The *Achille* being within musket reach, a double-headed shot was added to each gun, already loaded with single thirty-two pounders, and a broadside was poured in with most destructive effect; the action with the *Vengeur* being at the same time continued. Five or six rounds brought all the masts of the *Achille* by the board, and scattered her crew like mice upon the ocean.

About an hour after the *Brunswick* had disabled this new assailant, the *Ramillies*, commanded by Captain Harvey's brother, came up to her assistance. After pouring two tremendous broadsides into the *Vengeur*, the *Ramillies* made sail for another French ship bearing down upon them, and went off engaging her.

Soon after the departure of the *Ramillies*, the *Brunswick* swung clear of the *Vengeur*, tearing away three anchors from her bow. A steady raking fire carried the fore and main-mast of the latter by the board, and she had otherwise sustained so much damage, that after a conflict of two hours and a half, she was obliged to yield. All our boats having been shot to pieces, no relief could be afforded by us to our vanquished opponent, which foundered soon after the action. Though every possible exertion was made, only two hundred of the crew were saved; the rest, in number about six hundred, went to the bottom in the ship.

The *Brunswick* was herself reduced to a perfect wreck, and of her crew forty-seven were killed, and one hundred and eighteen badly wounded.[1] In this forlorn state it was deemed impossible to

---

[1] Among these was her gallant commander, Captain Harvey, who was wounded early in the action by a musket ball, which carried away part of his right hand; but this he carefully concealed and bound up the wound with his handkerchief. Some time afterwards he received a violent contusion in the loins, which extended him almost lifeless on the deck. Rallying his strength, however, he still continued at his post, directing the engagement, till his right arm was shattered to pieces. Faint from loss of blood he was now compelled to retire; but when assistance was offered to conduct him below, he refused it. "I will not," said he, "have a single man leave his quarters on my account; my legs still remain to bear me down to the cock-pit." Casting an affectionate look on his brave crew, he thus addressed them: "Persevere my brave lads in your duty. Continue the action with spirit, for the honor of our king and country, and remember my last words: The colours of the *Brunswick* shall never be struck." It was found necessary to amputate his arm the same evening, and after sustaining the most excruciating pain; he expired at Portsmouth on the 30th of June.

rejoin the British fleet, and judged necessary, in order to save the ship, to bear away for port.

During the whole of this engagement, in which I was either actor or spectator, I felt not in the least intimidated. Just before the coming up of the *Ramillies*, I received a severe wound above the ankle of my left leg, from a grapeshot, that struck on the aftermost brace of the gun, and rebounding on the deck, lodged in my leg; notwithstanding which I attempted to rise three times, but without effect, and in the last effort part of the bone projected through the skin, in such a manner as wholly to prevent my standing, if I had been able to rise. To complete my misfortune, I received another wound by a musket-ball, that went completely through my thigh, a little above the knee of the same leg, and lay in this crippled state till the engagement was over; every person on board not wounded, being too much occupied to yield me the least assistance. I remained in this situation during the rest of the action; but at length was conveyed, with many other wounded, to the cock-pit; where the surgeon, after making me suffer the most excruciating pain, could not extract the grape-shot from above my ankle, so completely was it lodged, and surrounded by the swelling which soon took place, and prevented his endeavours, through fear of injuring the tendons, among which he declared that it lay.

On the 12th of June we reached Spithead, but the severity of my wounds obliged me to keep close to my birth, and I was thus deprived of the gratification of being hailed with those of my gallant messmates, who, on their arrival, were greeted with the loudest acclamations of applause, by their grateful countrymen. With the first convenient opportunity, I was conveyed to Haslar hospital, at Gosport, and placed under the care of surgeon Dodd, as outpatient, there not being sufficient room, from the number of wounded seamen, to admit me into the hospital. During the time I lay under his hands, I lodged at No. 2, Riemes Alley, Gosport, and supported myself with money I had received from Captain Harvey prior to the engagement. After four months attendance, I obtained a partial cure; for surgeon Dodd, though the utmost of his skill was exerted, could not extract the ball, it having lodged, as before stated, among the tendons; to have cut among which, he said, would make me a cripple for life.

At length, little remaining but the scars which I shall carry to my grave, and having obtained in a great measure the use of my leg, I was discharged from the hospital, and soon after entered on board the *Vesuvius* bomb, Capt. Tomlinson, then belonging to the squadron under the command of Sir Sydney Smith, lying at Spithead, and immediately commenced a cruise, in hopes of making prizes. After cruising some weeks on the French coast without success, we steered for the Mediterranean, and, on our arrival at Gibraltar, came to an anchor, and there remained for three days. During this interval we received an order to join the squadron under Sir Sydney Smith; on which we immediately weighed, and proceeded according to directions. Nothing worth notice occurred un til we fell in with Sir Sydney and the ships under his command, in company of which we proceeded off Havre-de-Grace, where we were soon after separated in a gale.

While on board the *Vesuvius*, we encountered a most tremendous storm, in which I was employed on an occasion that I can never think of, without being astonished at the hardships which, in youth, a human being is capable of sustaining. It was necessary for some one on board, to go to the jib-boom, to catch the jib-sheet, which in the gale had got loose. The continual lunging of the ship rendered this duty particularly hazardous, and there was not a seaman on board, but rejected this office. I was acting in the capacity of Midshipman, though I never received pay for my service in this ship, but as a common man. This circumstance I mention only, to shew that it was not my particular duty to undertake the task; which on the refusal of several who were asked, I voluntarily undertook. Indeed the preservation of us all depended on this exertion. On reaching the jib-boom, I was under the necessity of lashing myself fast to it; for the ship every minute making a fresh lunge, without such a precaution I should inevitably have been washed away. The surges continually breaking over me, I suffered an uninterrupted wash and fatigue for six hours, before I could quit the post I occupied. When danger is over, a sailor has little thought or reflection; and my messmates, who had witnessed the perilous situation in which I was placed, passed it off with a joke, observing, "that I had only been sipping sea-broth;" but it was a broth of a quality, that though most seamen relish, yet few I imagine would like to take in the quantity I was compelled to do.

Continuing on the French coast with intent to rejoin Sir Sidney, we fell in with two privateers near Dunkirk; from whom, observing their superior force, Captain Tomlinson endeavoured to make sail. The Frenchman observing his determination, crowded all the sail he could make, in chase; and we instantly commenced a running fire, which continued seven hours; at the end of which their superior weight of metal brought us to; we were in consequence immediately boarded. What became of Captain Tomlinson, the vessel, and part of the crew, I know not, as myself, and William

Richards, a young midshipman, were separated from the rest, and carried on board one of the privateers that captured us. We imagined that the rest were conveyed on board the other; but I have since reason to think the *Vesuvius* was recaptured, as she is now again in the British service.

When on board the privateer, we were deprived of our dirks, and conveyed to Dunkirk, where we were lodged in the prison of St. Clare, in Church Street, which had a little before belonged to the nuns of St. Clare, some of whom, since the revolution, have settled in England. Here I experienced the hardships of a French prison for the tedious space of eighteen months; in the course of which time Richards and myself projected a plan for our escape, by getting to the top of the prison, in order to jump off; but being observed by a sentinel on duty, we were both confined in separate dungeons, where it was so dark, that I never saw day-light, during the space of eleven weeks; and the only allowance I received, was bread and water, let down to me from the top of the cell. My bed consisted only of a little straw, not more than half a truss, which was never changed. For two days I was so ill in this dreadful place that I was unable to stir from my wretched couch to reach the miserable pittance; which, in consequence, was drawn up in the same state as it had been let down. The next morning a person, who I suppose, was the keeper of the place, came into the dungeon without a light, (which way he came I know not, but suppose by a private door, through which I afterwards passed to be released) and called out to me, "Are you dead ?" To this question I was only able to reply, by requesting a little water, being parched almost to death by thirst, resulting from the fever which preyed on me: he told me he had none, and left me in a brutal manner, without offering the least relief. Nature quickly restored me to health, and I sought the bread and water with as eager an inclination as a glutton would seek a feast. About five weeks after my illness, an exchange of prisoners taking place, I obtained my liberty, but did not see any thing of Richards till after my arrival in England, where I met him by chance, near Covent-Garden.

During my residence in the prison of St. Clare, I observed among the rest of the prisoners, a very ingenious man, a German, who employed his time, and obtained more comforts in this place, than most others, by working gold wire in a particular manner, and which he disposed of, in the various shapes of bracelets, rings, and ornamental chains for ladies dresses. This man seemed fearful lest I should learn his method of workmanship, and was angry whenever I particularly noticed him at his work; notwithstanding,

I contrived by frequent sight of the method he used, to bring the secret with me to England.

On my deliverance from prison, I was extremely weak, though in excellent spirits, but could scarcely bear the light for some days afterwards, it having an effect on my eyes, as if every thing round me was chalk. I had thoughts of returning to England by the means of those who effected my release, but was diverted from this intention by an unexpected circumstance.

Following my fellow prisoners just released, and from the pain in my leg, being considerably behind them, it was my chance to overhear the conversation of a gentleman making inquiries in English, of some seafaring men (by appearance) in Church Street, near the market, respecting any lad they knew, willing to make a voyage to America, in quality of ship's steward. I immediately accosted him, and proffered my service, being destitute of necessaries, and preferring such a situation, if I could obtain it, to a return to England with the rest of my countrymen lately exchanged. The gentleman immediately asked me my present situation at Dunkirk, which I briefly explained; in consequence of which I accompanied him back to the prison of St. Clare, where finding from the keepers of the prison that I had given him a true relation, he engaged me in the above capacity to perform the voyage to New-York, and thence to England (which he informed me would be his next voyage) for 50 l. and all I could make, at the same time advancing me sufficient cash in part, to fit me out. His name was Captain John Field, of the *Ariel*, merchantman, New-York, on board which vessel I immediately embarked; and during our short stay at Dunkirk, was employed in correcting the ship's books, paying the men, victualling the ship, and taking in the cargo. Our vessel was chiefly laden with bale-goods, among which was French lace to the value of 5000 l. We set sail for New-York, in the month of August 1796, and arrived after a successful and expeditious voyage of not more than a month, at the place of our destination, which, on going on shore I mistook for London, and particularly remarked a church, so like that in Covent-garden, that I was absolutely confirmed in the idea. I was detained little more than a fortnight at New-York, and was chiefly employed in taking an account of the goods delivered to the respective owners; after which duty, I accepted an invitation to accompany my Captain in an excursion to Providence, in Rhode Island, where his family resided. During this journey, and indeed the whole of the voyage, I was treated rather as a friend and companion, by Captain Field, than a person in his pay, and under his command.

On our arrival at Rhode Island, we found Captain Field's family in good health; it consisted of his wife, four children and a niece. Here I spent the most agreeable fortnight of my life; as the Captain neither paid not received any visits, but I made one of the party: Mrs. Field also appeared equally attached to me, which made the short time I continued among this worthy family, appear to me but as a dream, so few and transient were my days of happiness. Among other visits, we made one to Mr. Field, the Captain's father, a very agreeable and worthy gentleman. The only circumstance of an unpleasant nature that occurred during my stay in America, arose from the strong partiality which the Captain's niece conceived to my company, and which proceeded to such an extent, as to induce her to make me an offer of her hand in marriage. I made several excuses, but could not divert her attention from what she proposed. Mrs. Field at length becoming acquainted with the circumstance, made great objection to my youth and inexperience of the world; but neither my excuses, nor Mrs. Field's remonstrances had any weight, opposed to the young lady's inclination, which she fondly cherished to the last hour of my residence at Rhode Island. She requested before Mrs. Field, that I would make her a present of my picture; for which purpose I sat for a miniature at New York, in the full uniform of an American officer. For this picture I paid eighteen dollars. The time of our departure for England being arrived, I took my leave, not without regret, of Mrs. Field, and family; but had scarcely proceeded two miles on the way to New York, before I was summoned back, being overtaken by a servant, who informed the Captain and myself, that we must return, as the young lady was in strong fits. We returned, and found her still in a fit, out of which, with great difficulty, we recovered her; and by making her a promise of a speedy return from England, she very reluctantly allowed me to depart.

Our stay at New York was but short; the mate, in the absence of Captain Field and myself, having taken charge of the cargo consigned to England, and obtained the necessary invoices of the goods; chiefly manufactured cotton and camblets. This, had I remained on board, would have been part of my duty; but through the indulgence of the captain, it was performed by another. We proceeded on our voyage to England with a favourable wind, and arrived at Cowes, in the Isle of Wight, without meeting with any thing particular on the way. Our provisions falling short, we took in some fresh, and after waiting three days for a convoy, proceeded to the river Thames, where we safely cast anchor on the 20th of November, 1796, and came to a mooring in the tier off Churchhole, Rotherhithe. We delivered our cargo, and began to take in a fresh one, as it was Captain Field's intention to stay no longer in England than was absolutely necessary for shipping an outward bound cargo. The many acts of friendship which I had experienced from this gentleman, determined me to accompany him in any voyage which he might undertake; particularly as he had often informed me that if I continued with him a voyage or two more, he would resign the command of the vessel to me; it being his intention to retire from the sea service in a short time. He told me that he had an idea of making a trading voyage up the Mediterranean, and commissioned me to purchase some maps, charts, &c. necessary for such an undertaking, which I in consequence bought (at Faden's, who then resided at the corner of St. Martin's Lane, Strand,) by his direction.

Being short of men to work the ship, the Captain had engaged two fresh hands, who came on board the afternoon of the same day, myself being the only officer on board; I took the description of their persons, and entered their names on the ship's books, being employed at the same time in settling my accounts in the cabin, and having some loose cash, and bank-notes lying on the desk. After giving them orders to assist in swabbing the decks the first thing in the morning, I dismissed them. Soon after twelve o'clock at night, I was awakened by a violent noise at the upper cabin door, with a crash, as if some part of it had given way. Alarmed at the moment, I searched for a tinder-box, to strike a light, but through hurry could not lay my hand on it. Almost at the same instant I caught hold of a brace of pistols, which hung on the side of the cabin fire-place; these, to my great surprise, I found unloaded. A second attempt of a more violent nature than the first, being made at the inner door, I recollected a sword which hung over the captain's birth, and which I took down, at the instant the cabin door had given way, by a wrench from an iron crow, or some such instrument. Knowing the situation of the door, I advanced towards it, with the sword in my hand, and immediately made a thrust which I knew must wound deep, from the difficulty I found in drawing it back. I heard neither groan, nor noise; but found that the intruder, whoever he was, had retired. I now sought the tinder-box, and struck a light, secured the door, and sat up the remainder of the night. The first thing in the morning the men observed a quantity of blood on the deck, in a track from the cabin door, which they noticed as being broken, and asked me if any thing particular had happened; to which I made no reply; but on finding Thomas Honarton, one of the new engaged hands, to be absent, I inquired after him, and was informed that he was unwell from an accident he had met with the night before in getting into his birth.

I made no other inquiries; but waited until the captain should come on board, which he did about eleven o'clock the same morning; and on entering the cabin, he noticed the shattered condition of the door. When I informed him of the particulars, adding, that the man whom I suspected, Thomas Honarton, still remained in the ship; the captain instantly ordered him to be brought forward, when his thigh was discovered to be dreadfully swelled, and the marks of the wound shewed a sword or some such weapon to have passed through his thigh. He could make no defence to my accusation of his attempt to rob the cabin, and breaking the door. Captain Field finding his wound dangerous, sent him to St. Thomas's hospital, where he escaped prosecution, by the ship's sailing before he could obtain a cure. The other man engaged, named Mac Gregory, we rather suspected of being a deserter. He denied it, but one of the lads had an opportunity one night, of observing his back to be marked, as if he had been flogged, which confirmed our suspicion; but not being able to get the ship cleared, for want of hands, we were glad of him.

A few days after this affair, the mate, John Jones, (a native of New Providence) and myself, agreed on a little excursion on shore, previous to our leaving England, to which purpose we put on a plain seaman's dress, knowing the prejudice of most of the lower people about Wapping, against officers of any description, whom in general they consider as little better than spies on their actions. But while about to land at St. Catherine's, we were attacked by a press-gang, whom we resolutely opposed; I in my defence taking up one of the scullers of the boat, with which I struck one or two who attempted to secure me. In this contest I received a wound on my head by a cutlass, a large seam from which remains to the present hour. After a long struggle, during which I was tumbled out of the boat up to my armpits in water, the mate and myself were both secured. Fortunately for him, he had his warrant as an American officer about him, which procured his discharge, when taken on board the tender. On my examination, being unprepared for such an event, I had inadvertently left my protection as an American on board the *Ariel*, behind me. This circumstance, with the treachery of Jones, who informed the regulating captain that I was an Englishman, thereby thinking to get rid of a dangerous rival, (for he was particularly attached to the niece of Captain Field, but had lost all hope of success with her, from her known partiality for me) and moreover stated I was the best seaman on board their vessel. This declaration, joined with the want of the certificate I had left in the *Ariel*, occasioned my detention on board the tender for three days and nights. In this situation my indignation at the treachery of

Jones, agitated me beyond any thing I had hitherto suffered; and I thought of various schemes, but without putting any in practice, to effect my deliverance. At length there being a sufficient number of impressed men collected to clear the tender for the reception of others, myself and the rest of the men confined were brought upon deck, in order to be sent to different ships. Finding I had nothing to prevent this, but a disclosure of what I had so long kept within my own breast, I accosted the inspecting officers, and told them I was unfit to serve his Majesty in the way of my fellow-sufferers, being a female. On this assertion they both appeared greatly surprised; and at first thought I had fabricated a story to be discharged, and sent me to the surgeon, whom I soon convinced of the truth of my assertion. The officers upbraided each other with ignorance at not discovering before, that I was a woman, and readily gave me a discharge.

Resolved never to go on board the *Ariel*, after the disclosure of my sex, I wrote to Captain Field, without mentioning the way in which I obtained a discharge from the tender, only requesting he would meet me as soon as possible at a house at the corner of Tower Street, Tower Hill. Being on board at the time, my letter had not been dispatched long, before he gave me the meeting, and was astonished, at my disclosing to him the manner in which I obtained my liberty. It was some time before I could convince him that I was really a woman; having for such a length of time known me experience hardships so opposite to the delicacy of the female sex. He endeavoured to prevail on me to accompany him in his intended voyage, but no arguments could induce me (after acknowledging former favours received) to accompany him, or indeed for the present to think of the sea-service, in any way whatever. Finding his applications fruitless, he honourably paid me every shilling due on our engagement, and besides made me a very handsome present. After this interview I saw him but twice, nothing material passing between us, except his earnest desire of my disguising my sex, and resuming my former situation, which he could never prevail on me to accede to.

I had not been released above a day or two from the tender, when, in November 1796, the King was attacked on his way to the Parliament-house, by the mob, and the glasses of his carriage were broken in pieces. The horse-guards had just left him proceeding along the park in his private carriage from the gate of St. James's Palace. I had climbed a tree opposite to the small gate that leads to the Green Park, so that I had a complete view of the whole of this extraordinary scene. Just as the carriage was passing, it was most furiously attacked. The coach-door was opened, the coachman thrown off his box, and the three footmen were pulled down from behind, and one desperado had even seized his Majesty by the collar, and was in the act of pulling him out, while others of the mob were spitting in his face. Just at this moment was heard the cry of "Help! for God's sake! The King is in danger! The King will be killed!" At this cry, Lieutenant Beauclerc, commanding the troop of horse, who had just left the court at the King's Palace, ordered his men to wheel and galloped off to rescue his Majesty from the hands of his infuriated assailants. He struck with his sword on the shoulder, the man who had hold of the king, but the villain contrived to escape. As I was in the tree, I was asked if I knew any of the persons concerned in this outrage, and on my replying that I should certainly recognise the man who had been struck, if I were to see him again, I was ordered to follow to Buckingham House, which I did among the horse soldiers. No person was then apprehended; but as I was afterwards going along Chandos Street to Bow Street, to give a description of the fellow, I saw the very man led between two others, and pointed him out to the officer, by whom he was secured; but his companions escaped. He was so badly wounded, that he was immediately sent to the hospital, where I believe he died, for no examination ever took place, though I was bound over to appear against him.

With money in my pocket, I was undetermined how to act, but for the present took a lodging in East-Smithfield. I frequented the theatres, and houses about Covent-garden, where I became known to persons of every description as a good companion. Among others, I had formed an acquaintance with Haines, the well-known highwayman, who was some time afterwards hung in chains on Hounslow Heath, for shooting one of the Bow Street officers, when about to apprehend him. I did not know that this man followed so dangerous an occupation; but one evening, when my cash was nearly exhausted, I met him at a house in Covent-garden, known by the name of the Finish. Being out of spirits, he questioned me as to the cause; I told him, I had lived so freely since I came on shore, that my cash was quite exhausted, and I was racking my imagination to get a fresh supply. He clapped his hand on my shoulder and exclaimed, "D_____n it, my fine fellow, I'll put you up to the best way in the world to get the supply you stand in need of." We left the house, and while walking, he proposed that I should join him on an excursion to take a purse on the road; and observing that my sailor's habit was not calculated for the occasion, he furnished me with money to buy buckskin small clothes, &c. necessary for the purpose. The road we were to take was not settled, but our meeting was fixed for the next night; I purchased the buckskin small clothes at Ford's, in the Strand, and a pair of boots from Newcomb, in Pall Mall. At the hour appointed, I met Haines at a livery stable behind the New Church, in the Strand, and found him in company with six more persons, all of whom I understood had met on the same business, though intending to take different roads. I was to accompany Haines, who furnished me with a pair of pistols, which he told me cost three guineas. When every thing was ready for our departure, a sudden recollection of the danger and dishonour of this undertaking, providentially occurred to my mind; and I informed Haines how very reluctant I was to break an engagement, or my word in any particular, yet when I considered the probable consequences of the business in question, I could not think of accompanying him, however far I had gone on the occasion. At the same time I remarked, it was not the danger of the enterprise that I dreaded, but the certain shame attached to a dishonourable action; the principles of a state of warfare I should not mind, but never deliberately would act the part of a Pirate. He endeavoured to divert my resolution, seemed highly exasperated, and shewed an inclination to quarrel, which I think was only suppressed by a knowledge of the situation in which he stood. I left the place without farther opposition, congratulating myself on so narrow an escape. Though I saw Haines afterwards, he never took the least notice of the affair, and I took care for the future what company I connected myself with.

During my residence in East-Smithfield, I made several applications at the Navy-pay office, Somerset-House, for money due to me for service on board the *Brunswick* and the *Vesuvius* bomb, in which I was taken by the French, besides prize-money to which I was entitled by the captures on the first of June. At length I was directed to apply respecting the prize-money to the agent, in Arundel Street, Strand, whither I immediately went, and was desired to call another time. Being vexed at the disappointment, I returned to Somerset-House; where, through many disappointments, I made use of language which gave offence to some of the gentlemen, and was immediately conveyed to Bow Street, on the 31st of December, 1796. Here I underwent a long examination, which lasted till near twelve o'clock, before the sitting magistrate, now Sir Richard Ford, to whom I produced my discharge from the tender, and other documents to prove the sufferings and hardships which I had undergone, so much to his satisfaction, that I obtained a discharge, and was requested to attend the Monday following at two o'clock, which I did, and found several magistrates assembled. Having undergone a long private examination, the consequence was, a subscription was immediately made, and by the recommendation of some gentlemen present, I was placed in a lodging at the house of Mrs. Jones, Falcon-court, Shoe-lane, with a strict injunction, if possible, to break me of the masculine habit to which I was so much used. I received twelve shillings a week for my support till I could obtain the money due to me from Government. That sum was regularly paid me from the above subscription, by a Mr. Pritchard of New-Inn, who was present at my last examination, and to whom Mrs. Jones was laundress.

I had not yet changed my seaman's attire; but during the stay I made with Mrs. Jones, I resumed the dress of my own sex, though at times I could not entirely forget my seafaring habits, but frequently dressed myself, and took excursions as a sailor. In less than a month, I received the greater part of the money due to me from the Navy-pay-office, which I cheerfully shared with the family of Mrs. Jones; who, notwithstanding, treated me in an ungrateful manner, misrepresenting me to the gentlemen who had raised the subscription, as a person on whom their bounty was thrown away, and more inclined to masculine propensities, such as smoking, drinking grog, &c. than what became a female, though I never took any of the latter, but she was always invited to a part, and of which I never found her backward in taking a good allowance. Whenever I dressed myself as a sailor, I sought the company of some messmates I had known on board the *Brunswick*, and as long as my money lasted, spent it in company with the brave fellows, at the Coach and Horses, opposite Somerset-House, a place where they mostly frequented.

I removed from Mrs. Jones's to Chichester Rents, Chancery-lane, and lodged with a very decent woman, named Higgins, where the grape-shot which had remained in my leg from the time of our engagement in the *Brunswick*, June 1794, worked itself out in February 1797. The reason I imagine, proceeded from the wounds breaking out afresh, in consequence of my too free use of spirituous liquors, since my residence on shore. The ball, to which there adhered a quantity of flesh, I kept by me for some time, but was obliged at last to throw it in the fire, from the offensive smell of the flesh, which soon putrefied. My leg, notwithstanding the ball was out, continued so bad, that I applied for admission to St. Bartholomew's hospital, and went in as a female, though I frequently wore, while under cure, my sailor's dress, and was in consequence taken, by strangers, for a man in the woman's ward. I remained in Watt's ward, under surgeon Blake four months, and during the time had several pieces of shattered bone taken from my leg; at length it being to all appearance well, I was discharged. The cure, however, did not prove of any long duration, the bone being very much injured, and my blood continuing in a bad state, it soon broke out again. In this situation, without any place of refuge, or means of subsistence, I was advised to petition his Royal Highness the Duke of York for relief; and accordingly applied to a gentleman, who drew up a petition, stating the various hardships which I had undergone by sea and land. Having obtained the signatures of her Grace the Duchess of Devonshire, and Sir William Pulteney, I left it at the Horse Guards, with Captain Nowell, secretary to his Royal Highness. In less than a fortnight, I called at the Horse Guards, and received from Captain Nowell five guineas, with my petition signed by his Royal Highness, as well as her Royal Highness the Duchess of York, and directions, when I called, that I should present it to her Majesty. I afterwards got it signed by Sir James Pulteney; and through Mr. Dundas, meant to have presented it to her Majesty; taking the opportunity of a court day to give it to him for that purpose, as he was passing to the royal apartments. He remarked it was not intended for him, I told him no, but I wished him to present it to her Majesty from myself, and accordingly left it with him.

Not hearing any thing in consequence of my petition, and the money I had received from his Royal Highness the Duke of York, being expended, the idea struck me that if I could obtain a machine similar to the one I observed the German use in the prison of St. Clare, with which he manufactured the gold wire, I might obtain a comfortable subsistence. For that purpose I called on Mr. Loyer, a jeweller, in Denmark Street, St. Giles's, in order, if possible, to get a machine made from my description. Mr. Loyer, from my instructions, soon produced an instrument that every way answered the purpose; and having informed him of the use for which it was intended, he informed me, if I would manufacture it in his house, he had no doubt he could from his connection, dispose of enough to keep me constantly employed. I made no objection to his proposal, and worked gold wire in various shapes, so much to his satisfaction, that I continued in his employ some time. Mr. Loyer keeping a number of persons employed, I worked in the same apartment with some others; among whom was a German, named Hieronimo, who, observing the manner in which I worked, afterwards practised it as part of his profession, and worked on the same, during the time I continued in Mr. Loyer's employ. Finding the money I received not adequate to support me in a proper manner, my wounded leg getting so bad as to put me to considerable inconvenience, I applied to Mr. Loyer for an advancement of price, which, he objecting to, knowing that he had Hieronimo to do the same kind of work if I left him, we parted. Being jealous lest I should learn every thing in the jewellery business, having been able to work in more branches than that for which he engaged me, he removed me for some time previous to my quitting him, to a separate apartment from the shop, where I worked by myself.

About the time of my working at Mr. Loyer's, I formed an acquaintance in my male dress, with a person who informed me he was Vice-grand of a lodge of Odd Fellows, held at the Harlequin, near the stage-door of Drury-lane Theatre. This person discovering in me, a conviviality, suitable to such an undertaking, proposed my becoming one of their members; and as there was to be a meeting of the Lodge that evening, he said he would propose me as a new member. On my ready acquiescence, we adjourned to the place, where I went through the whole of the forms used on such occasions, and became a free member of the society of Odd Fellows, Lodge 21. Neither the person who introduced me, nor any of the members knew my sex. It is the boast of free-masonry, that they never had more than one female belonging to their institution (namely, Queen Elizabeth); and I think I may fairly challenge any Lodge of Odd Fellows, to produce another female member: it being generally thought that there is not a female in England (myself excepted) belonging to this society.

At the time of my employ by Mr. Loyer, I put on my seaman's dress and accompanied the procession, when their Majesties went to St. Paul's, and the different colours of the enemy, were carried to be hung up in that Cathedral Church, as trophies of the victories obtained over their arms, by Howe, St. Vincent, and Duncan. I was one of Lord Howe's attendants with his colours, and, rode on the car, and the chains of the bracelets which her Majesty wore on the occasion, were made by me, at Mr. Loyer's, by order from Messrs. Gray and Constable, Jewellers, of Sackville Street, Piccadilly.

On my quitting Mr. Loyer's, my leg getting worse, I obtained admission into St. George's hospital, and experienced a tedious confinement of seven months, being carefully attended by surgeons Keate and Griffiths. While thus situated, I was enabled to enjoy many comforts which this charitable institution does not supply, from the benevolent attention of Mrs. Emma Raynes, a lady to whom I shall ever confess my obligations, as, immediately on my obtaining a discharge from the hospital, she provided me with a decent lodging in Tottenham Court Road, and supported me for a considerable time at her own expense, though I had no other claim to her protection than my necessitous condition. Previous to my finding a friend in this lady, it was judged by several in the hospital, from the low state I was reduced to, (my bones coming almost through the skin) that I should not survive the illness under which I laboured, from the pain of my wounded limb, and I procured some little necessaries from a subscription made by the young gentlemen, pupils, who attended the hospital; one of whom, named Scaife, in joke, I imagine, offered me half-a-crown a week while I lived, to have my body when dead. However he might mean it, I know not, but this circumstance produced in me such an aversion to physic, that while I remained under cure, I would take no more medicine, fearing it would hasten my death; and I remarked that my wound healed faster than before. Weary of the hospital, I solicited a discharge, though my leg was by no means well; and through the kindness of Mrs. Raynes, had every necessary provided for my use. Unwilling to remain a burthen on the generosity of this lady, longer than I could possibly help myself, I came to a resolution of making my sufferings known to some persons of distinction, having heard nothing relative to the petition I had left in the hands of Mr. Dundas, to be presented to her Majesty. I wrote immediately to his grace the Duke of Norfolk, whose humane and charitable disposition is so well known, that it is totally unnecessary for me to enlarge on that subject. The result of my application was successful, as I received a very handsome present from his grace.

This seasonable relief was to me of the greatest service, though it contributed to place me under a very embarrassing circumstance. Fearing that my little fund would be exhausted before I could obtain another supply, I endeavoured, as far as my circumstances would admit, to make as decent an appearance as possible, that I might more readily appear before the illustrious personages who had recommended the presentation of my petition to her Majesty, and to obtain, if possible, a knowledge, whether it had been presented by Mr. Dundas, or not. At this time I had removed from the lodging provided me by Mrs. Raynes to another near Rathbone Place; and having at times, previous to my removal, worn a little powder in my hair whenever I had occasion to call at the houses of Noble persons, to whom I had made my case known, I was informed against as an unqualified person, having no licence, through the malice of my last landlady's sister, and in February 1799, received a summons to attend the Commissioners of the Stamp Office, from the solicitor, Mr. Estcourt, to answer to the accusation. Without money or a friend to come forward on my behalf, I attended on the day mentioned, in the notice which I had received, and set up in my defence to the accusation, that I had never worn powder as an article of dress though I had frequently made use of powder in defence of my King and country. This assertion from a female excited the curiosity of the Commissioners; who questioned me, under what circumstance, I could make use of powder in the way understood from my speech; when I related the several incidents of my life, in the land, as well as sea service, likewise my examination at Bow Street, after applying for my pay at the Navy Office. On concluding my defence, and remarking the distress of my present situation, the Commissioners, and other gentlemen present made a handsome collection, and presented me with it to the extreme mortification of the informer, who rather expected a share of the penalty, which she supposed I should be under the necessity of paying, than, that her spite against me should turn out so much to my advantage. On the contrary, my late landlady, her sister, expressed herself greatly pleased with the fortunate turn in my favour; and her sincerity I did not doubt, from the many little kindnesses I had before experienced from her. Mr. Estcourt gave me a letter to Evan Nepean, Esq. of the Admiralty, on what subject I knew not, but imagined it to be in relation to myself; which, though I delivered it at the Admiralty office, I never afterwards heard any thing of. Considering in what way to obtain a sum which might enable me to establish myself in a little comfort, I thought of the petition which I had long since left in the hands of Mr. Dundas; and as it was originally recommended to be presented to her Majesty, by the message I had received from the Duke of York, I resolved to wait on his Royal Highness at Oatlands, to inform him that I had never received an answer to his recommendation. On my arrival I sent in my name and business, by one of the attendants on his Royal Highness; and received in answer a guinea, and a message that his Royal Highness would make an immediate enquiry concerning where the petition lay; and as I had left a direction where I lodged in town, I received a few days afterwards, a quantity of female apparel from Oatlands, sent, as I imagine, by order of her Royal Highness the Duchess of York.

The long silence which I have kept with regard to Mr. Sucker, particularly as he was the only person, who could have informed me of many circumstances relative to my family and interests, will naturally strike many of my readers. I need not offer as an excuse for my negligence in this particular, that I had been so much occupied by a variety of circumstances, each following the other with such rapidity as wholly to prevent me, had it been my intention, from seeking an earlier explanation. I had in a great measure been induced to defer my application to Mr. Sucker, in consequence of

Messrs. Winter and Hay, of Long Acre, through the recommendation of Justice Bond, having taken the trouble of writing to Mr.
Wilson of Trevallyn several times, for the particulars relating to
my birth and expectations; but as no answer was obtained to either of the letters sent, I thought it best to apply to Mr. Sucker in
person. During the suspense in which I remained with respect to
the success of my petition, I determined to pay this gentleman a
visit, and went to Shrewsbury, by the mail; and put up at the Talbot, kept at that time by Mr. Purslow. I then proceeded to Newport, Mr. Sucker's residence, in a return chaise; but finding a difficulty of being introduced to him as a female, as I did not chuse to
send in my name, I returned to Shrewsbury, and procured an en-
sign's uniform of a person in Dog Lane, who dealt in cloaths from
London. Unwilling to change my dress at Mr. Purslow's, where I
was known, I went to the Raven Inn, in Raven Street, where I sub-
stituted for female attire, the dress which I had procured the loan
of, in which I walked to the Elephant and Castle, in Mardol, and
hiring a horse, rode back to Newport. On my arrival at Mr.
Sucker's house, I sent a message in by a servant, that a gentleman
wished to speak with Mr. Sucker, and in return received an answer
to send in my name and business; I replied, that I waited on him,
having known Captain Bowen of the 82d regiment, and had something particular to communicate; on which I was immediately introduced to him, and though labouring under considerable agitation, I asked him if he knew a Miss Talbot, or could inform me
what had become of her. He said he had known her well, but that
she died abroad in the year 1793, of which he was well informed by
letters in his possession. I told him I doubted the fact, and wished
to see the letters mentioned, which he evaded. I then asked him if
she had any particular mark, or if he had known her well enough
to swear to her person, if she were alive? He replied that he could
identify her, among a thousand, that she was a twin, and had a deficiency on the left side of her forehead, I immediately put my hair
aside, and pointed my finger, to the part of my forehead he had
described, and briskly drawing my sword, declared he was my
prisoner, and should account to me for the property of which I
supposed that he had defrauded me. I informed him that I was
Miss Talbot, and had visited him, for this express purpose, knowing, that when I was entrusted to his care, he had a sufficient in-
demnification for what trouble or expense he might be put to, and
had no doubt something considerable in trust for my use? He appeared surprised and confounded, trembled exceedingly, and after
repeatedly declaring that he was a ruined man, abruptly quitted
the room. I was myself greatly agitated, but conceiving myself so

much injured, I immediately went to Shrewsbury, in order to consult a lawyer how to proceed. Mr. Lox-dale, to whom I intended to apply, being unfortunately from home, I returned to Newport with a determination if possible, to obtain from Mr. Sucker, some information respecting my family, connections, and expectations. When I arrived at Newport, I learnt to my great disappointment, that Mr. Sucker had suddenly retired from his house, and in less than three days from the time, was found dead in his bed at Longford, near Newport, without any previous appearance of illness. Thus frustrated in gaining the intelligence I so much needed, I left the place in great distress of mind, with so scanty a sum in my pocket, that I was prevented from proceeding to Mr. Wilson's at Trevallyn, which I otherwise should have done, though his wilful neglect to answer the letters sent by Messrs. Winter and Hay, left me in great doubt as to the reception he might have given me. I now again took the road to London, where I soon arrived without any other prospect than the uncertain hope of better success with my petition, and thinking some money was still due to me for pay, I applied to Lord Spencer, then first Lord of the Admiralty, and saw his Lordship, who presented me with a guinea, and ordered me some refreshment.

My existence now chiefly depended on the liberality of many noble and generous persons, to whom I was necessitated to make my case known; and the frequent walks I was obliged to take when thus employed, caused the wounds of my leg to break out afresh, so as wholly to deprive me of the power of walking, many pieces of the shattered bone occasionally coming out of my leg. On this, I obtained admission into Middlesex hospital, and about a fortnight afterwards received a message from Mr. Justice Bond, to attend if possible at Bow Street, to confront a female, who, in the dress of a light horseman, had assumed the name of John Taylor, and represented herself in a way to be mistaken for me. I accompanied the person who brought me the letter to Bow Street, and saw a fine looking woman about five feet ten inches high, whom Mr. Bond desired me to interrogate as to the situation she had occupied on board the *Brunswick*, where she reported to have been wounded. A very few questions brought her to a confession, that she was not the person she had pretended, and not giving a satisfactory account of herself, she was committed to the House of Correction for three months, as a vagrant. William Richards, my fellow prisoner in France, chancing to pass in Bow Street, I called to him from the coach, and he went in with me into the office and offered to make oath as to my identity; but Mr. Bond informed him that he was sufficiently satisfied who was the impostor. Several persons in the office informed me that this woman had been imposing on the public in my name for some time past, and congratulated me on her detection.

On my return from Bow Street, while getting out of the coach at the door of my lodging where I called previous to my return to the hospital, I was followed into the passage by a hair-dresser, named Spraggs, of Cleveland Street, who mistaking me for a lodger in the same house with whom he had a dispute respecting a wig which she had purchased of him, struck me a violent blow which brought me to the ground, and cut my head in a shocking manner, and materially hurt my wounded leg by kicking me in the passage. I afterwards learnt that the cause of this violence was as follows: Spraggs had sold a wig to a lady, and she was prevented from paying him, by the assertion of another hairdresser of the name of Kennedy, that the wig was not the property of Spraggs, but belonged to him. Spraggs in consequence when he applied for payment, was informed of this circumstance, and not receiving the money as he expected, he brought an action in the Marshalsea court, but was non-suited, by not attending to prove the wig his property. Thus disappointed, he took the above method of revenge, and in his rage mistook the person. My friends advised me to procure a warrant against him for the assault, and I immediately returned to Bow Street, where a warrant was granted me. Spraggs however kept out of the way for several days, but at last it was served on him, and he was obliged to find bail for his appearance at the Quarter Sessions, Clerkenwell. This business detained me till it was too late to return to the hospital that night, so that I was obliged to wait till the regular day of taking in patients, before I could regain my former place. When the trial came on at Clerkenwell, I was still in the hospital, but having been apprized of the time when it was to come on, I obtained leave of absence from Surgeon Miners, and attended three days before my cause came on. Mr. Sylvester, the present Recorder of London, pleaded in my behalf without taking the least gratuity; on the contrary, when I attended him to state the case, he made me a handsome present. Very little defence was attempted on the part of Spraggs, who was found guilty of the assault, and sentenced to pay me 10l. for the injury he had done. I then returned to the hospital, and through the skill and attention of Surgeon Miners, was once more enabled to use my wounded leg, though by no means given to understand that I had obtained a radical cure. Soon after quitting the hospital, I received a notice to attend at the War Office, where I was directed to deliver a letter addressed to Lord Morton, at Buckingham House. I had no doubt that this letter related to the petition which I had left for her Majesty's inspection, and which I imagined his Royal Highness the Duke of York had sought after, agreeably to the message I received at Oatlands. I went to Buckingham House, and saying I had a letter from the War Office for Lord Morton, was immediately introduced to his Lordship, who, on reading it, informed me that it related to my petition, and conducted me to another apartment, where I saw a lady seated, whose hand Lord Morton desired me to kiss; after which, I returned with his Lordship to the apartment where I had found him, and received five guineas from his Lordship's hands, on quitting Buckingham House.

The Lady whose hand I kissed did not ask me a question, or speak a word: I imagined it might be her Majesty, though Lord Morton had not mentioned any thing concerning her title or rank. I was soon afterwards confirmed in this conjecture, for having an opportunity of seeing her Majesty in public, I recognised in her the lady whose hand I had the honour of kissing at Buckingham House. Lord Morton directed me to apply to the War Office, where I was informed that I must attend on a future day, in my sailor's dress, to receive a half-year's payment of her Majesty's bounty, which I afterwards did, in the name of John Taylor. This was in August, 1799.

On my quitting Middlesex Hospital, Surgeon Miners informed me, that my leg was not in a state to bear much walking, and indeed the obligation I was under to attend in person, on many occasions, soon rendered it as bad as ever. I was recommended by John Bond, Esq. a Magistrate, of Hendon, in Middlesex, to go a second time into Middlesex Hospital. Surgeon Miners was at Mr. Bond's at the time I was thus advised, and informed me that I must in all probability have my leg amputated. With this impression on my mind I again entered the hospital, and only escaped from if without the loss of a limb, by a singular, though in the first part, unfortunate circumstance: I had, previous to going into the hospital, taken under my care a motherless child about three years of age, which when out of my power now to attend, was protected by two young women, who soon after having an engagement to dine on board the Sophia, a West-Indiaman, lying off Hermitage Stairs, unfortunately took their little charge on the party. Not being sufficiently attended to, the child fell overboard and was drowned. The intelligence no sooner reached me at the hospital, then frantic at the loss, although my leg was surrounded with bandages preparatory to amputation, I the next morning by seven o'clock, October 24th, 1799, quitted the hospital, after taking off the screw bandage, and walked to Hermitage Stairs, in such distraction of mind, that I felt neither pain nor impediment in my leg the whole way. But on my arrival where the ship lay, I could gain no information concerning the body, notwithstanding I offered every thing I had in the world as a reward to any person who should find it. All my exertions were ineffectual, the child was never seen afterwards; but it was suggested, and on reasonable grounds, that he was not drowned, but carried to the West Indies; for a black boy on board, as well as he could be understood, gave me to understand, that he was not drowned, but carried away. His name was George Lacon Griffin, and he was heir to a considerable estate in Shropshire, as I was informed by his father, Mr. George Griffin, carver and gilder, Charing Cross, who entrusted him to my care; being himself under pecuniary embarrassment, and in confinement at that time, on account of a bill which he had accepted for a friend.

I had not left Middlesex Hospital more than a fortnight, before I experienced new trouble and inconvenience in my leg; which, previous to my so sudden departure, on the melancholy loss of the unfortunate child, had been doomed to amputation, by the universal opinion of the surgeons; and to the general conversation on this subject, I attribute a spurious account of my adventures, which at this time found its way into the Morning Herald. As I did not wait for a discharge from Middlesex Hospital, I felt a reluctance to apply there again for relief, but obtained an order to the St. Mary-le-bone Infirmary, and was of course admitted. Here I continued almost four months; and after many pieces of the shattered bone had been extracted, and the flesh by continued rest, a little grown over, I consulted with Mr. Phillips, the principal surgeon, whether I was not in a situation to quit the Infirmary. He told me that with care, and the use of bandages, which he would give me, I might do as well out as where I was, but desired I would walk as little as possible, while I found the least pain, as it would retard the healing of the flesh round the bone. Having obtained the bandages of Mr. Waller, the house surgeon, I thought of quitting the Infirmary immediately, but having made myself use ful towards the latter part of the time I was there, in keeping account of clothes, and marking a variety of articles, for the use of the Infirmary and parish, Dr. Hooper, the principal of the house, objected to my departure. I persisted, nevertheless, in my purpose, and in consequence came away; as the Doctor threatened to report me to the Board, I told him I would save him the trouble, and went the following Friday, and stated the whole affair myself, which being satisfactory to the gentlemen present, I received two guineas, and left the place highly pleased. One of the gentlemen said, he knew Mrs. Tapperley, of Chester well, and that he had a daughter under her care, at the time I was with her, adding, that he knew I was related to the family whose name I bore. He followed me out, when I withdrew, and made me a present of a guinea; and I have since, whenever he met me, experienced some mark of his liberality.

Having engaged a lodging in that neighbourhood, I removed the whole of my wearing apparel, which in all situations I had hitherto taken the utmost care of, to this place. But as if I was to be stripped and persecuted through life, one morning while in bed, I was robbed of every thing I possessed in the world, and but for the kindness of some ladies at the next house, should have been without an article to wear. A woman who lived with a trumpeter of the Dragoon Guards, was soon afterwards taken up on suspicion of robbing another person, and having in her possession a great quantity of false keys, and duplicates of property in pawn, I attended her examination at Marlborough Street, and having discovered that several of the duplicates described my property, I was desired to attend on her trial, as a witness; but on application to the pawnbrokers, with whom she had pledged the different articles, I was informed that they had been taken away, on an affidavit being made of the loss of the duplicates. She was, however, found guilty of the robbery for which she was apprehended, and sentenced to be transported for seven years.

Many professions presented themselves to my choice, as the means of obtaining a livelihood, but none appeared more congenial to my mind than the theatrical line, to which I was ever particularly attached. Knowing a person belonging to the Thespian Society, held in Tottenhamcourt Road, I procured an introduction to perform a character, and attempted that of Floranthe, in *The Mountaineers*, which I got through with considerable applause. Mr. Talbot, afterwards of Drury-lane Theatre, performed the part of Octavian, and Miss Mortimer of Covent-garden, played Agnes. I afterwards performed the parts of Adeline, in the *Battle of Hexham*; Lady Helen, in *The Children in the Wood*; Juliet, in *Romeo and Juliet*; Irene, in *Barbarossa*; Thyra, in *Athelstan*; the Queen, in *Richard the Third*; Mrs. Scout in *The Village Lawyer*, and Jack Hawser in *Banyan Day*. Finding this pursuit, however, more pleasant than profitable, I was compelled to relinquish it, and solicit assistance towards my support, from several respectable persons to whom I had made known my adventures and my sufferings.

I must not omit a circumstance which had nearly involved me in a situation, more dangerous than any to which I had hitherto been exposed. When my adventures began to attract the attention of the first characters in the kingdom, I received several sums of money from persons, who at the time, did not discover to whom I was obliged. One evening a gentleman called at my lodgings, and on being introduced to my apartments, asked me if I was the person who had suffered so many hardships abroad? I replied in the affirmative; when he informed me Colonel Gerrit Fisher, of the 9th regiment of foot, had been particularly inquiring concerning me, and he had no doubt it would produce something considerable to my advantage. He soon took his leave, and about a month afterwards, called in my absence, and left with Mrs. Cornish, of Suffolk Street, at whose house I lodged, an order signed by Colonel Fisher, on Messrs. Cox and Co. Craig's Court, Charing Cross, for nine guineas, saying at the same time, it was the amount of money received in subscription for my use, by Colonel Fisher. He also left a complimentary note, in which he styled himself Captain Grant, and was accompanied by a person who was introduced to me as a servant of Colonel Fisher's, and confirmed what Grant said. This order came as I then thought, providentially to my aid, but it being holiday time, I waited a few days, after which, in company with Mrs. Cornish, I presented it for payment as directed, but was informed that Colonel Fisher was out of town, and that it could not then be paid. Very much disappointed, I returned home, and as I did not hear when the Colonel was expected in town, it was some time before I thought of calling on him respecting the transaction, which at length I did, on the 2d of February, 1802, at his house in Manchester Square. On saying that I wished to speak with Colonel Fisher on business, he came into the passage, and understanding in part what I had to say, introduced me into the parlour, where I saw a lady seated, whom I afterwards found to be Mrs. Fisher. I now presented the note to him, and asked him if it was his hand-writing. He read it, and enquired how I came by it, when I told him it was left at my apartments by a gentleman, who said it was the amount of what Colonel Fisher had raised in subscription for me. The Colonel requested a description of the gentleman's person, and gave me pen and ink to write it, on which I first described the gentleman who had called, and reported Colonel Fisher's interesting himself on my account, and was about to write down the particulars, when Mrs. Fisher prevented me, by saying to the Colonel, "It surely must be Gardiner." To this he made no reply, but putting the order into his waistcoat pocket, said he would take care of it, though he did not give me a shilling.

A few days afterwards, he called at my lodgings, and seeing Mrs. Cornish, asked her who, and what I was, and whether she did not think I had forged the order? Mrs. Cornish then related the same particulars I had before given him, respecting the manner in which the order came into my possession. He then left the house, telling Mrs. Cornish if she had not given a good account of the way the draft was left, he should have prosecuted us both for a forgery. I afterwards called at his house, and sent up my name by a servant, who returned with the message, that my business required no answer, since which time, I have never heard any thing of him or his order.

Whether or not the order was in Colonel Fisher's handwriting, or a trick played on me by the man who styled himself Captain Grant, I never could learn, but as the clerks of Cox and Co. must have been acquainted with the Colonel's writing, and never attempted to stop the draft, which they certainly would have done, on the slightest suspicion of forgery, I cannot bring myself to think it was so. Indeed the Colonel himself never denied it to be his writing, but only inquired how I came by it.

With the certainty of my income from her Majesty's bounty, I removed to the neighbourhood of Whitechapel, some time previous to my waiting on Colonel Fisher; and having been ever more remiss in my own accounts than those of others, Mrs. Nicklin, my landlady, brought me in a bill for lodging, &c. amounting to £11 3s. 6d. Being incapable of paying, I was arrested at her suit in the court of Exchequer, and after remaining at a lock-up house, in Carey Street, Lincoln's-Inn-Fields, a week, and being sufficiently tired of the expense, I was removed to Newgate, though not before I had been enabled by a friend to make an offer of six guineas in part of the debt, which was rejected. A new scene in life now opened to my view, and finding many of my fellow prisoners of a congenial temper with my own, I frequently joined in parties of conviviality that would scarcely be supposed to exist in this place. These pleasures, however, were confined to a certain time, as my station in the women's ward, compelled a separation by ten o'clock, at which hour, the respective wards are locked.

At one of these meetings I was very near being turned out of the prison, as a stranger. After passing a few pleasant hours in the midst of our merriment, the time of separation arrived; when returning to the woman's side, I was followed in by Mr. White, the principal turnkey, who asked my business, and mistaking me for a stranger, visiting some of the prisoners, conducted me into the lobby in order to turn me out. On my remonstrance that I was a prisoner, and telling my name, he threatened to send me to the felons' side, for attempting an escape in disguise; to which purpose he went and informed Mr. Kirby, the keeper, who shortly after coming into the lobby, I explained to him the whole of the transaction, adding, that having been used to a male dress in defence of my country, I thought I was sufficiently entitled to wear the same whenever I thought proper; at the same time shewing him the wounds I had received. He directed Mr. White to conduct me to the women's side as usual, and in a day or two, sent for me to relate to him the whole of my adventures, with which he seemed so well pleased, that he sent for me two or three times afterwards when he had company, from whom I received some handsome presents.

I was advised to petition the Society for the relief of persons confined for small debts, and having obtained the necessary form of a letter, I sent it, with respectable vouchers as to the truth of my memorial. This had so good an effect, that five pounds was sent to Mr. Kirby for the purpose of settling the debt, but if the plaintiff refused that sum, it was to be returned to that charitable institution. Mrs. Nicklin, was however too good a judge to refuse so good an offer, and accordingly took the money, which was given to her friend Mr. Edmonds, on bringing my discharge. His expenses must have swallowed the greatest part of the above sum; and my landlady was well off in not being troubled herself by her own attorney, which must have been the case, if she had refused the sum offered, as I was determined to have sued her as soon as I could, for the sixpences.

My time in Newgate was rendered more comfortable than I had any reason to expect, from the constant attention of a female who had lived with me some time previous to my being arrested: for when no longer in my power to support her in the way I had been accustomed, instead of quitting me, she remained in the prison, and by needle-work which she obtained, contributed greatly to my support. She has remained a constant friend in every change that I have since experienced.

Soon after I quitted Newgate, my troubles again commenced. A Mr. E_____, not far from Pump-Court, in the Temple, having employed me to wash, mend, &c. till he was indebted to me thirty-eight pounds for that, and money which I had obtained by pledging my wearing apparel to lend him (though I have reason to think he is a man of property) I was under the necessity of arresting him to recover the amount. I had received five pounds, and a letter from him at the same time, saying, "he would settle with me honourably." He did not, however, keep his word, and being at this time in the greatest distress, for want of money and clothes, I took lodgings at the house of Mr. Joseph Bradley, Little St. Mary-le-bone Street, who has been for many years butler to a gentleman in Gloucester Place, Hyde Park Corner. Being in arrear for one week's rent, five shillings and sixpence, Mrs. Bradley, his wife, stopped not only my trunk, containing the whole of my letters and papers, but some needlework which I had to do for another person, which had she suffered me to carry home, would have nearly paid her demand. I summoned her for the work to Marlborough Street, but the Magistrate saying, they had a right to stop all they could lay their hands on, I was advised to arrest Mr. Bradley in an action of trover, as being deprived of the work, which they still hold, with my letters and papers, which would have proved my debt against Mr. E_____. I employed Mr. Worley, an attorney, in Wells Street, Oxford Road, who immediately sued out a writ against Bradley, which by some means was not served on him that term; before the next, he was arrested at my suit, and gave bail to Mr. Weekly the officer, for his appearance, which was entered at the commence-ment of the term, in order to go to trial. My attorney, Mr. Worley, on whom I called several times, informed me, that he would let me know, when I should be wanted to attend, and in the mean time said, if I would procure two pounds, he would establish me as a pauper, that I might proceed, without a necessity for more money. The above sum a gentleman advanced me for the purpose, and on my paying it into Mr. Worley's hands, he said, he would immedi-ately proceed in the cause, and told me it would come on that term. The money I gave him on Wednesday, April 11th, 1804, and called by his appointment on Friday the 13th; not seeing him, I called repeatedly, with no better success, till the morning of the 17th, when he told me my action had suffered a *non-pros* on the 7th of March. Though I had repeatedly seen him before and since that time, he never informed me of the circumstance till that mo-ment; greatly shocked and disappointed, I told him I should in-form the gentleman from whom I had received the money, of the whole transaction. The latter accordingly waited on Mr. Worley, and was informed that the money which I had given him, he had carried to my account, and no other redress was I ever able to ob-tain.

Nothing but troubles and misfortunes for the two last years of my life having occurred, and followed me step by step, I have only to apologise to my readers, for any deviation from the paths of propriety, which have only been occasioned by the greatest neces-sity, and the deepest distress. I trust that I shall gain their pity, rather than censure, when I assert, that had I been brought up in a workhouse, or any other situation to have earned my bread in the most humble manner, I should have preferred it, to the number of misfortunes and difficulties, I have been doomed to encounter, as my wounds and other afflictions have rendered me incapable of almost every exertion to procure a livelihood.

Having described as minutely as possible, the leading circumstances of my adventures, I submit the whole to the decision of my readers, with a solemn assurance, that in no particular have I advanced any thing but matters of fact; which, if they should in any way serve as a lesson to future guardians and those under their care, in avoiding the troubles I have experienced, will answer one end to which they were made public by an unfortunate sufferer,

MARY ANN TALBOT

Here terminates the account given by the writer of her chequered life up to the commencement of the year 1804. The remainder of her history is short, and not much less gloomy than the preceding portion. Misfortune still seemed to pursue her with unrelenting severity. One night in September, in the last mentioned year, she was thrown from a coach which fell into a hole left in Church Lane, Whitechapel, by the negligence of the firemen belonging to one of the offices, and besides various contusions, sustained such a serious injury in the fracture of one of her arms, as to be deprived of the use of it for some months. Various applications, accompanied with the attestations of several respectable inhabitants of the place, who saw the accident, were made in her behalf to the Directors of the Fire Office in question, who were certainly bound in law and equity to make some compensation; but inferring probably from the lowness of her circumstances her inability to obtain legal redress, they peremptorily refused to afford any relief.

In this helpless situation she was received into the house of the publisher, with whom, after her recovery from the effects of the accident, she continued to reside above three years in the capacity of a domestic. In 1807, a general decline, induced partly by the sufferings and hardships she had undergone, and partly, no doubt, by free and irregular living, rendered her, in a great measure, incapable of following her usual occupations. Towards the end of the year, she was reduced so low, that she resolved, in the hope of a favourable change, to remove to the house of an acquaintance in a distant part of the country: but nature was completely exhausted, and in a few weeks she expired on the 4th of February 1808, having just completed her 30th year.

The history of this unfortunate young woman naturally suggests some important reflections. It belongs to a class, which, perhaps, affords one of the strongest arguments in favour of a future state. The reader here beholds a female born to better prospects, reduced, while yet a child, by a series of circumstances, over which she could have no control, and without any concurrence of her will, to a state of degradation, which drew down upon her all the train of calamities that successively embittered the remainder of her existence. Can it then be imagined, that the Being, whom we are taught to consider as love itself, has formed any of his creatures expressly to be miserable? It were blasphemy to harbor such an idea. How then can they be compensated for sufferings, persecution, and a thousand evils incident to this mortal life, unless by the felicity of an hereafter, by the enjoyments of a state "where the wicked cease from troubling, where the weary are at rest."

It has been remarked, that females who have assumed the male character, have in general renounced with their sex, the virtues which distinguish it, and, with the dress and manners of the other, have adopted only its vices. This censure, though in general well founded, must not, however, be admitted without certain exceptions. In the subject of these pages, if long habits of association had blighted the delicacy and modesty which are such ornaments to a female; she had nevertheless contracted (if however she did not possess from nature) all that blunt generosity of spirit and good-nature peculiar to British seamen, accompanied likewise, it is true, with all their thoughtlessness and improvidence. She retained, notwithstanding her long metamorphosis, much of the sensibility of her sex; and to a friend or acquaintance, she was ever willing, when able, to render either pecuniary assistance or personal service. But here let us pause, and

No farther seek her merits to disclose,
Or draw her frailties from their dread abode
(There they alike in trembling hope repose)
The bosom of her Father and her God.

Coming in 2008-2009
The Fireship Press
Lady Warrior Series

Autobiographies of women who served in combat roles
LONG before it was accepted... or acceptable.

Lady Redcoat: (Winter, 2008)
  Mrs. Christian Davies - British Army (1693)

Lady Tars: (Available Now)
 Hannah Snell - Royal Marines (1745)
 Mary Lacy - Sailor/Shipwright - Navy (1760)
 Mary Anne Talbot - Royal Navy (1792)

Lady Patriot: (Fall, 2008)
  Debora Sampson - Soldier - American
    Revolutionary Army (1780)

Lady Rebel: (Available Now)
  Loreta Velazquez - Confederate Officer (1860)

Lady Tommy: (Spring, 2009)
  Dorothy Lawrence - British Army (1914)

www.FireshipPress.com

If you liked this book,
you'll love

Lady Rebel: The Story of Loreta Velazsquez

By Loreta Velazsquez

520 Pages - 6" X 9" Paperback

**Wife • Mother • Combat Officer • Confederate Spy.
One of the most remarkable figures of the Civil War:
Loreta Velazsquez.**

Take a Confederate officer who recruits 236 men in four days, who fought in the First Battle of Bull Run, became a spy, fought in the siege of Fort Donelson, was wounded, again served as a spy, fought in the Battle of Shiloh, wounded again, served as a spy again, and finished the war attempting to organize a rebellion of Confederate prisoners of war.

Such a person would be hailed as one of the South's great heros. Well, there was such a person, only he was a she. Her name is Loreta Velazsquez and, disguised as "Lt. Harry T. Buford," did all those things and more. This is her story.

The book is not without controversy, even today. When it was first published Confederate General Jubal Early said the book was an obvious fiction. Modern historians have said the events were so improbable that they can't be true. But the History Channel says the book IS true and did a one-hour TV special on the subject called *Full Metal Corset*.

You can believe it or not. Take your choice. Either way it's an exciting, informative, read.

A part of the Fireship Press *Lady Warrior Series*

Concise • Readable • Authoritative

www.FireshipPress.com

Printed in the United Kingdom by
Lightning Source UK Ltd., Milton Keynes
137065UK00002B/28/P